oks are to be return
the last date

20. OCT. 1976

30. NOV. 1976
-8. OCT. 1980
15. OCT. 1984
-8. JUN 1990

17. JUN. 1994

Sou
Envi

compile

LONDON · GEORGE P

Peter S. Berry, B.A., M.Ed., M.I. Env. Sc., is Lecturer in General Studies at Reading College of Technology, Honorary Secretary of the Conservation Society and Education Officer for the Conservation Society Conservation Trust's Joint Education Working Party

© 1975 PETER S. BERRY

Set by H. Charlesworth & Co. Ltd., Huddersfield and printed in Great Britain by J. W. Arrowsmith Ltd., Bristol

ISBN 0 540 00991 1

Contents

Introduction

This book has been produced in response to a clear demand from teachers and lecturers for information on the types and sources of teaching material available in Environmental Studies/Science.

These subjects are growing increasingly important in an age when awareness of the influence that the environment has on man, and man has on the environment is becoming ever more necessary. An apparently bewildering number of books, films, etc. has become available on various environmental topics in the last few years, and this book is an attempt to classify them. Although some of the items listed have been labelled by their producers as suitable for work in more traditional disciplines, such as Geography or Biology, they have been included because their contents lend themselves directly to work in this new, and rapidly growing, field.

The book has been divided into three parts. Part I classifies the material under twenty-nine environmental topics; Part II lists the sources from which the materials may be obtained; and Part III provides other important background information.

In addition to listing authors, titles and publishers an indication has been given, wherever possible, of the approximate age-range for which the material is best suited. A guide to the cost of purchasing or hiring the material has been included (see page x), and a brief indication of the subject-matter of the various items has been added where the content is not otherwise obvious from the title or classification. Cross-references have also been added to indicate where other related material may be found.

All books listed in Part I and published by commercial organizations may be ordered from Conservation Books, 288 London Road, Earley, Reading, RG6 1AH, who operate the Conservation Society Book Service and provide a special service for schools. Inspection copies, however, should be obtained direct from the publishers concerned. Other items published by non-commercial and voluntary bodies (e.g. Oxfam, V.C.O.A.D., J.E.W.P., W.O.W., W.D.M., Shelter, C.E.E., etc.) should be ordered direct from the bodies concerned. Generally such non-commercial bodies do not send out inspection copies, and require payment to be made with the order.

The reader will quickly realize that not all the twenty-nine sections in Part I are the same length. This is a reflection of the amount of material available on each topic. In case of the better-documented topics, such as *Ecology* (2) and *Natural History* (3), it has been necessary to undertake a certain amount of selection, but there are other, more specialized topics, such as *Noise* (22) and *Leisure* (28), where the amount of material available is much more limited.

Every effort has been made to ensure that this sourcebook is as complete, up-to-date, and accurate as possible. It is, however, in no sense intended as a commercial catalogue, and neither the author nor the publishers can guarantee the supply situation of the material listed. The reader is advised to contact the suppliers quoted for the latest information. The author would be pleased to receive notification of any alterations and also details of any other relevant material not included in the current edition.

Peter S. Berry

Abbreviations in Text

A – L	price guide (see page x)	**f/s.**	filmstrip
b/w.	black and white	**s/f.**	single-frame filmstrip
col.	colour	**transp.**	overhead projector
d/f.	double-frame filmstrip		transparency
f.	number of frames	**U.P.**	University Press
	(filmstrip)		

A.A.	Automobile Association
A.C.E.	Advisory Centre for Education
A.I.D.	Animals in Danger Corps
A.N.I.B.	Australian News and Information Bureau
B.A.C.A.N.	British Association for the Control of Aircraft Noise
B.B.C.	British Broadcasting Corporation
B.B.O.N.T.	Berkshire, Bucks. and Oxon Naturalists' Trust
B.E.E.	Bulletin of Environmental Education
B.F.I.	British Film Institute
B.P.	British Petroleum
B.S.S.R.S.	British Society for Social Responsibility in Science
C.A.	Consumers' Association
C.A.L.L.	Cambridge Aids to Learning Ltd.
C.C.P.R.	Central Council for Physical Recreation
C.E.E.	Council for Environmental Education
C.E.G.B.	Central Electricity Generating Board
C.F.L.	Central Film Library
C.G.	Common Ground
C.I.A.V.	C. I. Audio Visual Ltd.
CoEnCo	Committee for Environmental Conservation
C.O.I.	Central Office of Information
C.P.R.E.	Council for the Protection of Rural England
C.R.A.C.	Careers Research Advisory Centre
C.S.V.	Community Service Volunteers
C.U.P.	Cambridge University Press

C.U.S.C.	Council for Urban Studies Centres
C.Y.A.	Conservation Youth Association
D.E.L.T.A.	Directory of Environmental Literature and Teaching Aids
D.E.S.	Department of Education and Science
D.H.S.S.	Department of Health and Social Security
E.A.I.	Eco-Action
E.A.V.	Educational Audio Visual Ltd.
E.C.O.	Environmental Communicators' Organization
E.F.V.A.	Educational Foundation for Visual Aids
E.P.	Educational Productions
E.S.A.	Educational Supply Association
E.U.P.	English Universities Press
F.A.O.	Food and Agriculture Organization of the United Nations
F.F.H.	Freedom From Hunger Campaign
F.O.E.	Friends of the Earth Ltd.
F.P.A.	Family Planning Association
F.S.C.	Field Studies Council
G.A.	Geographical Association
G.L.C.	Greater London Council
Guild	Guild Sound and Vision Ltd.
H.M.S.O.	Her Majesty's Stationery Office
I.C.I.	Imperial Chemical Industries
I.M.E.	Institution of Municipal Engineers
I.P.P.F.	International Planned Parenthood Federation
I.T.D.G.	Intermediate Technology Development Group
I.U.C.N.	International Union for the Conservation of Nature
I.W.P.C.	Institute of Water Pollution Control
J.E.W.P.	Joint Education Working Party (Conservation Society)
M. & E.	Macdonald and Evans
M.I.T.	Massachusetts Institute of Technology
N.A.E.E.	National Association for Environmental Education
N.A.V.A.L.	National Audio-Visual Aids Library
N.C.B.	National Coal Board
N.C.S.S.	National Council of Social Service
N.C.W.	National Council of Women
N.E.R.C.	Natural Environment Research Council
N.F.E.R.	National Foundation for Educational Research
N.H.R.	National Housewives Register
N.I.A.E.	National Institute of Adult Education

N.P.W.A.	National Pure Water Association
O.E.C.D.	Organization for Economic Co-operation and Development
O.U.P.	Oxford University Press
P.C.E.T.	Pictorial Charts Educational Trust
P.F.B.	Petroleum Films Bureau
R.A.C.	Royal Automobile Club
R.E.E.D.	Review of Environmental Education Developments
R.G.S.	Royal Geographical Society
R.I.B.A.	Royal Institution of British Architects
R.I.C.S.	Royal Institute of Chartered Surveyors
R.S.A.	Royal Society of Arts
R.S.P.B.	Royal Society for the Protection of Birds
R.S.P.C.A.	Royal Society for Prevention of Cruelty to Animals
S.A.G.E.	Schools Action Group for the Environment
S.C.E.P.	Study of Critical Environmental Problems
S.E.A.G.	Schools Eco-Action Group
S.E.E.	Society for Environmental Education
S.P.N.R.	Society for the Promotion of Nature Reserves
T. & C.P.A.	Town and Country Planning Association
U.N.A.	United Nations Association
U.N.E.S.C.O.	United Nations Educational, Scientific and Cultural Organization
U.N.I.C.E.F.	United Nations International Children's Emergency Fund
U.N.O.	United Nations Organization
U.T.P.	University Tutorial Press
V.C.O.A.D.	Voluntary Committee on Overseas Aid and Development
V.E.N.I.S.S.	Visual Education National Information Service for Schools
V.P.S.	Visual Programmed Systems
W.D.M.	World Development Movement
W.E.A.	Workers' Educational Association
W.H.O.	World Health Organization
W.O.W.	War on Want
W.U.L.	World University Library
W.W.F.	World Wildlife Fund
Y.H.A.	Youth Hostels Association

Price Guide

Owing to fluctuating prices, hire charges, etc. the following code letters have been used to give an indication of the costs.

A	Up to 10p	**G**	£3 – £4
B	10p – 25p	**H**	£4 – £5
C	25p – 50p	**J**	£5 – £10
D	50p – £1	**K**	£10 – £20
E	£1 – £2	**L**	£20 and over
F	£2 – £3		

Where two code letters are given (e.g. **C/E**), there are two editions or versions available. In the case of books, the cheaper is usually in paperback.

Prices quoted do not necessarily include postage and packing.

PART ONE

Classification of Teaching Material

The topics covered in most environmental studies syllabuses (*see pages* 2–173) have been classified under twenty-nine headings. Cross-references given at the beginning of each section refer to others which include related material; for example, material on *Planning* (Section 12) will also be found under *Urbanization* (10), *Land Use* (11) and *Transport* (18).

In each topic the teaching material has been arranged as follows:

Books (General) – arranged alphabetically by author, these are suitable for general reference, teachers, libraries, and students in further and higher education. A number of advanced research texts has also been included.

Books (Atlases) – these have been included in Section 1 only, and have been arranged alphabetically by title.

Books (School) – arranged alphabetically by authors, these are suitable for class use. Many of the books listed as suitable for '17 years +' will also be of value in further and higher education.

Films – arranged alphabetically by title. Some of the films listed are also available for purchase, but a guide is given to their hire charges only. These hire charges usually refer to the cost for one day; charges for longer periods are generally at a lower rate. Some films become heavily booked, and plenty of advance notice is essential. Where alternative sources are quoted, it is often worth approaching both. Savings in hire charges are frequently possible in this way. All the films listed are available in 16 mm (sound).

Filmstrips/Slides/Filmloops/Transparencies – arranged alphabetically by title. Most of these are available for purchase only.

Wallcharts/Posters – arranged alphabetically by title.

Games/Kits/Workcards – arranged alphabetically by title.

Organizations – arranged alphabetically. For details of addresses, etc. see pages 195–221.

Journals/Periodicals – arranged alphabetically by title. For details of publishers, subscriptions, etc. see pages 222–233. Many of these are highly specialized.

Articles – a selection of recent articles from the more readily-available periodicals has been included at the end of each section.

1   GENERAL ENVIRONMENTAL TOPICS

BOOKS (GENERAL)

Adler, I. & Adler, R., *The Earth's Crust* ('The Reason Why' series)
Dobson   1964   Price **D**
Adler, I. & Adler, R., *Oceans* ('The Reason Why' series)   Dobson
1963   Price **D**
Aldous, T., *Battle for the Environment*   Collins/Fontana   1972
Price **C**
Alfven, H. & K., *Living on the Third Planet*   Freeman   1973   Price **F**
Allsopp, B., *Civilization, the Next Stage: The Importance of Individuals
in the Modern World*   Oriel Press   1969   Price **D/E**
Barbour, I. G., *Earth Might be Fair*   Prentice-Hall   1972   Price **F**
Barr, J. (ed.), *The Environmental Handbook: Action Guide for the U.K.*
Pan/Ballantine   1971   Price **C**
Barret, E. C. & Curtis, L. F. (eds.), *Environmental Remote Sensing*
(Collection of essays on Landscape, land use and climate)
Arnold 1974   Price **J**
Ben-David, J., *Scientists' Role in Society*   Prentice-Hall   1971
Price **E/G**
Benjamin, B., Cox, P. R. & Peel, J. (eds.), *Resources and Population*
(Symposium of Eugenics Society)   Academic Press   1973
Price **F**
Bonham-Carter, V., *The Survival of the English Countryside*   Hodder
& Stoughton   1971   Price **G**
Borgstrom, G., *Too Many: An Ecological Over-view of the Earth's
Limitations*   Collier-Macmillan   1969   Price **D/F**
Brain, R., *Introducing the Primitive Environment – Survival on the
Edge of our Civilization* (Life styles)   Philip   1972   Price **F**
Brierley, J. K., *Biology and the Social Crisis*   Heinemann   1967
Price **D/E**
Brooks, P., *The House of Life. Rachel Carson at Work*   Allen & Unwin
1973   Price **H**
Brower, D. R., Collins, L. & Schweitzer, M., *Only a Little Planet* (A
photo-essay on the natural environment by F.O.E.)   Ballantine
1973   Price **E**
Brown, M., *The Social Responsibility of the Scientist*   Collier-
Macmillan   1971   Price **F/H**
Burch, W. R. *et al.*, *Social Behaviour, Natural Resources and the
Environment*   Harper & Row   1972   Price **F**
Burton, I. & Kater, R. W. (eds.), *Readings in Resource Management and
Conservation*   Chicago U.P.   1965   Price **G**
Calder, N., *The Environment Game*   Panther   1969   Price **C**
Calder, N., *Nature in the Round: A Guide to Environmental Science*
Weidenfeld & Nicolson   1973   Price **G**
Carpenter, J. R., *Ecological Glossary*   Collier-Macmillan   1971
Price **G**

2

Chermayeff, S. & Tzonis, A., *Shape of Community: Realization of Human Potential*   Penguin   1971   Price **D**
Chisholm, M. (ed.), *Resources for Britain's Future* (Series reprinted from *Geographical Magazine*)
David & Charles   1972   Price **F**
Penguin   1972   Price **D**
Chisholm, M. & Rodgers, B. (eds.), *Studies in Human Geography*
Heinemann   1972   Price **E/G**
Clarke, R., *We All Fall Down: The Prospects of Biological and Chemical Warfare*   Penguin   1969   Price **C**
Clarke, R., *We All Fall Down: the prospects of biological and chemical warfare*   Penguin   1969   Price **C**
Commoner, B., *Science and Survival*   Pan/Ballantine   1971   Price **C**
Commoner, B., *The Closing Circle: The Environmental Crisis and its Cure*   Cape   1972   Price **F**
Darling, F. F., *Wilderness and Plenty* (Reith Lectures 1969)
B.B.C.   1970   Price **E**
Pan/Ballantine   1971   Price **C**
Dasmann, R. F., *Planet in Peril: Man and the Biosphere Today*
Penguin   1972   Price **C**
Dawson, J. A., & Doornkamp, J. C., *Evaluating the Human Environment. Essays in Applied Geography*   Arnold   1973   Price **F/H**
de Blij, H., *Man Shapes the Earth: A Topic*   Geography (Includes landscape, climate, population, industrialization, urbanization, etc.)   Hamilton/Wiley   1974   Price **J**
Dept. of Environment, *The Human Environment – the British View*
H.M.S.O.   1972   Price **E**
Derrick, *Delicate Creation*   Stacey   1972   Price **E**
Dorst, J., *Before Nature Dies*   Collins   1970   Price **G**
Douglas, J. D., *Technological Threat*   Prentice-Hall   1971   Price **E/G**
Drake, E. T. (ed.), *Evolution and Environment: A Symposium*
Yale U.P.   1968   Price **J**
Dumont, R. & Rosier, B., *The Hungry Future*   Methuen   1970   Price **D**
Ebling, F. J. & Heath, G. W. (eds.), *The Future of Man*   Academic Press   1972   Price **F**
Ehrenfeld, D. W., *Conserving Life on Earth*   O.U.P.   1973   Price **H**
Ehrlich, P. R., *The Population, Resources, Environment Crisis: Where Do We Stand Now?* (1972 Presidential Address)   Conservation Society   1972   Price **B**
Ehrlich, P. R. & Harriman, R. L., *How to Be a Survivor: A Plan to Save Spaceship Earth*   Pan/Ballantine   1971   Price **C**
Ehrlich, P. R. & Holdren, A. H., *Human Ecology: Problems and Solutions*   Freeman   1973   Price **E**
English, P. W. & Mayfield, R. C., *Man, Environment, and Space: Concepts in Contemporary Human Geography*   O.U.P.   1972   Price **F**

3

Epstein, S. & Williams, V., *The Sea*   Dobson   1961   Price **D**
Ericson, D. B. & Wollin, G., *The Ever-Changing Sea*   Paladin   1971
   Price **D**
Fleming, D. F., *The Issues of Survival*   Allen & Unwin   1972
   Price **F**
Forrester, J. W., *World Dynamics* (Man and Ecology)   Wiley   1971
   Price **H**
F.O.E., *The Stockholm Conference: Only One Earth*   Earth Island
   1972   Price **D/F**
Goldsmith, E. (ed.), *Can Britain Survive?*   Stacey   1971
   Price **D/G**
Goldsmith, E. *et al.*, *Blueprint for Survival* (Reprinted from *Ecologist*)
   Stacey   1972   Price **E**
Goldsmith, M. (ed.), *The Predicament of Man* (3rd International
   Symposium of Science Policy Foundation)   Inforlink
   Price **J**
Gresswell, P., *Environment: An Alphabetical Handbook*   Murray
   1971   Price **G**
Hall, C., *How to Run a Pressure Group*   Dent   1974   Price **E**
Harrison, G., *Earthkeeping*   Hamilton   1972   Price **F**
Helfrich, H. W. (ed.), *The Environmental Crisis: Man's Struggle to Live
   with Himself*   Yale U.P.   1970   Price **D/G**
Helfrich, H. W. (ed.), *Agenda for Survival: The Environmental Crisis*
   Yale U.P.   1970   Price **E/H**
Henshaw, P. S., *This Side of Yesterday: Extinction or Utopia*   Wiley
   1971   Price **E/G**
Hettena, P. H. G. & Syer, G. N. (eds.), *Decade of Decision* (Report of
   Conservation Society's conference 'Conservation 1970')
   Academic Press   1971   Price **D**
Holliman, J., *Consumer's Guide to the Protection of the Environment*,
   2nd edn.   Pan/Ballantine   1974   Price **D**
House, J. W. (ed.), *The U.K. Space. Resources, Environment and the
   Future* (Study in applied geography)   Weidenfeld & Nicolson
   1973   Price **J**
Hussey, M., *Environment File*   Open University   1972   Price **E**
Irving, R. M. & Priddle, G. B., *Crisis* (Readings on the deterioration of
   the environment)   Macmillan   1972   Price **J**
Jarrett, H. (ed.), *Environmental Quality in a Growing Economy*
   Johns Hopkins   1966   Price **D**
Johnson, C. E. (ed.), *Eco-Crisis*   Wiley   1971   Price **E**
Jones, M. M. *et al.*, *Chemistry, Land and Society*   Saunders   1972
   Price **J**
Khare, R., Kolka, J. & Pollis, C. (eds.), *Environmental Quality and
   Social Responsibility*   Wisconsin U.P.   1972   Price **E**
King, G. E. (ed.), *Conflict and Harmony. A Source-Book of Man and
   his Environment* (Over 300 extracts)   Philip   1972   Price **G**
King-Hele, D., *The End of the 20th Century?*   Macmillan   1970
   Price **D**

4

Leach, G., *The Biocrats* (Modern bio-medicine) Penguin 1972 Price **D**
Littleton, T. (ed.), *Approaching the Benign Environment* ('Man and
     Society' series) Muller 1973 Price **E**
Lockwood, J. G., *World Climatology. An Environmental Approach*
     Arnold 1974 Price **J**
Loraine, J., *The Death of Tomorrow* Heinemann 1972 Price **G**
Love, G. A. & R. M., *Ecological Crisis: Readings for Survival* Harcourt
     Brace 1971 Price **E**
Maddox, J., *The Doomsday Syndrome*
     Macmillan 1972 Price **F**
     Penguin 1974 Price **C**
Masters, G. M., *Introduction to Environmental Science and Technology*
     (Includes sections on ecology, pollution and energy and raw
     materials) Wiley 1974 Price **J**
McCamy, L. J., *The Quality of the Environment* Free Press 1973
     Price **G**
McHale, J., *World Facts and Trends* (Statistics on man and environ-
     ment) Collier-Macmillan 1973 Price **D/F** Price **F**
McLaughlin, T., *Coprophilia or a Peck of Dirt* Cassell 1971 Price **F**
Meadows, D. H. et al., *The Limits to Growth: A Report for the Club
     of Rome's Project on the Predicament of Mankind* Earth
     Island 1972 Price **E**
Meadows, D. L. (ed.), *Towards Global Equilibrium: Collected Papers*
     Wiley 1973 Price **J**
Montefiore, H., *Doom or Deliverance? The Dogmas and Duties of a
     Technological Age* Manchester U.P. 1972 Price **C**
Mossman, A. S., *Towards Conservation* (Comprehensive survey of world
     environmental problems) Intertext 1974 Price **E**
Murdoch, W. W. (ed.), *Environment: Resources, Pollution and Society*
     Sinauer 1971 Price **F**
Newell, M., *The Value of Life* (Selected readings on environment,
     pollution and conservation) Dent 1973 Price **C**
Nicholson, M., *The Environmental Revolution: A Guide for the New
     Masters of the World*
     Hodder & Stoughton 1970 Price **H**
     Penguin 1972 Price **D**
Paterson, J. H., *Land, Work and Resources* Arnold 1972 Price **E/G**
Pole, N. (ed.), *Environmental Solutions* Eco-Publications 1972
     Price **D**
Polunin, N. (ed.), *The Environmental Future: Proceedings of the 1st.
     International Conference on Environmental Future* Macmillan
     1972 Price **J**
Porteous, A., *Maintaining the Environment* Open University 1972
     Price **E**
Radest, H. B. (ed.), *To Seek a Humane World. How Can Man Direct his
     Future Evolution?* (Proceedings of the Fifth Congress of the
     International Humanist and Ethical Union) Pemberton 1972
     Price **D/F**

Ravetz, J. R., *Scientific Knowledge and its Social Problems*   O.U.P.
   1971   Price J
Rigg, J. B., *Textbook of Environmental Study*   Constable   1968
   Price F
Rogers, P. (ed.), *The Education of Human Ecologists* (Symposium at
   Huddersfield Polytechnic)   Knight   1973   Price G
Russell, B., *Has Man a Future?*   (Nuclear warfare)   Penguin   1972
   Price C
Schwab, M. (ed.), *Teach-in for Survival* (Proceedings of seminar by
   Movement for Survival)   Robinson & Watkins   1972
   Price E/F
Slesser, M., *The Politics of Environment*   Allen & Unwin   1972
   Price E/G
Stone, P. B., *Did We Save the Earth at Stockholm?* ('The People and
   Politics in the Conference on the Human Environment')   Earth
   Island   1973   Price E
Storr, A., *Human Aggression*   Penguin   1970   Price C
Strahler, A. N. & A. H., *Introduction to Environmental Science*
   (Physical and natural environment)   Wiley   1974   Price J
Taylor, G. R., *The Doomsday Book*   Thames & Hudson   1970
   Price F
Thorold, O., *The Environmental Law Handbook*   Earth Island   1972
   Price F
Udall, S., *Agenda for Tomorrow*   Harcourt Brace   1972   Price D/F
Urban, G. R. & Glenny, M. (eds.), *Can We Survive our Future?*
   Bodley Head   1972   Price F
Vickers, G., *Freedom in a Rocking Boat*   Penguin   1970   Price C
Wagner, K. A., *et al., Under Siege: Man, Men and Earth* (Comprehensive
   study of the environment and man's battle against its abuse)
   Intertext   1973   Price J
Waller, R., *Be Human or Die: A Study in Ecological Humanism* (Phil-
   osophy and the ecological crisis)   Knight   1973   Price G
Wallis, H. F., *The New Battle of Britain*   Knight   1972   Price D/F
Walters, A. H., *Ecology, Food and Civilization: An Ecological History
   of Human Society*   Knight   1973   Price F
Ward, B. & Dubos, R., *Only One Earth: The Care and Maintenance of a
   Small Planet*
   Deutsch   1972   Price F
   Penguin   1972   Price C
Watt, K. E. F., *The Titanic Effect: Planning for the Unthinkable*
   Sinauer   1974   Price E
Weale, M. (ed.), *Environmental Issues*, 3rd edn.   Ely Resource and
   Technology Centre   1974   Price D
Weiner, J. S., *A Guide to the Human Adaptability Proposals*, 2nd edn.
   Blackwell Scientific   1969   Price D
Woods, B. (ed.), *Eco-Solutions: A Casebook for the Environmental
   Crisis* (A series of articles on the effect the environment has on
   people)   General Learning Press   1972   Price J

Environment (11 articles from *New Society*)   New Society   1972
Price **B**
The Environment: A Radical Agenda   B.S.S.R.S.   1973   Price **B**
Environment Today (21 articles from *New Scientist*)   New Scientist
1972   Price **C**
An Environmental Directory (Index to societies)   Civic Trust   1972
Price **C**
Natural Environment Research Council (Report)   H.M.S.O.   1971
Price **D**
The Protection of the Environment   H.M.S.O.   1970   Price **B**
Resources and Man: A Study and Recommendations   Freeman   1969
Price **E/F**
U.K. Conference on the Human Environment 1972 (Memorandum to
the Secretary of State for the Environment)   Conservation
Society   1972   Price **A**

BOOKS (ATLASES)

Atlas Advanced, 1st edn. Collins-Longman   1968   17 years +
Price **F**
Atlas of Britain and Northern Ireland
O.U.P.   1963   Price **L**
Atlas of Europe
Bartholomew/Warne   1974   Price **H**
Atlas of the British Isles
Readers' Digest/Hodder & Stoughton   1967   Price **J**
Atlas of the Earth, The (Combined world atlas and environmental
encyclopaedia)
Philip   1972   Price **K**
Atlas One (Metric edition)
Collins-Longman   1970   Primary   Price **C**
Atlas Two, 2nd edn.
Collins-Longman   1971   Secondary   Price **C**
Atlas Three
Collins-Longman   1972   C.S.E.   Price **D**
Atlas Four, 1st edn.
Collins-Longman   1969   G.C.E. 'O'   Price **D**
Collins Clear School Atlas
Collins   Secondary   Price **B**
Collins Pocket Atlas
Collins   13 years +   Price **C**
Collins World Atlas, The
Collins   1970   Price **E**
Commercial Course Atlas, rev. edn.
Philip   9–16 years +   Price **D**
Concorde World Atlas (Mainly political)
Philip   9–16 years +   Price **H**
Concise Oxford Atlas
O.U.P.   1970   Price **F**

Daily Telegraph Atlas, The (Includes space supplement)
    Collins   Price **E**
Elementary Atlas
    Philip   9–16 years   Price **C**
Exploration Universe Atlas (Environmental Studies atlas for children)
    Holmes McDougall   1972   Price **E**
First Venture Atlas
    Philip   Primary   Price **B/C**
Graphic Atlas, new edn.
    Collins   Price **D**
Great World Atlas (Includes World Feature section) Readers' Digest/
    Hodder & Stoughton   1965   Price **H**
International Atlas, The
    Philip   1969   Price **K**
Library Atlas, The
    Philip   1973   Price **J**
Little Oxford Atlas
    O.U.P.   1972   Price **D**
Middle School Atlas
    Philip   9–16 years   Price **C**
Modern School Atlas
    Philip   9–16 years +   Price **D**
New School Atlas
    Philip   9–16 years   Price **D**
Observer Atlas of World Affairs, The
    Philip   1971   Price **F**
Oxford Atlas
    O.U.P.   1970   Price **F/H**
Oxford Economic Atlas of the World (Includes a statistical supplement)
    O.U.P.   1972   Price **G/J**
Oxford Home Atlas of the World
    O.U.P.   1971   Price **E**
Oxford Junior Atlas
    O.U.P.   1967   Price **C**
Oxford Regional Economic Atlas of Western Europe
    O.U.P.   1971   Price **F/G**
Oxford School Atlas
    O.U.P.   1971   Price **D**
Oxford World Atlas
    O.U.P.   1973   Price **G/J**
Penguin World Atlas, The (Includes environmental maps)
    Penguin   1974   Price **E**
Pergamon General World Atlas
    Pergamon   Secondary   Price **E**
Primary Atlas
    Philip   1971   Primary   Price **B**
Secondary School Atlas
    Philip   9–16 years   Price **C**

Shorter Oxford School Atlas
 O.U.P. 1972 Price **D**
Study Atlas, The, 18th edn.
 Collins—Longman Price **D**
Times Atlas of the World, The
 Bartholomew 1968 Price **L**
Times Concise Atlas of the World, The
 Times Newspapers 1972 Price **J**
University Atlas, 15th edn.
 Philip 1973 16 years + Price **H**
Venture Atlas
 Philip 9—16 years Price **C**
Visible Regions Atlas, The, 18th edn.
 Collins-Longman Price **C**
Visual Atlas
 Philip 9—16 years Price **C**
World Atlas
 Pergamon 1968 Price **L**
World Wide Atlas
 Collins 1970 Price **C**

BOOKS (SCHOOL)

Allsop, K., *Fit to Live In? The Future of Britain's Countryside*
 ('Connexions' series) Penguin 1970 Secondary Price **C**
Andrews, K., *Beneath the Oceans* ('Visual Books' series; includes
 projects) Macdonald Educational 1972 C.S.E. Price **D**
Baines, J. D., *The Environment* Batsford 1974 Secondary
 Price **E**
Bassey, M., *European Environment 1975—2000: A Simulation*
 Conservation Trust 1972 17 years + Price **C**
Bernard, R., *Looking at Landscape* ('Nelson's Geography Studies'
 series) Nelson 1968 13—18 years Price **C**
Boon, G. S., *Environment* ('Viewpoint Britain' series) Evans 1974
 11—16 years Price **D**
Brain, R., *Into the Primitive Environment. Survival on the Edge of our
 Civilization* (The survival of cultural identity) Philip 1972
 16 years + Price **F**
Brooks, P. F., *Problems of the Environment* (Includes suggested
 activities) Harrap 1974 14 years + Price **F**
Critchlow, K., *Into the Hidden Environment. Oceans: Lifestream of
 our Planet* Philip 1972 16 years + Price **F**
Davis, A., *Inside the Earth* ('Visual Books' series) Macdonald Educa-
 tional 1972 C.S.E. Price **D**
Ferris, B. & Toyne, P., *World Problems* Hulton 1970 14 years +
 Price **E**
Gatland, K. W., *Exploring Space* ('Visual Books' series) Macdonald
 Educational 1972 C.S.E. Price **D**

Harris, A., Harrison, C. & Smithson, P., *Man's Environment* ('Visual Books' series; includes projects)   Macdonald Educational   1972   C.S.E.   Price **D**

Jones, C. *et al.*, *The Balance of Nature* ('Pollution' series)   Dent   1973   14 years +   Price **E**

Jones, C. *et al.*, *The Dangerous Atom* ('Pollution' series)   Dent   1973   14 years +   Price **E**

Lines, C. J. & Bolwell, L. H., *Discovering Your Environment*
  1. *Understanding Local Maps*
  2. *About the Weather*
  3. *People at Work*
  4. *Using Local Maps*
  5. *About Buildings and Scenery*
  6. *People on the Move*
  7. *History in a Village*
  8. *History in Towns*
  9. *History along Roads and Waterways*
  10. *Crafts and Industries in the Past*
     Ginn   1968/71   9–13 years   Price (each) **C**

Long, M. & Roberson, B. S., *World Problems: a Topic Geography*   E.U.P.   1969   C.S.E./G.C.E.   Price **D**

Mackillop, A., *Talking about the Environment*   Wayland   1973   14 years +   Price **E**

Mackintosh, R. D. *et al*, *Environment* ('Living Geography' series)   Holmes McDougall   1969   9–13 years   Price **D**

Masini, G., *S.O.S. Save the Earth*   Collins   1972   9 years +   Price **E**

Matthews, B. & P.,. . . *Happily Ever After?* (Current world problems)   Arnold   1973   14–16 years   Price **D**

Riley, D. & Spolton, L., *Climate and its Causes* ('Nelson's Geography Studies' series)   Nelson   1972   13–18 years   Price **C**

Robson, R., *Man and His Environment* ('Nelson's Geography Studies' series)   Nelson   1972   13–18 years   Price **C**

Searle, G., *Project Earth: An Action Guide for Young People*   Wolfe   1972   8 years +   Price **F**

Tinker, J., *You and Your Environment* (Teachers' notes)   Pedigree Petfoods   1973   Price free

Walker, W. J., *Environmental Problems* ('Location and Links' series)   Blackwell   1973   11–16 years   Price **D**

FILMS

Choice, The
  I.C.I.   29 min., col.   Hire free
Environment in the Balance (1970)
  S.P.N.R.   30 min., col.   Hire **G**
  Shell   Hire free
Interview with Paul Ehrlich
  B.B.C./Concord   40 min., b/w.   Hire **F**

Landscape of Choice
    B.B.C.   25 min., col.   Hire **J**
Limits to Growth, The (1972)
    Concord   60 min., col.   Hire **J**
Multiply and Subdue the Earth (1970) (Man's misuse of the
    environment)
    Concord   50 min., col.   Hire **J**
Shadow of Progress, The (1970) (Pressure on resources and environ-
    ment by population)
    B.P.   27 min., col.   Hire free
Tilt (1972) (Serious problems facing the world – cartoon)
    Concord   14 min., col.   Hire **E**
    Canada House   Hire free

FILMSTRIPS/SLIDES/FILMLOOPS/TRANSPARENCIES
Britain in the Future
    C.P.R.E.   50 slides   Hire **C**
Our Environment (1970)
    Visual Information (36)   37 f., col.   Price **E**
Population and Resources
    1. *Population*
    2. *Renewable and Non-Renewable Resources*
    D. Wyllie   37 f., col.   Price **F/G** each
Science and Natural Resources (1970)
    9171 *Can the Biologist Meet the Demand?*
    9172 *Can the Chemist Renew the Supply?*
    9173 *Can the Physicist-Engineer Strike a Balance?*
    Encyclopaedia Britannica   34 f., col.   Price (each) **F**
Twentieth Century Environment: Its Origins and Growth (Deals with
    the built environment)
    EB1 *Small Beginnings*
    EB2 *Natural Growth*
    EB3 *A Conscious Effort*
    EB4 *Backyard Environments*
    EB5 *Garden Environment*
    EB6 *Tomorrow is Today*
    Visual Publications   d/f., col.   Price (each) **F**

WALLCHARTS/POSTERS
Eco-Posters (Slogans, suitable as car stickers)
    Overpopulation is Suicide
    Zero Population Growth
    Give Earth a Chance
    Liberty, Equality, Ecology
    Support Your Local Planet
    Overpopulation is Everybody's Baby
    No Mining in Snowdonia
    Eco-Posters   Price **A**

Environmental Control
   C.O.I.   Price **A**
Only One Earth
   T. & C.P.A.   Price **B**
Packaging and the Environment
   Your Environment   Spring 1972   Price **A**
Technology — Exciting or Frightening?
   P.C.E.T.   Secondary   Price **D**
Tomorrow and You (Leisure, food, planning and education)
   P.C.E.T.   Secondary   Price **D**
You and Your Environment (Resources, pollution, landscape and
   ecology)
   Pedigree Petfoods   1973   Price free

GAMES/KITS/WORKCARDS

Environmental Studies: 1. A Piece of Land (workcards)
   Blackwell   9–12 years   Price **E**
Lifescape Series
   1. Haikin, P., *The Way Things Are*
   2. Holme, A., *Home, Neighbourhood and Community*
   3. Haveron, F., *Communications*
   4. Inglis, E., *The World of Work*
   6. Madon, M., *Environment: the Changing Countryside*
   8. Clark, E., *Community Care*
   9. Artley, A., *Taking Part and Dropping Out*
  10. Browne, K., *The Way Things Might Become*
   Architectural Press   1972/3   Price (each) **E**
Man in his Environment (Role-playing game)
   Coca-cola   1971   10–15 years   Price **J**
Relationships (Modular Learning Programme)
   C.I.A.V. (SE 4)   13–17 years   Price **G**
Teaching About Spaceship Earth (Role-playing simulation)
   V.C.O.A.D.   11–13 years   Price **C**
World and Men, The (Seminar Cassettes — 'Life on Earth' series)
   Foulsham (SS 108)   54 min.   Price **F**
You and Your Community (4 audio-visual filmstrips on Homes, Travel,
   Work, Leisure)
   Coca-Cola   1974   8–13 years   Price **J**

ORGANIZATIONS

British Society for Social Responsibility in Science (B.S.S.R.S.)
Centre for Environmental Studies
Committee for Environmental Conservation (CoEnCo)
Community Service Volunteers (C.S.V.)
Conservation Society
Consumers' Association (C.A.)
Council for Environmental Education (C.E.E.)

Department of Environment
Enterprise Youth
Environmental Communicators' Organization
Environmental Consortium
Environment Centre
Eugenics Society
Friends of the Earth (F.O.E.)
Geographical Association (G.A.)
Howey Foundation
Institute of Biology
Institution of Environmental Sciences
International Union for the Conservation of Nature (I.U.C.N.)
International Youth Federation for Environmental Studies and
    Conservation
National Association for Environmental Education (N.A.E.E.)
National Union of Students – Conservation Project
Natural Environment Research Council
People
Prince of Wales's Committee
Professional Institutions Council for Conservation
Research Institute for Consumer Affairs
Royal Geographical Society (R.G.S.)
Schools Eco-Action Group (S.E.A.G.)
Scottish Development Department
Society for Environmental Education (S.E.E.)
Survival
Watch

JOURNALS/PERIODICALS
AMBIO, A Journal of the Human Environment
Background Notes on Social Studies
Bulletin of Environmental Education (BEE)
Communus
Conservation News
Crisis Paper
Ecologist, The
Environment and Industry
Environment Film Review, The
Environment This Month, The
Environmental Studies
Environmental Times
Epoch
Geographical Journal
Geographical Magazine
Geography
Good Earth
Human Ecology

Information for Survival
International Journal of Environmental Studies
Journal of Biosocial Science
Journal of Environmental Management
Nature
Naturopa
N.E.R.C. News Journal
New Scientist
New Society
Plain Truth
Towards Survival
Undercurrents
U.N.E.S.C.O. Courier
Which?
World Survey
Your Environment

ARTICLES

'Blueprint for Survival' issue   *BEE*   February 1972
Southwood, T. R., 'The Environmental Complaint − Its Cause,
    Prognosis and Treatment   *Biologist*   May 1972
'A Blueprint for Survival'   *Ecologist*   January 1972
'Stockholm Conference' issue   *Ecologist*   June 1972
Hodgson, R. I., 'First Threat to the Environment'   *Geographical
    Magazine*   January 1971
Nicholson, M., 'Environment on Record'   *Geographical Magazine*
    November 1971

2 ECOLOGY

See also Sections 3 Natural History (*page* 30), 4 Soils and Soil
Erosion (*page* 47) and 25 Conservation (*page* 145)

BOOKS (GENERAL)
Adler, I. & Adler, R., *Insects and Plants* ('The Reason Why' series)
   Dobson   1964   Price **D**
Allaby, M., *The Eco-Activists*   Knight   1971   Price **E/G**
Allee, W. C., *et al.*, *Principles of Animal Ecology*   Saunders   1949
   Price **J**
Allsopp, B., *Ecological Morality*   Muller   1972   Price **E**
Anderson, M. S., *Geography of Living Things* ('Teach Yourself'
   series)   E.U.P.   1951   Price **D**
Andrewartha, H. G., *Introduction to the Study of Animal Populations*
   Chapman & Hall   1970   Price **F**
Andrews, W. E. *et al.*, *Guide to the Study of Freshwater Ecology*
   Prentice-Hall   1972   Price **E/F**
Ashby, M., *Introduction to Plant Ecology*, 2nd edn.   Macmillan
   1969   Price **F**
Barlow, K. E., *The Disciplines of Peace*, 2nd rev. edn.   Knight   1971
   Price **F**
Barnes, R. S. K., *Estuarine Biology* ('Studies in biology' series)
   Arnold   1974-in preparation   Price **D/E**
Barnett, S. A., *'Instinct' and 'Intelligence': The Behaviour of Animals
   and Man*, rev. edn.   Penguin   1970   Price **D**
Bateson, G., *Steps to an Ecology of Mind*   Intertext   1972   Price **G**
Benthall, J., *Ecology, the Shaping Enquiry*   Longman   1972
   Price **E/G**
Bishop, O. N., *Natural Communities*   Murray   1972   Price **E**
Boughey, A. S., *Ecology of Populations* ('Current Concepts in
   Biology' series)   Collier-Macmillan   1968   Price **E**
Boughey, A. S., *Fundamental Ecology*   Intertext   1971   Price **E**
Bresler, J. B. (ed.), *Human Ecology: Collected Readings*   Addison-
   Wesley   1966   Price **J**
Brown, G. W. (ed.), *Desert Biology*
   Volume 1   1968   Price **K**
   Volume 2   1974   Price **L**
   Academic Press
Campbell, B. & Binford, S., *Human Ecology*   Heinemann   1972
   Price **G**
Carpenter, J. R., *Ecological Glossary*   Collier-Macmillan   1971
   Price **G**
Chinery, M. & Larkin, D., *Patterns of Living: Foundations of Ecology*
   Low & Marston   1966   Price **E**
Chisholm, A., *Philosophers of the Earth*   Sidgwick & Jackson   1971
   Price **F**
Clapham, W. B., *Natural Ecosystems*   Collier-Macmillan   1973   Price **E**

15

Clark, L. R. *et al.*, *The Ecology of Insect Populations in Theory and Practice*　Methuen　1970　　Price **G**

Clarke, G. L., *Elements of Ecology*　Wiley　1965　　Price **J**

Clowes, R., *The Structure of Life*　Penguin　1970　　Price **D**

Colinvaux, P. A., *Introduction to Ecology*　Wiley　1973　　Price **H/J**

Cox, C. B. *et al.*, *Biogeography: An Ecological and Evolutionary Approach*　Blackwell　1973　　Price **F/G**

Cragg, J. B. (ed.), *Advances in Ecological Research*　Academic Press　1971　　Price **J**

Creed, E. R., *Ecological Genetics and Evolution: Essays in Honour of E. B. Ford*　Blackwell Scientific　1971　　Price **J**

Darnell, R. M., *Organism and Environment: A Manual of Quantitative Ecology*　Freeman　1971　　Price **F**

Debach, P. (ed.) & Schlinger, I., *Biological Control of Insect Pests and Weeds*　Chapman & Hall　1964　　Price **J**

Ehrlich, P. R. & A. H., *Population, Resources, Environment: Issues in Human Ecology*, 2nd edn.　Freeman　1972　　Price **F/H**

Elton, C. S., *The Ecology of Invasions by Animals and Plants*　Methuen　1958　　Price **E**

Elton, C. S., *The Pattern of Animal Communities*　Methuen　1966　　Price **J**

Elton, C. S., *The Ecology of Animals*　Chapman & Hall　1969　　Price **D**

Eyre, S. R. & Jones, G. R. J., *Geography as Human Ecology. Methodology by Example*　Arnold　1966　　Price **F**

Fabun, D., *Dimensions of Change*　Collier-Macmillan　1972　　Price **F/G**

Faegri, K. & Van Der Pijl, L., *Principles of Pollination Ecology*, 2nd edn.　Pergamon　1971　　Price **J**

Farb, P., *Ecology* ('Life Nature Library' series)　Time-Life　1965　　Price **G**

Ford, E. B., *Ecological Genetics*　Chapman & Hall　1971　　Price **H**

Ford, J. M., *Living Systems: Principles and Relationships*　Canfield Press　1972　　Price **H**

Ford, R. F. & Hazen, E. (eds.), *Readings in Aquatic Ecology*　Saunders　1972　　Price **F**

Gimingham, C. H., *Ecology of Heathlands*　Chapman & Hall　1972　　Price **H**

Goodhue, D. *et al.*, *The Study of Life*　Pitman　1972　　Price **F**

Graham, M., *A Natural Ecology*　Manchester U.P.　1973　　Price **E**

Griffin, D. M., *Ecology of Soil Fungi*　Chapman & Hall　1972　　Price **F**

Hall, G., *Ecology: Can We Survive under Capitalism?*　International　1972　　Price **D**

Hazen, W. E., *Readings in Population and Community Ecology*, 2nd edn.　Saunders　1970　　Price **F**

Holdgate, M. W., *Antarctic Ecology* (2 volumes)   Academic Press
    1970   Price (each) **J**
Holdren, J. P. & Ehrlich, P. R. (eds.), *Global Ecology: Readings
    towards a Rational Strategy for Man*   Harcourt Brace   1971
    Price **F**
Holmes, R. L., *Reproduction and Environment* ('Contemporary
    Science Paperbacks' series)   Oliver & Boyd   1968   Price **C**
Howard, J. A., *Aerial Photo-Ecology*   Faber   1971   Price **J**
Huffaker, C. B. (ed.), *Biological Control*   Plenum   1971   Price **J**
Hutchinson, G. E., *The Ecological Theater and the Evolutionary Play*
    Yale U.P.   1966   Price **F**
Hynes, H. B. N., *The Ecology of Running Waters* (A comprehensive
    examination of stream limnology)   Liverpool U.P.   1970
    Price **J**
Jensen, W. A. & Salisbury, F. B., *Botany: An Ecological Approach*
    Prentice-Hall   1972   Price **J**
Kershaw, K. A., *Quantitative and Dynamic Plant Ecology*, 2nd edn.
    Arnold   1973   Price **F/J**
Klopfer, P. H., *Behaviour Aspects of Ecology*   Prentice-Hall   1972
    Price **H**
Koob, D. D. & Buggs, W. E., *The Nature of Life*   Addison-Wesley
    1972   Price **H**
Kormondy, E. J., *Concepts of Ecology* ('Concepts of Modern Biology'
    series)   Prentice-Hall   1969   Price **F**
Krebs, C. J., *Ecology: The Experimental Analysis of Distribution and
    Abundance*   Harper & Row   1973   Price **H**
Lack, D., *Ecological Adaptation for Breeding in Birds*   Chapman &
    Hall   1968   Price **H**
Lack, D., *Ecological Isolation in Birds*   Blackwell Scientific   1971
    Price **H**
Lack, D., *The Natural Regulation of Animal Numbers*   O.U.P.   1970
    Price **E/G**
Laycock, G., *Alien Animals* (The effect of the introduction of an
    alien animal on a habitat)   Pan/Ballantine   1970   Price **C**
Leutscher, A., *Field Natural History: a Guide to Ecology*   Bell   1969
    Price **G**
Leutscher, A., *The Ecology of Water Life*   Franklin Watts   1971
    Price **E**
Lewis, T. & Taylor, L. R., *Introduction to Experimental Ecology*
    Academic Press   1967   Price **F**
Macan, T. T. & Worthington, E. B., *Life in Lakes and Rivers*   Fontana
    1972   Price **D**
Macfadyen, A., *Ecology*   Arnold (in preparation)
McConnaughey, B. H., *Introduction to Marine Biology*   Kimpton
    1970   Price **H**
McHale, J., *The Ecological Context*   Studio Vista   1971   Price **G**
McLean, R. C. & Ivimey Cook, W. R., *Practical Field Ecology*   Allen
    & Unwin   1969   Price **E**

Mills, D. H., *An Introduction to Freshwater Ecology* Oliver & Boyd 1972 Price **D**

Milne, L. & M., *The Arena of Life. The Dynamics of Ecology* Allen & Unwin 1972 Price **J**

Moss, R. P., *Biogeography* Macmillan 1972 Price **E/G**

Nelson, G. E. & Ray, J. D. (eds.), *Biologic Readings for Today's Students* Wiley 1971 Price **E**

Nelson, J. G. & Chambers, M. J. (eds.), *Vegetation, Soils and Wildlife* Methuen 1970 Price **G**

Nelson-Smith, A., *Oil Pollution and Marine Ecology* Elek Science 1972 Price **G**

Nybakken, J. W., *Readings in Marine Ecology* Harper & Row 1971 Price **H**

Odum, E. P., *Fundamentals of Ecology*, 3rd edn. Saunders 1971 Price **J**

Oglesby, R. T. *et al.*, *River Ecology and Man* Academic Press 1972 Price **J**

Opie, J., *Americans and Environment: The Controversy over Ecology* Heath 1972 Price **E**

Perkins, E. J., *The Biology of Estuaries and Coastal Waters* Academic Press 1974 Price **K**

Phillipson, J., *Ecological Energetics* ('Studies in Biology' series) Arnold 1966 Price **D/E**

Pringle, J. W. S. (ed.), *Biology and the Human Sciences* (Herbert Spencer lectures) O.U.P. 1972 Price **E/F**

Ranwell, D. S., *Ecology of Salt Marshes and Sand Dunes* Chapman & Hall 1972 Price **H**

Reid, K., *Nature's Network* ('Interdependence in Nature' series) Aldus Books 1969 Price **E**

Rorison, I. H., *Ecological Aspects of the Mineral Nutrition of Plants* Blackwell Scientific 1969 Price **J**

Rudd, R. L., *Pesticides and the Living Landscape* Faber 1964 Price **F**

Ruttner, F., *Fundamentals of Limnology* O.U.P. 1963 Price **G**

Sadleir, R. M. F. S., *The Ecology of Reproduction in Wild and Domestic Mammals* Methuen 1969 Price **H**

Scientific American, *The Biosphere* Freeman 1970 Price **E/G**

Scientific American, *Ecology, Evolution and Population Biology* Freeman 1974 Price **H**

Seddon, B., *Introduction to Biogeography* Duckworth 1971 Price **E/G**

Smith, J. M., *The Theory of Evolution*, 2nd edn. Penguin 1966 Price **C**

Smith, R. L. (ed.), *The Ecology of Man: An Ecosystem Approach* Harper & Row 1972 Price **G**

Southwick, C. H., *Ecology and the Quality of the Environment* Van Nostrand Reinhold 1972 Price **F**

Southwood, T. R. E., *Ecological Methods* Chapman & Hall 1966 Price **H**

Spedding, C. R. W., *Grassland Ecology*   O.U.P.   1971   Price **F**
Tait, R. V., *Elements of Marine Ecology*   Butterworth   1972
   Price **G**
Thorson, G., *Life in the Sea*   W. U. L.   1972   Price **E/F**
Tortora, G. J. & Becker, J. F., *Life Science*   Collier-Macmillan
   1972   Price **G**
Treshow, M., *Environment and Plant Response*   McGraw-Hill   1970
   Price **J**
Tubbs, C. R., *The New Forest: An Ecological History*   David &
   Charles   1968   Price **E**
Usher, M. B., *Biological Management and Conservation*   Chapman &
   Hall   1973   Price **J**
Van Dyne, G. M., *The Ecosystem Concept in Natural Resource
   Management*   Academic Press   1969   Price **J**
Waller, R. (ed.), *Human Ecology*, 2nd rev. edn.   Knight   1971
   Price **F**
Waller, R. (ed.), *Just Consequences* (Health problems and nutrition)
   Knight   1972   Price **F**
Walters, A. H., *Ecology, Food and Civilization: An Ecological History
   of Human Society*   Knight   1973   Price **F**
Watson, A., *Animal Populations in Relation to their Food Resources:
   10th Symposium of the British Ecological Society*   Blackwell
   Scientific   1970   Price **J**
Watt, K. E., *Ecology and Resource Management: A Quantitative
   Approach*   McGraw-Hill   1967   Price **J**
Weatherley, A. H., *Growth and Ecology of Fish Populations*
   Academic Press   1972   Price **H**
Weiner, J. S. & Lourie, J. A., *Human Biology: A Guide to Field Methods*
   Blackwell Scientific   1969   Price **J**
Weiss, D. E. *et al.*, *Nature in the Balance*   Heinemann   1972
   Price **E**
Whittaker, R. H., *Communities and Ecosystems* ('Current Concepts in
   Biology' series)   Collier-Macmillan   1970   Price **E**
Williamson, M., *The Analysis of Biological Populations*   Arnold
   1972   Price **F/H**
Wood, E. J. F., *Marine Microbial Ecology*   Chapman & Hall   1965
   Price **F**
Wynne-Taylor, J., *The Civilized Alternative: A Pattern for Protest*
   (Ethics of ecology)   Centaur Press   1972   Price **E**
Young, J. Z., *An Introduction to the Study of Man*   O.U.P.   1971
   Price **J**

'The Emergence of Man' series, especially:
   Life Before Man   (1973)
Time-Life   Library   Price **G**

'Life Nature Library' series, especially:
   Ecology (rev. edn., 1971)

The Earth (rev. edn., 1970)
Evolution (rev. edn., 1973)
Animal Behaviour (rev. edn., 1970)
The Desert (rev. edn., 1972)
The Mountains (rev. edn., 1973)
The Poles (rev. edn., 1971)
The Sea (1969)
The Land and Wildlife of Australasia (rev. edn., 1973)
The Land and Wildlife of North America (1971)
The Land and Wildlife of Asia (rev. edn., 1973)
The Land and Wildlife of South America (rev. edn., 1971)
The Land and Wildlife of Tropical Asia (rev. edn., 1972)
The Land and Wildlife of Eurasia (rev. edn., 1973)
    Time-Life   Library   Price (each) **G**

'The World's Wild Places' series, including:
The Amazon (1973)
The Grand Canyon (1973)
    Time-Life   Library   Price (each) **G**

BOOKS (SCHOOL)

Armstrong, P. H., *Discovering Ecology* ('Discovering' series)   Shire
    Publications   1973   Price **C**
Beidleman, R. G., *Dynamic Equilibrium* (Patterns of Life' series)
    Murray   1969   15–18 years   Price **D**
Billings, W. D., *Plants and the Ecosystems*   Macmillan   1965
    11 years +   Price **D**
Billington, E. T., *Understanding Ecology*   Kaye & Ward   1971
    11 years +   Price **D**
Brown, A. L., *Ecology of Fresh Water*   Heinemann   1971
    17 years +   Price **E**
Carter, G. & Cox, R., *How We Behave* ('Social Biology' series)   Ginn
    1975   C.S.E.   Price **E**
Carthy, J. D., *Ecology: The Patterns of Nature*   Collins   9–16 years
    Price **E**
Cloudsley-Thompson, J. L., *Animals of the Desert* ('Natural Science
    Picture Books' series)   Bodley Head   1969   8–12 years
    Price **D**
Cloudsley-Thompson, J. L. & Chadwick, M., *Life in Deserts*   Foulis
    1964   17 years +   Price **G**
Cushing, D. H., *The Productivity of the Sea* ('Oxford Biology Reader'
    series)   O.U.P.   1974   17 years +   Price **B**
Dale, A., *Patterns of Life*   Heinemann   1951   C.S.E./G.C.E.   Price **D**
Darlington, A., *Ecology of Refuse Tips*   Heinemann   1969
    17 years +   Price **E**
De Beer, G., *Adaptation* ('Oxford Biology Reader' series)   O.U.P.
    1972   17 years +   Price **B**

Dowdeswell, W. H., *An Introduction to Animal Ecology*   Methuen
    1966   17 years +   Price **D**
Dowdeswell, W. H., *Practical Animal Ecology*   Methuen   1968
    17 years +   Price **D**
Friederlander, C. P., *Heathland Ecology*   Heinemann   1960
    17 years +   Price **D**
Grant, M. P., *Biology and World Health*, rev. edn.   Abelard-Schuman
    1971   10 years +   Price **E**
King, H. F., *Life Around Us*   Heinemann   1968   C.S.E./G.C.E.
    Price **D**
Knowles, F., *Man and Other Living Things. An Introduction to Human
    Biology*   Harrap   1959   15–18 years   Price **E**
Miles, P. M. & H. B., *Biological Field Studies*
    Seashore Ecology
    Freshwater Ecology
    Town Ecology
    Woodland Ecology
    Chalkland and Moorland Ecology
    Hulton   1967/8   11 years +   Price (each) **D**
Miles, P. M., Miles, H. B. & Graham, V. E., *Tropical Freshwater
    Ecology*   Hulton   1970   11 years +   Price **D**
Neal, E. G., *Woodland Ecology*   Heinemann   1958   17 years +
    Price **D**
Perrott, E., *Biology: An Environmental Approach*
    1. *The World of Life: The Biosphere*   Price **D/E**
    2. *Diversity Among Living Things*   Price **D/E**
    3. *Patterns in the Living World*   Price **D/E**
    4. *Looking into Organisms*   Price **E/F**
    5. *Man and His Environment*   Price **E/F**
    Murray   1972   15 years +
Price, J. T., *The Origin and Evolution of Life*   E.U.P.   1971
    17 years +   Price **E**
Proctor, E., *Looking at Nature*
    1. *Nature Awake and Asleep*
    2. *Nature at Home*
    3. *Working with Nature*
    4. *Looking at Life*
    Black   1961/71   Price (each) **D**
Riley, D., *Natural Regions and their Vegetation* ('Nelson's Geography
    Studies' series)   Nelson   1972   13–18 years   Price **C**
Riley, D. & Young, A., *World Vegetation*   C.U.P.   1966   17 years +
    Price **D**
Robinson, H., *Biogeography*   M. & E.   1972   17 years +
    Price **F**
Sankey, J., *Chalkland Ecology*   Heinemann   1966   17 years +
    Price **E**
Sears, P. B., *Biology of the Living Landscape*   Allen & Unwin   1964
    15 years +   Price **E**

Southward, A. J., *Life on the Sea Shore*   Heinemann   1965
   17 years +   Price **E**
Vevers, G., *Life in the Sea* ('Natural Science Picture Books' series)
   Bodley Head   1963   8–12 years   Price **D**
Watson, G. G., *Fun with Ecology*, rev. edn.   Kaye & Ward   1971
   10–14 years   Price **D**
The Nuffield Junior Science Project
   Teachers' Guide One
   Teachers' Guide Two
   Apparatus
   Animals and Plants
      Collins   1967   Teachers   Price (each) **E**
   Autumn into Winter
   Science and History
   Mammals in Classrooms
      Collins   1965/7   5–13 years   Price (each) **C**
'Studies in Biology' series   Arnold   17 years +   Price (each) **D/E**

FILMS

Above the Timberland (1960) (Alpine tundra)   Canada House
   16 min., col.   Hire free
Adaptation to Environment (1968)   11–15 years
   N.A.V.A.L. (606 D38)   18 min., col.   Hire **F**
Animals of the Rocky Shore   11 years +
   Rank (20.0689)   11 min., b/w.   Hire **D**
Between the Tides (1958)
   British Transport (BT 314)   22 min., col.   Hire **G**
Brownsea – An Island Sanctuary
   S.P.N.R./Dorset Trust   20 min., col.   Hire **G**
Changing Forest, The (1958) (Canada)
   C.F.L. (C 540)   18 min., col.   Hire **E**
Conservation and the Balance of Nature (1966)   13 years +
   N.A.V.A.L. (600 D78)   18 min., col.   Hire **E**
Distribution of Plants and Animals, The (1966)   13 years +
   N.A.V.A.L. (605 D53)   9 min., col.   Hire **E**
Diversity of Living Things
   B.B.C.   20 min., b/w.   Hire **E**
Edge of the Barrens (1964)   (Tundra)   10 years +
   N.A.V.A.L. (606 D34)   13 min., col.   Hire **E**
Estuary, The   11 years +
   Rank (21.7495)   14 min., col.   Hire **G**
Hidden World, The
   F.S.C.   19 min., col.   Hire Free
Interdependence of Pond Life, The (1936)   13 years +
   N.A.V.A.L. (605 A3)   9 min., b/w.   Hire **D**
Life Beside the Sea
   McGraw-Hill (613914)   8 min., b/w.

Life in Parched Lands   12 years +
   McGraw-Hill (657263)   30 min., col.   Hire J
Life in the Desert (1956)   11 years +
   N.A.V.A.L. (605 D31)   10 min., col.   Hire E
Life in the Forest (1956)   11 years +
   N.A.V.A.L. (605 D33)   10 min., col.   Hire E
Life in the Grasslands (1956)   11–15 years
   N.A.V.A.L. (605 D32)   11 min., col.   Hire E
Life in a Woodlot (1960)
   Canada House   16 min., col.   Hire free
Living Environment, The (1964)   13–16 years
   N.A.V.A.L. (605 D42)   8 min., col.   Hire E
Living Pattern, The (1963) (Wildlife in Britain)
   National Benzole   30 min., col.   Hire free
Nature in Trust
   S.P.N.R./Lincs. Trust   35 min., col.   Hire J
Nitrogen Cycle, The   11 years +
   Rank (20.4596)   17 min., b/w.   Hire E
Place for Wildlife, A
   S.P.N.R./Scottish Wildlife Trust   25 min., col.   Hire G
Plants and Animals Living Together (1950)   9–13 years
   N.A.V.A.L. (600 A9)   20 min., b/w.   Hire E
Plant Succession
   McGraw-Hill (653211)   15 min.,b/w.
   McGraw-Hill (65311)   15 min., col.
Price of Life, The
   Rank (21.1284)   11 min., col.   Hire F
Rival World, The (1955) (Insects)
   Shell   26 min., col.   Hire free
River of Life (River Usk)   11 years +
   Rank (71.7339)   35 min., col.   Hire J
Science Extra – Biology (1972)
  A Place to Live (Habitats)
  Living in Rivers
  Life in the Soil
  Living on Others (Parasites)
  Polluted Waters
  Man's Environment
  Servicing the Blood Stream
  To the Limit
  Patterns of Behaviour
  Understanding Behaviour
  Signs and Signals
   B.B.C.   Each 20 min., b/w.   Hire (each) G
Sea, The   11 years +
   N.A.V.A.L. (605 D51)   17 min., col.   Hire F
Seashore, The (1959)   11–16 years
   N.A.V.A.L. (605 D38)   20 min., col.   Hire F

Seashore Ecology (1965)   9—15 years
   N.A.V.A.L. (605 D45)   16 min., col.   Hire F
Spruce Bog, The — An Essay in Ecology
   C.F.L.   22 min., col.   Hire E
Survival in the Sea   12 years +
   McGraw-Hill (657265)   30 min., col.   Hire J
Threat in the Water, The (1968) (Bilharzia)
   Shell   30 min., col.   Hire free
Today and Tomorrow
   S.P.N.R./Gloucs. Trust   30 min., col.   Hire G
Tree, The (1964)   8—11 years
   N.A.V.A.L. (600 D12)   10 min., col.   Hire E
Wealth of the Chalk, The
   S.P.N.R./Wilts. Trust   35 min., col.   Hire G
Wild Highlands (1961)
   British Transport (BT. 409)   21 min., col.   Hire G
Wildlife in Trust
   S.P.N.R./B.B.O.N.T.   20 min., col.   Hire F
Wood, The
   B.B.C.   50 min., b/w.   Hire J
Woodland Ecology (1965)   14—17 years
   1. *The Flora*   14 min., col.
   2. *The Fauna*   19 min., col.
   N.A.V.A.L. (605 D43/4)   Hire (each) F
World in a Marsh
   Guild   22 min., col.   Hire F

FILMSTRIPS/SLIDES/FILMLOOPS/TRANSPARENCIES
Beginnings of Life
   Visual Information (141)   35 f.   Price D
Biology: an Environmental Approach
   Social Behaviour in Chickens
   Mimicry
   The Peppered Moth and Population Study
   Behaviour of Purple Bacterium
   Planarium Behaviour
   Imprinting
   Regeneration in Acetabularia
   Chemical Communication
   Mating Behaviour in the Cockroach
   Murray   Filmloops   Price (each) J
Change of Habitat, A
   Slide Centre (S764)   12 slides, col.   Price E
Earth Without Man, The
   GC 101 *Equatorial Lands*
   GC 102 *Hot Grasslands — I*
   GC 103 *Hot Grasslands — II*

GC 104 *Hot Deserts*
GC 105 *Mediterranean Lands*
GC 106 *Cold Lands – I*
GC 107 *Cold Lands – II*
GC 108 *Monsoon Lands*
  Visual Publications   d/f. or s/f., col.   Price (each) **F**
Ecology
  Milliken   12 transp./4 masters   Price **G**
Ecology and Man – Set 1
  Introduction to Ecology
  Changes in Eco-Systems
  Energy in Relationships
  Habitats and Niches
  Populations and Biomass
  Adaptations to Environment
  McGraw-Hill (613375)   6 X c.45 f.   Price (each) **G**
Ecology and Man – Set 2
  The Forest Biome – I
  The Forest Biome – II
  The Grassland Biome
  The Desert Biome
  Freshwater Ecology
  Seacoast Ecology
  McGraw-Hill (613382)   6 X c.45 f.   Price (each) **G**
Ecology and Man – Set 3
  Man-Managed Ecosystems
  The Management of Water
  The Management of Soil
  The Ecology of Farming
  Competitive Land Use
  Human Ecology
  McGraw-Hill (613390)   6 X c.45 f.   Price (each) **G**
Ecology Series
  Physical Environment
  The Field as a Community
  The Pond as a Community
  The Forest as a Community
  The City as a Community
  Ecological Succession
  McGraw-Hill (633510)   6 X c.45 f.   Price (each) **F**
Elementary Biology for Schools (Series of 14 filmstrips)
  Visual Information (401–425)   Price (each) **D**
Forest Community Series, The
  Building the Soil
  Where Tress Grow
  How Trees Grow
  Forests for the Future
  Forest Plant and Animal Relationships

Enemies of the Forest
   McGraw-Hill (694710)   6 X c.52 f.   Price (each) **G**
Freshwater Life (1965)   10–16 years
   FL 1 *Living in Freshwater*
   FL 2 *Life in a Pond*
   FL 3 *Life in a River and Stream*
   FL 4 *Life in a Canal*
   Visual Publications   s/f., col.   Price (each) **E**
How Plants Breed
   Visual Information (140)   46 f., b/w.   Price **D**
How Plants Feed
   Visual Information (147)   66 f., b/w.   Price **D**
Interdependence of Living Things
   Introduction to Ecology
   The Web of Life
   Animal and Plant Communities: Forest
   Animal and Plant Communities: Field
   Animal and Plant Communities: Pond
   Animal and Plant Communities: City
   McGraw-Hill (405590)   6 X c.40 f.   Price (each) **F**
Know the Land (1962)   11–15 years
   KL 1 *The Soil and the Plant*   KL 8 *Wet Places*
   KL 2 *The Climate and the Plant*   KL 9 *Heaths and Bogs*
   KL 3 *Plant Anatomy*   KL 10 *Chalk Hills*
   KL 4 *Plants and their Habitats*   KL 11 *Woods*
   KL 5 *Fields*   KL 12 *Moors and Mountains*
   KL 6 *Hedges*   KL 13 *Sea Coast*
   KL 7 *Dry Places*   KL 14 *Field Work*
   Visual Publications   s/f., col.   Price (each) **E**
Life in a Hedgerow
   C.G.   37 f., b/w.   Price **E**
Life in a Stream
   C.G.   40 f., b/w.   Price **E**
Life in a Pond   9–15 years
   Visual Information (538)   58 f., b/w.   Price **D**
Life in Ponds
   Marian Ray   f/s., col.   Price **F**
Life on the Seashore
   C.G.   35 f., b/w.   Price **E**
Life on the Seashore (1966)   9 years +
   E.P.   35 f., col.   Price **E**
Living Things through the Ages   8 years +
   11161/11191 *How Plants and Animals have Changed*
   11162/11192 *Age of the Earth and of Living Things*
   11163/11193 *How Living Things are Adapted*
   11164/11194 *How Adaptation helps Living Things Survive*
   Encyclopaedia Britannica   4 X c.48 f., col.
   Price (each) **F**

Mutual Aid and Communal Life
   Visual Information   30 f., b/w.   Price **D**
Natural Regions of the World
   Visual Information (533)   82 f., b/w.   Price **E**
Nature Reserves in Miniature (1972)
   Ecology of a Sand-dune
   Ecology of a Bramble Bush
   Ecology of a School Garden
   E.P.   f/s., col.   Price (each) **F**
Plant and Animal Ecology
   Visual Information (408)   66 f., b/w.   Price **D**
Plant and Animal Relationships   8 years +
   10791 *The Grassland: Story of the Major Community*
   10792 *The Swamp: Some Relationships between Organisms*
   10793 *The Desert: An Example of Adaptation*
   10794 *The Seashore: A Continuously Changing Environment*
   10795 *The Pond: How Living Things change their Environment*
   10796 *The Forest: A Stable Community*
   Encyclopaedia Britannica   6 X c.45 f., col.   Price (each) **F**
Plants and the Earth   8 years +
   Visual Information   42 f., b/w.   Price **D**
Principles of Biology – Set 1
   1. *Energy and Life*
   2. *Fundamental Life Processes*
   3. *Interdependence of Living Things*
   4. *Structure of Living Things – I*
   5. *Structure of Living Things – II*
   6. *Behaviour of Living Things*
   McGraw-Hill (401867)   6 X c.40 f.   Price (each) **E**
Principles of Biology – Set 2
   7. *Effects of Environment*
   8. *Heredity and Environment*
   9. *Factors in Survival*
   10. *Factors in Health and Disease*
   11. *Origins of Living Things*
   12. *Descent with Change*
   McGraw-Hill (401874)   6 X c.40 f.   Price (each) **E**
Terrestrial Food Chain
   Macmillan (SB/K/7)   Filmloop   Price **H**

WALLCHARTS/POSTERS

Adel Beck (Ecological study of a Yorkshire valley)
   P.C.E.T.   5 charts   Price **D**
Cellograph Nature Wall Pictures   Primary
   Philip & Tacey
   12 pictures/display board   Price **J**
   Accessories   Price **H**

Cross-Section Through Plant Communities
    E.P.   Secondary   Price D/E/F
Food Cycle, The
    P.C.E.T.   Secondary   Price D
Life on the Seashore
    P.C.E.T.   All ages   Price D
Natural Environment, The
    P.C.E.T.   Price D
Photosynthesis
    P.C.E.T.   15–18 years   Price D

GAMES/KITS/WORKCARDS

Conservation (Social Education Kit; includes worksheets, information sheets; filmstrips)
    Macmillan   14–15 years   Price K
Countryside, The (A.C.E. study kit)
    E.S.A.   Price E
Extinction: The Game of Ecology (Educational board game)
    Freeman   Price J
Nature in Your Town (Includes wallcharts, books)
    Humane Education Centre   10–13 years   Price D
Science – Ecology
    Milliken (4C 912)   12 transp./4 masters   Price G
Stillitron Science and Technology Unit, The (Programmed Learning System)
    Stillitron   Price K
Survival (How the balance of nature is threatened by man)
    Galt   8 years +   Price E

ORGANIZATIONS

British Ecological Society
British Naturalists' Association
Campaign for Biological Sanity
Council for Nature
Institute of Biology
Landscape Research Group
Marine Biological Association of the U.K.
School Natural Science Society
Society for the Promotion of Nature Reserves (S.P.N.R.)

JOURNALS/PERIODICALS

Biologist
Conservation Review
Ecologist
Freshwater Biology

Journal of Animal Ecology
Journal of Applied Ecology
Journal of Ecology
Nature

ARTICLES

Robertson, J. C., 'Man's Place in the Ecological Pattern'   *Geographical
Magazine*   January 1970
Cole, M., 'Plants, Animals and Environment'   *Geographical Magazine*
January 1972
Howe, G. M., 'Environment for Disease'   *Geographical Magazine*
August 1972
Teather, E. K., 'The Hedgerow: An Analysis of a Changing Landscape
Feature'   *Geography*   April 1970
Anderson, P., 'Planning a Wood'   *Ecologist*   October 1973

3   NATURAL HISTORY

See also Sections 2 Ecology (*page* 15) and 25 Conservation (*page* 145)

BOOKS (GENERAL)

Agricultural Research Council, *The Effects of Air Pollution on Plants and Soils*   H.M.S.O.   1967   Price **C**

Ary, S. & Gregory, M., *The Oxford Book of Wild Flowers*   O.U.P. 1960/70   Price **E/F**

Baker, J. (ed.), *The Shell Treasury of the Countryside*   Dent   1965   Price **C**

B. B., *The Pegasus Book of the Countryside*   Dobson   1964   Price **E**

Brierley, J. K., *A Natural History of Man*   Heinemann   1970   Price **E**

Bucksbaum, R., *Animals without Backbones* (2 volumes)   Penguin 1951   Price (each) **B**

Burton, M., *The Shell Natural History of Britain*   Joseph   1970   Price **F**

Burton, M., *Wild Animals of the British Isles*   Warne   1968   Price **F**

Bustard, R., *Sea Turtles*   Collins   1973   Price **G**

Campbell, W. D., *Birds of Town and Village* (in Britain)   Hamlyn 1968   Price **G**

Christian, R., *The Nature Lover's Companion*   Methuen   1972   Price **G**

Courtney, B. & Zimmerman, J. H., *Wildflowers and Weeds. A Guide in Full Colour*   Van Nostrand Reinhold   1972   Price **G**

Darling, F. F. & Boyd, J. M., *The Highlands and Islands* ('New Naturalist' series)   Collins   1969   Price **E**

Dasmann, R. F., *Wildlife Biology*   Wiley   1964   Price **G**

Dickens, M. & Storey, E., *The World of Butterflies*   Osprey   1974   Price **E**

Dickens, M. & Storey, E., *The World of Moths*   Osprey   1972   Price **F**

Ettlinger, D. M. T., *Natural History Photography*   Academic Press 1974   Price **K**

Eyre, S. R., *Vegetation and Soils – A World Picture*   Arnold   1968   Price **F**

Eyre, S. R., *World Vegetation Types*   Macmillan   1971   Price **E/G**

Finch, I., *Town and Country*
   Autumn Trees
   Pond Animals
      Longman   1969   Price (each) **D**

Fisher, J., *Shell Nature Lover's Atlas of England, Scotland and Wales*   Ebury Press/Joseph   1966   Price **C**

Fisher, J., *The Shell Bird Book* (Includes details of bird reserves)
Joseph   1966   Price E
Fisher, J., Simon, N. & Vincent, J., *The Red Book: Wildlife in Danger*
Collins   1969   Price H
Fitter, R., *Vanishing Wild Animals of the World* (World Wildlife Fund)
Kaye & Ward   1968   Price E
Fitter, R., *Wildlife in Britain*   Penguin   1963   Price C
Fleure, H. J. & Davies, M., *A Natural History of Man in Britain* ('New
Naturalist' series), new edn.   Collins/Fontana   1971
Price D/G
Fogg, G. E., *The Growth of Plants*   Penguin   1970   Price C
Gilmore, J. & Walters, M., *Wild Flowers: Botanizing in Britain* ('New
Naturalist' series)   Collins   1969   Price F
Grigson, G. & Fisher, J., *The Shell Nature Book* (includes 60 colour
plates)   Dent   1964   Price F
Guggisberg, C. A. W., *Man and Wildlife*   Evans   1971   Price G
Heinzel, H. *et al.*, *The Birds of Britain and Europe*   Collins   1972
Price E
Hickin, N. E., *The Natural History of an English Forest*   Hutchinson
1971   Price E/G
Hyams, E., *Animals in the Service of Man: 10,000 Years of Domestica-
tion*   Dent   1972   Price F
Hyams, E., *Plants in the Service of Man: 10,000 Years of Domestication*
Dent   1971   Price F
Jackman, L., *The Field: Its Wildlife and Plants throughout the Year*
Evans   1972   Price F
Jackson, D. F. (ed.), *Algae and Man*   Plenum   1964   Price J
Keighley, G., *The Pegasus Book of Trees*   Dobson   1971   Price E
Lawson, G. W., *Plant Life in West Africa*   O.U.P.   1966   Price E
Lucas, J., *A Source Book of Wild Animals*   Ward Lock   1971
Price D
Matthews, H. L., *British Mammals* ('New Naturalist' series)   Collins
1968   Price E
Mowat, F., *Never Cry Wolf*   Pan/Ballantine   1971   Price C
Muus, B. J. & Dahlstrom, P., *Collins Guide to the Freshwater Fishes of
Britain and Europe*   Collins   1972   Price F
Page, F. J. T. (ed.), *Field Guide to British Deer,* 2nd edn.   Blackwell
Scientific   1971   Price E
Perry, G. A., *Plant Life*   Blandford Press   1965   Price D
H.R.H. The Prince Philip, Duke of Edinburgh & Fisher, J., *Wildlife
Crisis*   Hamilton   1970   Price H
Polunin, O., *Flowers of Europe: A Field Guide*   O.U.P.   1969
Price J
Reade, W. & Stuttard, R. M. (eds.), *A Handbook for Naturalists*
Evans   1968   Price E
Reay, R. C., *Insects and Insecticides* ('Contemporary Science Paperbacks'
series)   Oliver & Boyd   1969   Price C
Sage, B. L., *Alaska and its Wildlife*   Hamlyn   1973   Price F

Schomberg, G., *The Penguin Guide to British Zoos*   Penguin   1970
     Price **C**
Scott, N., *The Pegasus Book of Ponds and Streams*   Dobson   1969
     Price **E**
Scott, N., *The Pegasus Book of the Sea*   Dobson   1965   Price **E**
Snow, D. W., *The Status of Birds in Britain and Ireland*   Blackwell
     Scientific   1971   Price **G**
Southwood, T. R. E., *Life of the Wayside and Woodland*, rev. edn.
     Warne   1963   Price **E**
Steers, J. A., *The Sea Coast* ('New Naturalist' series)   Collins   1969
     Price **E**
Stonehouse, B., *Animals of the Arctic*   Ward Lock   1971
     Price **F**
Tansley, A. G., *Britain's Green Mantle: Past, Present and Future*, 2nd
     edn.   Allen & Unwin   1968   Price **G**
Vesey-Fitzgerald, B., *The Vanishing Wildlife of Britain*   MacGibbon
     & Kee   1969   Price **E**

Book of the British Countryside (Alphabetical guide)   A.A./Drive
     Publications   1973   Price **J**
East African Mammals. An Atlas of Evolution in Africa
     Academic Press
     Volume I   1971   Price **K**
     Volume II (part A)   1974   Price **K**
     Volume II (part B)   1974   Price **K**
'Fontana New Naturalist' series   Collins/Fontana   Price (each) **D**
'Life Nature Library' series, especially:
     The Fishes (rev. edn., 1973)
     The Plants (rev. edn., 1971)
     The Insects (rev. edn., 1971)
     The Birds (1971)
     The Reptiles (rev. edn., 1971)
     The Mammals (rev. edn., 1973)
     The Primates (rev. edn., 1972)
     Animal Behaviour (rev. edn., 1970)
     The Desert (rev. edn., 1972)
     The Mountains (rev. edn., 1973)
     The Poles (rev. edn., 1971)
     The Sea (1969)
     The Land and Wildlife of Australasia (rev. edn., 1973)
     The Land and Wildlife of North America (1971)
     The Land and Wildlife of Asia (rev. edn., 1973)
     The Land and Wildlife of South America (rev. edn., 1971)
     The Land and Wildlife of Tropical Asia (rev. edn., 1972)
     The Land and Wildlife of Eurasia (rev. edn., 1973)
     Time-Life   Library   Price (each) **G**
'Natural History' series   Blandford Press   Price **D–F**
'New Naturalist Library' series   Collins   Price **D–G**

32

BOOKS (SCHOOL)

Allen, G. & Denslow, J., *Freshwater Animals*   O.U.P.   1971
   7—12 years   Price **D**
Bracegirdle, C., *Zoos are News* (Origin, purpose and work of zoos,
   including conservation and ecology)   Abelard-Schuman   1972
   10 years +   Price **E**
Bulla, C. R., *A Tree is a Plant*   Black   1962   7—9 years   Price **D**
Burton, M., *Animals of Australia*   Abelard-Schuman   1969
   10 years +   Price **E**
Burton, M., *Animals* (Adaptation of animals to their environment)
   O.U.P.   1966   Price **E**
Burton, M., *More Animals*   O.U.P.   1968   Price **E**
Burton, R., *Animals of the Antarctic*   Abelard-Schuman   1970
   10 years +   Price **E**
Cansdale, G., *British Wild Animals* ('Ladybird Nature' series)   Wills
   & Hepworth   1958   7—9 years   Price **B**
Jenkins, A. C., *Wild Life in Danger* ('The World we are Making' series)
   Methuen   1970   14 years +   Price **E**
Lauber, P., *The Look-it-up Book of Mammals*   Collins   8 years +
   Price **E**
Leigh-Pemberton, J., 'Ladybird Nature' series
   Garden Birds
   Sea and Estuary Birds
   Heath and Woodland Birds
   Pond and River Birds
   Birds of Prey
   Wills & Hepworth   1967/70   7—10 years   Price (each) **B**
Leigh-Pemberton, J., *Disappearing Mammals* ('Ladybird Conservation'
   series)   Wills & Hepworth   1973   7—10 years   Price **B**
Littlewood, C. & Ovender, D. W., *The World's Vanishing Animals*
   Foulsham   1969   11 years +   Price **D**
Matschat, C. H., *Animals of the Valley of the Amazon*   Abelard-
   Schuman   1966   10 years +   Price **E**
Matthews, H. L., *The Whale*   Allen & Unwin   1969   14 years + Price **J**
May, C. P., *Animals of the Far North*   Abelard-Schuman   1965
   10 years +   Price **E**
Mellanby, J., *Wildlife in Danger* ('Project Earth' series)   Wayland
   1974   13—16 years   Price **F**
Moses, H. G., *Animals of Many Lands*
   1. *Golden Eagle of Scotland*
   2. *The River Horse of Africa*
   3. *The Worker Elephant of India*
   4. *The Kangaroos of Australia*
   5. *Lions of the Grasslands*
   6. *Camels of the Desert Lands*
   7. *Reindeer of the North*
   8. *Bears of the Forest*
   Chapman   1969   7—9 years   Price (each) **B**

Osmond, E., *Animals of Central Asia*   Abelard-Schuman   1968
    10 years +   Price E
Prescott, B., *Who Lives in Your Garden?*   Faber   1971   8–10 years
    Price E
Riedman, S. R., *World Provider: The Story of Grass*   Abelard-
    Schuman   1961   10 years +   Price E
Royston, O., *Living Creatures of an English Home*   Routledge   1971
    11 years +   Price E
Scott, N., *Pond Life* ('Ladybird Nature' series)   Wills & Hepworth
    1966   7–9 years   Price B
Selsam, M. E., *Animals as Parents*   World's Work   1970   11 years +
    Price E
Selsam, M. E., *How Animals Live Together*   World's Work   1970
    11 years +   Price E
Selsam, M. E., *The Courtship of Animals*   World's Work   1970
    11 years +   Price E
Selsam, M. E., *The Language of Animals*   World's Work   1970
    11 years +   Price E
Shepherd, W., *Let's Look at Trees* ('Let's Look At. . .' series)   Muller
    1964   8–12 years   Price D
Silvérstein, A. & V., *A World in a Drop of Water*   Blackie   1970
    9 years +   Price D
Silverstein, A. & V., *Rats and Mice*   Blackie   1971   10–12 years
    Price E
Smith, G. A., *Woodland Animals*   Abelard-Schuman   1971
    10 years +   Price E
Snow, D. W., *A Study of Blackbirds*   Allen & Unwin   1958
    13 years +   Price E
Tinbergen, N., *Curious Naturalists*, rev. edn. ('Extensions' series)
    Penguin   1974   Secondary   Price D
Van Gelder, R. G., *The Biology of Mammals*   Allen & Unwin   1971
    14 years +   Price E/F
Vesey-Fitzgerald, B., *British Wild Flowers* ('Ladybird Nature' series)
    Wills & Hepworth   1957   7–9 years   Price B
Wilson, R. W., *Investigating Living Things*   Macmillan   1970
    11–15 years   Price D

'Animal Life Series'
    1. *Desert Animals*   3. *Animals at War*
    2. *Mountain Animals*   4. *Animals at Peace*
    Macdonald   1971   11 years +   Price (each) D
'Black's Picture Information Books'
    1. *Insects*   5. *Conservation*
    2. *Pond and Marsh*   6. *Flowers and their Visitors*
    3. *Seashore*   7. *Fungi*
    4. *Trees*   8. *Pests in the House*
    Black   1972/3   8–13 years   Price (each) D

'Collins Ecology' series
    Collins   9–16 years   Price (each) **E**
'Ladybird Natural History Books'
  Plants and How they Grow
  Animals and How they Live
  Birds and How they Live
    Wills & Hepworth   7–9 years   Price (each) **B**
'Macdonald Starters' series
  Bees   *Fish*
  Birds   *Snakes*
    Macdonald   6–8 years   Price (each) **C**
'National Trust Children's Series'
  All about Squirrels and Moles and Things
  All about Creatures on Islands and Things
  All about Pines and Oaks and Things
  All about Snails and Ladybirds and Things
    Dinosaur Publications   1972   Price (each) **B**
'The Observer's Pocket Series'   Warne   Price (each) **D**
'Read and Discover' series
  Birds in the Garden
  Insect Ways on Summer Days
  Furry Creatures of the Countryside
  Finding Wild Flowers
  Pond Life
    Hulton   7–9 years   Price (each) **C**
'Sterling Nature Series'
  A Fruit is Born
  A Bird is Born
  A Butterfly is Born
  A Tree is Born
    Sterling   1971   11–13 years   Price (each) **E**
'Wayside and Woodland' series   Warne   Price (each) **E/F**
'Young Naturalist' series
    Black   11 years +   Price (each) **D**
'The Young Specialist' series

1. *Dogs*	9. *Butterflies and Moths*
2. *Horses*	10. *Animals: Mammals*
3. *Birds*	11. *Molluscs*
4. *Weather*	12. *Reptiles*
5. *Trees and Shrubs*	13. *Reptiles*
6. *Pond Life*	14. *Cacti and Indoor Plants*
7. *Wildflowers*	15. *Marine Life*
8. *Seashore*	16. *Fungi*

    Burke Publishing   11 years +   Price (each) **D**

FILMS

Adventure has Wings (Bird-watching for young people)
    R.S.P.B.   18 min., col.   Hire **J**

Age of the Buffalo (Canada)   11 years +
    Rank (71.7871)   14 min., col.   Hire F
Amoeba, The   13 years +
    Rank (20.0561)   8 min., b/w.   Hire D
Avocets Return (Suffolk and Cornwall)
    R.S.P.B.   21 min., col.   Hire J
Awakening, The (Brown bears in Eastern Europe)   9 years +
    Rank (21.7755)   18 min., col.   Hire F
Badgers and their Cubs
    R.S.P.C.A.   13 min., col.   Hire free
Beneath the Seven Seas   11 years +
    Rank (70.3798)   35 min., b/w.   Hire G
Bird Neighbours
    R.S.P.B.   30 min., col.   Hire J
Birds of a Hampshire Garden
    R.S.P.B.   29 min., col.   Hire J
Birds of Teesmouth
    R.S.P.B.   38 min., col.   Hire J
Bird Sanctuary   9 years +
    Rank (20.0643)   18 min., b/w.   Hire E
Broadland Summer
    R.S.P.B.   30 min., col.   Hire J
Broadland Winter
    R.S.P.B.   36 min., col.   Hire J
Earthworm, The   13 years +
    Rank (20.0622)   17 min., b/w.   Hire E
Eye for the Country, An (Changing countryside in Lincolnshire)
    Lincs. Trust for Nature Conservation   Hire H
Discovering Dragonflies   9 years +
    Rank (21.7757)   9 min., col.   Hire F
Fasciola: the Liverfluke   13 years +
    Rank (20.0698)   19 min., b/w.   Hire E
Fox, The   9 years +
    Rank (21.7657)   11 min., col.   Hire F
Help Me (Saving birds after the Torrey Canyon)
    R.S.P.C.A.   10 min., col.   Hire free
High Life of the Rook
    R.S.P.B.   19 min., col.   Hire J
Hydra   13 years +
    Rank (20.0651)   19 min., b/w.   Hire E
Into your Hands (Wildlife and conservation in Australia)
    Concord   12 min., col.   Hire H
Introduction to the Frog   13 years +
    Rank (20.1000)   21 min., b/w.   Hire E
Living Pattern, The (1963) (Wildlife in Britain)
    National Benzole   30 min., col.   Hire free
Lonely Level, The (Ouse Washes)
    R.S.P.B.   38 min., col.   Hire J

Looking at Animals ('Science all Around' series)   9–11 years
    B.B.C.   20 min., b/w.   Hire **G**
Lune Valley
    R.S.P.B.   21 min., col.   Hire **H**
Monuments in Mangroves (Bird life off the coast of Florida)
    Rank (71.7864)   28 min., col.   Hire **F**
Octopus, The   9 years +
    Rank (21.7756)   14 min., col.   Hire **F**
Oliver Kite's Fawley (1968)
    C.F.L. (UK 2651)   23 min., col.   Hire free
    Esso   Hire free
Operation Osprey (Scotland)
    R.S.P.B.   14 min., col.   Hire **F**
Paramecium   13 years +
    Rank (20.0725)   15 min., b/w.   Hire **E**
Plants and Animals   7 years +
    Rank (21.7606)   9 min., col.   Hire **F**
Problems of Conservation – Wildlife
    N.A.V.A.L.   13 min., col.   Hire **E**
Ripples in the Reeds (Leighton Moss reserve)
    R.S.P.B.   13 min., col.   Hire **H**
Seal Sanctuary (Farne Islands)
    Rank   25 min., col.   Hire **H**
Secret World, The (Wildlife in London)
    Rank   28 min., col.   Hire **G**
Temples of Time (1971) (Wildlife in the Central Rockies)
    Canada House.   42 min., col.   Hire free
This Year, Next Year (English seasons)
    Rank   28 min., col.   Hire **H**
Tree is a Living Thing, A   Primary
    Guild   11 min., col.   Hire **F**
Trees in Britain (Life cycle of trees and life in trees)
    Guild (233 1956–5)   9 min., col.   Hire free
Weasel, The   9 years +
    Rank (21.7607)   12 min., col.   Hire **F**
Wildlife in the Rocky Mountains (1957)
    Canada House   14 min., col.   Hire free
Wild Wings (1965) (Slimbridge)
    British Transport (BT.628)   34 min., col.   Hire **G**
Winter Quarters (Norfolk Broads)
    Rank   23 min., col.   Hire **H**
World in a Marsh   11 years +
    Rank (71.7124)   18 min., col.   Hire **F**

FILMSTRIPS/SLIDES/FILMLOOPS/TRANSPARENCIES

Anatomy of the Flowering Plant, The
    E.P. (C 6429)   d/f., col.   Price **F**

Animals and Birds of the World
    268 *Part I*   269 *Part II*
    Hulton   f/s., col.   Price (each) F
Animals of Home and Farm
    E.P. (126)   f/s., b/w.   Price E
Animals of the Zoo
    E.P. (FC 0114)   f/s., col.   Price E
Ants
    Hulton (156)   f/s., b/w.   Price E
Arrangement of Floral Parts
    E.P. (C 6313)   f/s., col.   Price E
Basic Wildlife Slidefolios (Series of 36 folios)
    Slide Centre   8 slide folios   Price E each
Beetles
    E.P. (5118)   f/s., b/w.   Price E
Bird Gardens (Includes tape recording)
    R.S.P.C.A. (ST 2)   37 slides, col.   Hire free
Birds of Woodland and Coppice
    E.P. (C 6593)   f/s., col.   Price E
British Freshwater Fish
    E.P. (C 6542)   f/s., col.   Price E
British Fungi
    199 *Part I*   277 *Part II*
    Hulton   f/s., b/w.   Price (each) E
British Reptiles and Amphibians
    E.P. (C 6262)   f/s., col.   Price E
British Sea Birds (Series of 4 folios)
    Slide Centre   12 slide folios   Price (each) E
British Wild Orchids
    E.P. (C 6698)   f/s., col.   Price E
Bumble-Bee, The
    E.P. (FC 3004)   f/s., col.   Price E
Butterflies
    Hulton (15)   f/s., b/w.   Price E
Cat, The
    E.P. (128)   f/s., b/w.   Price E
Chick Embryology
    E.P. (C 6054)   f/s., col.   Price E
Classification of Plants
    Hulton (347)   f/s., b/w.   Price E
Climbing Plants
    E.P. (C 6178)   f/s., col.   Price E
Common Fungi
    E.P. (C 6175)   f/s., col.   Price E
Common Moulds
    E.P. (C 6525)   d/f., col.   Price E
Common Trees
    Visual Information (19)   51 f.   Price E

Common Wildflowers
    E.P. (C 6530)   f/s., col.   Price E
Conifer Trees
    Hulton (321)   f/s., b/w.   Price E
Coniferous Trees
    E.P. (C 6299)   f/s., col.   Price E
Cow, The
    E.P. (C 6510)   f/s., col.   Price E
Creatures of the Rocky Shore (Includes tape recording)
    R.S.P.C.A. (ST 4)   28 slides, col.   Hire free
Development of the Frog and Trout
    E.P. (C 6301)   d/f., col.   Price F
Discovering the Seashore
    Hulton (458)   f/s., col.   Price F
Dispersal of Fruit and Seed
    E.P. (C 6309)   d/f., col.   Price F
Dissection of the Frog
    Hulton (306)   f/s., b/w.   Price E
Domestic Animals
    E.P. (FC 0094)   f/s., col.   Price E
Edge of the Sea
    British Transport   47 f., col.   Hire free
Evolution of Social Life among Insects, The
    E.P. (C 6734)   f/s., col.   Price E
Families of Flowering Plants
    E.P. (C 6747)   f/s., col.   Price E
Farmyard Animals
    E.P. (C 6251)   f/s., col.   Price E
Ferns
    Hulton (121)   f/s., b/w.   Price E
Flowering Trees
    E.P. (C 6108)   f/s., col.   Price E
Flowers of Hedgerows and Clearings
    E.P. (C 6110)   f/s., col.   Price E
Flowers of Marsh and Pool
    E.P. (C 6403)   f/s., col.   Price E
Flowers of Meadow and Pasture
    E.P. (C 6260)   f/s., col.   Price E
Flowers of Moorland and Bog
    E.P. (C 6375)   f/s., col.   Price E
Flowers of the Coast
    E.P. (C 6506)   f/s., col.   Price E
Food Storage in Plants
    Hulton (346)   f/s., b/w.   Price E
Freshwater Fish
    Hulton (136)   f/s., b/w.   Price E
Furry Creatures of the Countryside
    14 *Part I*   63 *Part II*   64 *Part III*
    Hulton   f/s., b/w.   Price (each) E

Garden and Hedgerow Birds
  E.P. (5144)　　　f/s., b/w.　　　Price E
Grasses
  E.P. (C 6332)　　　f/s., col.　　　Price E
Growth and Structure of Wood, The
  E.P. (4706)　　　f/s., b/w.　　　Price E
Hawk Moths
  Hulton (359)　　　f/s., col.　　　Price F
Hedgerow, The
  E.P. (C 6348)　　　f/s., col.　　　Price E
Honey Bee, The
  E.P. (FC 3003)　　　f/s., col.　　　Price E
Horse, The
  E.P. (FC 0095)　　　f/s., col.　　　Price E
How Insects Fly
  E.P. (5162)　　　f/s., b/w.　　　Price E
How Plants make Food and Respire
  E.P. (C 6439)　　　f/s., col.　　　Price E
How to Watch Birds
  E.P. (4859)　　　f/s., b/w.　　　Price E
Insect Life
  E.P. (C 6076)　　　f/s., col.　　　Price E
Insects in the Garden
  E.P. (5260)　　　f/s., b/w.　　　Price E
Insects of Ponds and Streams
  E.P. (5178)　　　f/s., b/w.　　　Price E
Learning for Living　　　7–11 years
  1. *Flowers*　　　　　4. *Summer*
  2. *Our Animal Friends*　　5. *Autumn*
  3. *Spring*　　　　　6. *Winter*
  Rank　　c. 24 f., col.　　Price (each) F
Life Cycle of a Conker
  Hulton (17)　　　f/s., b/w.　　　Price E
Life Cycle of some Common Butterflies, The
  E.P. (C 6418)　　　f/s., col.　　　Price E
Life Cycle of the Flowering Plant
  E.P. (C 6486)　　　f/s., col.　　　Price E
Life Cycle of the Frog
  Hulton (16)　　　f/s., b/w.　　　Price E
Life History of the Fern
  E.P. (C 6308)　　　d/f., col.　　　Price F
Life History of the Liverwort and the Moss
  E.P. (C 6300)　　　d/f., col.　　　Price F
Life History of the Pine
  E.P. (C 6307)　　　d/f., col.　　　Price F
Life of a Robin
  Hulton (304)　　　f/s., b/w.　　　Price E
Life on the Seashore
  E.P. (C 6135)　　　f/s., col.　　　Price E

Locust, The
    E.P. (C 6736)   f/s., col.   Price **E**
Mammals of the British Isles
    E.P. (C 6402)   f/s., col.   Price **E**
Mammals of the Hedgerow (Includes tape recording)
    R.S.P.C.A. (ST 5)   26 slides, col.   Hire free
Microscopic Structure of Tissues (Rat and rabbit)
    Hulton (315)   f/s., b/w.   Price **E**
Morphology of the Leaf, The
    E.P. (C 6314)   d/f., col.   Price **F**
Naturalist in London's Country, The (1958)
    British Transport (BT. 542)   65 f., col.   Hire free
Nature During the Four Seasons (Series of 7 folios)
    Slide Centre   12 slide folios   Price (each) **E**
Nature in Spring
    E.P. (C 6180)   f/s., col.   Price **E**
Nature in Summer
    E.P. (C 6245)   f/s., col.   Price **E**
Nature in Autumn
    E.P. (C 6246)   f/s., col.   Price **E**
Nature in Winter
    E.P. (C 6247)   f/s., col.   Price **E**
Nests and Eggs of British Birds
    Slide Centre (S768)   24 slides, col.   Price **F**
Nests and Eggs of British Birds
    E.P. (C 6585)   f/s., col.   Price **E**
Our Birds
    E.P. (C 6055)   f/s., col.   Price **E**
Plants and their Foods
    E.P. (5064)   f/s., b/w.   Price **E**
Plant Families (Series of 14 folios)
    Slide Centre   12 slide folios   Price (each) **E**
Plant World
    405 *Part I*   406 *Part II*
    Hulton   f/s., col.   Price (each) **F**
Pollination
    Hulton (320)   f/s., b/w.   Price **E**
Pond Life
    E.P. (C 6676)   f/s., col.   Price **E**
Reptiles and Amphibians
    Hulton (83)   f/s., b/w.   Price **E**
Resident British Birds
    E.P. (C 6208)   f/s., col.   Price **E**
Rock Pools
    Hulton (457)   f/s., col.   Price **F**
Seed Germination
    E.P. (C 6290)   f/s., col.   Price **E**
Silk Worm, The
    E.P. (FC 0117)   f/s., col.   Price **E**

Some Common British Seaweeds
    E.P. (C 6620)   f/s., col.   Price E
Structure of the Flowering Plant
    Hulton (287)   f/s., b/w.   Price E
Summer Migrants
    E.P. (C 6203)   f/s., col.   Price E
Tiddlers, Tadpoles and their Kind (Includes tape recording)
    R.S.P.C.A. (ST 1)   27 slides, col.   Hire free
Trees in Britain
    200 *Part 1*   232 *Part II*
    Hulton   f/s., b/w.   Price E
Trees of Britain
    E.P. (C 6079)   f/s., col.   Price E
Tropical Leguminosae
    Hulton (494)   f/s., col.   Price F
Vegetative Reproduction
    E.P. (C 6675)   f/s., col.   Price E
Visit to the Zoo, A
    E.P. (C 6493)   f/s., col.   Price E
Wasp, The
    E.P. (C 6696)   f/s., col.   Price E
Weeds of Cultivated Land
    E.P. (C 6261)   f/s., col.   Price E
Wild Animals
    E.P. (127)   f/s., b/w.   Price E
Wild Animals
    Visual Information (256)   d/f.   Price E
Wildflowers
    302 *Part I*   303 *Part II*
    Hulton   f/s., col.   Price (each) F
Wild Fruits
    E.P. (C 6248)   f/s., col.   Price E
Wild Fruits of the Countryside (Series of 2 folios)
    Slide Centre   12 slide folios   Price (each) E
Wildlife and Vegetation (Australia)
    Visual Information (669)   76 f., b/w.   Price E
Woodland, The
    E.P. (C 6430)   f/s., col.   Price E

WALLCHARTS/POSTERS

Animal Life Chart (World's mammals)
    Tull   Price E
Animals in Danger
    Animals Magazine   Price D
Animals of Great Britain
    Galt   Price D
Bird Charts (Also available in sets of 4 in smaller format)
    Warne   8 charts   Price (each) C

Birds of Europe
    Galt   Price **D**
British Butterfly Chart
    Warne   Price **C**
British Sea Birds
    Animals Magazine   Price **D**
Fungi
    E.P. (BH 1/4)   4 charts   Price **F**
Junior Nature Study Series   8–10 years
    One   (ZDP 2/5)   4 charts   Price **E**
    Two   (ZDP 7/12)   6 charts   Price **F**
    Three   (ZDP 14/19)   6 charts   Price **F**
    Four   (ZEP 1/5)   5 charts   Price **F**
    Five   (ZEP 7/12)   6 charts   Price **F**
    Six   (ZCP 2/4)   3 charts   Price **E**
    E.P.
Mammal Charts (Also available as a set in smaller format)
    Warne   4 charts   Price (each) **C**
Nature Chart (British flora and fauna)
    Tull   Price **E**
Nature Class Pictures
    Macmillan   62 plates   Price **J**
               Reference book   Price **D**
Plants
    E.P. (BG 1/6)   6 charts   Price **G**
Project Charts (Bird projects)   Primary
    R.S.P.B.   5 charts   Price **D**
Small Birds
    E.P. (ZBP 2/5)   4 charts   Price **F**
Tree Posters (British trees)
    Gerrard   6 charts   Price (each) **C**
Trees
    E.P. (C 598)   2 charts   Price **D**
Useful Plants
    E.P. (BC 1/7)   7 charts   Price **G**
Wild Bird Chart (European birds)
    Tull   Price **E**

GAMES/KITS/WORKCARDS
Birds of Prey (Topic Kit; includes wallcharts, slides)
    R.S.P.B.   Price **F**
Ladybird Work Cards – Nature
    Wills & Hepworth   7–10 years   Price (per set) **E**
Science –
    4C 901 *Birds*
    4C 902 *Plants*
    4C 903 *Insects*

4C 904 *Amphibians and Reptiles*
4C 905 *Mammals*
    Milliken   12 transp./4 masters   Price (each) **G**
Science – Our Living World
    Milliken (107)   20 transp./20 masters   Price **H**

ORGANIZATIONS

Amateur Entomologists' Association
Anglers' Co-operative Association
Animals in Danger Corps
Arboricultural Association, The
Armagh Field Naturalists Society
Association of British Tree Surgeons and Arborists
Association of School Natural History Societies
Association of Tree Transplanters
Botanical Society of Edinburgh
Botanical Society of the British Isles
British Arachnological Society
British Broadcasting Corporation: Natural History Unit
British Butterfly Conservation Society
British Deer Society
British Ornithologists' Union
British Pteridological Society
British Trust for Entomology
British Trust for Ornithology
Conchological Society of Great Britain and Ireland
Conservation Corps
Crusade Against All Cruelty to Animals Ltd.
Fauna Preservation Society
Fermanagh Naturalists' Field Club
Forestry Commission
Humane Education Centre
Linnean Society of London
Malacological Society of London
Mammal Society of the British Isles
Men of the Trees
National Anglers' Council
Nature Conservancy
Northern Ireland Bird Records Committee
Northern Ireland Ornithologists' Club
Northwestern Naturalists' Union
Red Deer Commission
Route Naturalists Field Club
Royal Entomological Society of London
Royal Forestry Society of England, Wales and Scotland
Royal Scottish Forestry Society
Royal Society for the Protection of Birds (R.S.P.B.)

Scottish Ornithologists' Club
Scottish Wildlife Trust
Seabird Group
Southwestern Naturalists' Union
Wildfowl Trust
Wildlife Observation Society
Wildlife Youth Service
World Wildlife Fund (W.W.F.)
Young Crusaders
Zoological Society of London

JOURNALS/PERIODICALS

All Living Things
Animals
Bird Life
Bird Study
Birds
Birds and Countryside
Countryside
Geographical Magazine
Kingfisher
Living World, The
Mammal Review
National Geographic Magazine
Natural History
Naturopa
Oryx
R.S.P.B. Teachers' Newsletter
Trees
World of Wildlife
World Wildlife News

ARTICLES

Coleman, A., 'A Wildlife Atlas for England and Wales'   *Geographical Magazine*   October 1970

Baird, W. W. & Tarrant, J. R., 'Vanishing Hedgerows'   *Geographical Magazine*   May 1972

Grey-Wilson, C., 'Flowers from a Forbidden Frontier'   *Geographical Magazine*   July 1972

Zahal, P. A., 'Algae: The Life-givers'   *National Geographic Magazine*   March 1974

Breeden, K. and S., 'Eden in the Outback'   *National Geographic Magazine*   February 1973

Sisson, R. F., 'Life Cycle of a Coral'   *National Geographic Magazine*   June 1973

Edwards, W. M., 'Abundant Life in a Desert Land' *National Geopraphic Magazine* September 1973
Perring, F. & Walters, S. M., 'Europe's Flora Threatened' *Nature in Focus* Summer 1972
Wheeler, A., 'The Changing Fish Fauna of Europe' *Your Environment* Summer 1971
Herbert, A. & Wheeler, K., 'Nature on the Verge' *Your Environment* Spring 1973

4   SOILS AND SOIL EROSION

See also Section 2 Ecology (*page* 15)

BOOKS (GENERAL)

Agricultural Research Council, *The Effects of Air Pollution on Plants
    and Soils*   H.M.S.O.   1967   Price **C**
Buckman, H. O. & Brady, N. C., *The Nature and Properties of Soils*
    Collier-Macmillan   1968   Price **E**
Bunting, B. T., *The Geography of Soil*, 2nd edn.   Hutchinson   1967
    Price **D/E**
Comber, N. M. & Townsend, W. N.,   *An Introduction to the Scien-
    tific Study of Soil*   Arnold   1972   Price **E/F**
Cruickshank, J. G., *Soil Geography*   David & Charles   1972
    Price **E/H**
Eyre, S. R., *Vegetation and Soils – A World Picture*, 2nd edn.   Arnold
    1968   Price **G**
Hillel, D., *Soil and Water, Physical Principles and Processes*   Academic
    Press   1971   Price **J**
Hudson, N. W., *Soil Conservation*   Batsford   1971   Price **H**
MacBean, J., *The Soil*   Faber   1961   Price **E**
Nelson, J. G. & Chambers, M. J. (eds.), *Vegetation, Soils and Plant Life*
    Methuen   1970   Price **G**
Parkinson, D., *et al.*, *Methods for Studying the Ecology of Soil Micro-
    Organisms*   Blackwell Scientific   1971   Price **E**
Perry, G. A., *Soils*   Blandford Press   1965   Price **D**
Phillipson, J., *Methods of Study in Quantitative Soil Ecology: Popula-
    tion, Production and Energy Flow*   Blackwell Scientific
    1971   Price **H**
Rodale, R. & Furner, B. (eds.), *The Basic Book of Organic Gardening*,
    rev. edn.   Pan/Ballantine   1972   Price **C**
Russell, E. J., *The World of the Soil* ('New Naturalist' series)
    Collins/Fontana   1970   Price **D/F**
Townsend, W. N., *An Introduction to the Scientific Study of the Soil*,
    5th edn.   Arnold   1973   Price **F/H**

BOOKS (SCHOOL)

Morgan, M., *Soil Erosion and Conservation* ('Certificate Topics in
    Geography' series)   Collins   1969   15–16 years   Price **D**

FILMS

Generous Earth (1969) (Soil erosion and reclamation)
    C.F.L. (V 749)   51 min., col.   Hire **H**
Living Soil, The (1960) (Insect pests in the soil)
    Shell   20 min., col.   Hire free

Making of the Soil, The (1952)
C.F.L. (UK 1320)   35 min., col.   Hire **G**
Precious Soil, The
I.C.I.   38 min., col.   Hire free
World at Your Feet, The (1953)
C.F.L. (C 494)   23 min., col.   Hire **E**

FILMSTRIPS/SLIDES/FILMLOOPS/TRANSPARENCIES
Building the Soil ('The Forest Community' series)
McGraw-Hill   *c*.52 f.   Price **G**
Saving the Soil ('Conservation is Everybody's Business' series)
McGraw-Hill   f/s.   Price **F**
Soil (1960)
1. *Rocks and Erosion*   38 f., col.
2. *Plants and Decay*   35 f., col.
3. *Soil Profiles and their Formation*   37 f., col.
4. *The Composition of Soil*   35 f., col.
5. *Soil and Farming*   37 f., col.
Marian Ray   Secondary   Price (each) **F**
Soil, The
Visual Information (402)   29 f., b/w.   Price **D**
Soil and the Plant, The (1962) ('Know the Land' series)   11–15 years
Visual Publications   f/s.   Price **E**
Soil Conservation   11 years +
7361 *How Long Will it Last?*
7362 *How Soil is Formed*
7363 *Plant Life and the Soil*
7364 *Water and the Soil*
7365 *Animal Life and the Soil*
7366 *Minerals in the Soil*
7367 *How Man has Used the Soil*
7368 *How Man Conserves the Soil*
Encyclopaedia Britannica   Each *c*. 60 f.   Price (each) **E**
Soil Erosion (1951)   Secondary
Visual Information (671)   49 f., b/w.   Price **E**

WALLCHARTS/POSTERS
World of the Soil, The
P.C.E.T.   Secondary   Price **D**

GAMES/KITS/WORKCARDS
Soils (Curriculum Study Prints No. 34)   11 years +
Encyclopaedia Britannica   6 pictures   Price **H**

ORGANIZATIONS
Soil Association

JOURNALS/PERIODICALS

Ecologist
Journal of the Soil Association
Naturopa
Span

ARTICLES

Allaby, M., 'Living Soil'   *Ecologist*   November 1971
Pilpel, N., 'Structure of the Soil under Stress'   *Ecologist*   December 1971
Bean, C., 'We Need these Soil Tillers'   *Ecologist*   February 1972
Shewell-Cooper, W. E., 'The Story of the Soil'   *Epoch*   Spring/ Summer 1973
Young, A., 'Soil Survey Procedures in Land Development Planning'   *Geographical Journal*   February 1973
Brunsden, D., 'Calabria – An Environment on Edge'   *Geographical Magazine*   February 1973
Morgan, R. P. C., 'Nature Provides, Man Erodes'   *Geographical Magazine*   July 1974
Burnham, C. P., 'Discovering about Soils'   *Geography*   January 1973
Fournier, F., 'Soil Conservation in Europe'   *Nature in Focus*   Summer 1972
Brakel, J., 'Soil Biology'   *Nature in Focus*   Summer 1972
Muckenhausen, E., 'Soil Erosion by Water and Wind in Europe'   *Nature in Focus*   Summer 1972
Jamagne, M., 'Soil Cartography and Environmental Planning'   *Nature in Focus*   Summer 1972
Jones, D., 'Treat it with Respect. Modern Farming and the Soil'   *Your Environment*   Spring 1971

5   MAN AND ENVIRONMENT

See also Section 1 General Environmental Topics (*page* 2) and all
sections 7 to 28 (*pages* 62 to 167)

BOOKS (GENERAL)

Adler, R. *et al.*, *Spatial Organization*   Prentice-Hall   1971
Price H
Aldous, T., *Battle for the Environment*   Collins/Fontana   1972
Price C
Allsop, K., *Man and Environment: The Future of Britain's Country-
side*   Penguin   1970   Price C
Arvill, R., *Man and Environment: Crisis and the Strategy of Choice*,
rev. edn.   Penguin   1973   Price D
Association of American Geographers, *Habitat and Resources*
('Geography in an Urban Age' series; teachers' guide)   Collier-
Macmillan   1970   Price D
Barr, J., *The Assaults on our Senses*
Methuen   1970   Price F
Sphere   1971   Price C
Bates, M., *Man in Nature*, 2nd edn.   Prentice-Hall   1964
Price D
Black, J. N., *The Dominion of Man: The Search for Ecological Responsi-
bility*   Edinburgh U.P.   1970   Price F
Boughey, A., *Man and the Environment: An Introduction to Ecology
and Evolution*   Collier-Macmillan   1971   Price F/J
Bowen-Jones, H. (ed.), *Human Ecology in the Commonwealth*   Knight
1972   Price H
Bracey, H. E., *People and the Countryside*   Routledge   1970
Price G
Bresler, J. B., *Environment of Man*   Addison-Wesley   1968
Price E
Brown, L. R., *Man and his Environment: Food*   Harper & Row
1972   Price E
Brubaker, S., *To Live on Earth: Man and his Environment in Perspec-
tive*   Johns Hopkins   1972   Price G
Calder, N., *The Environment Game*   Panther   1969   Price C
Colvin, B., *Land and Landscape: Evolution, Design and Control*, 2nd
edn.   Murray   1970   Price H
Comfort, A., *Nature and Human Nature*   Penguin   1969
Price C
Commoner, B., *Science and Survival*   Pan/Ballantine   1971
Price C
Darling, F. F., *Wilderness and Plenty* (Reith Lectures 1969)
B.B.C.   1970   Price E
Pan/Ballantine   1971   Price C

Dawson, J. A. & Doornkamp, J. C., *Evaluating the Human Environment. Essays in Applied Geography*   Arnold   1973
Price F/H
Dept. of Environment, *How Do You Want to Live?* (Report of the Working Party on the Human Habitat)   H.M.S.O.   1972
Price E
Detwyler, T. R. (ed.), *Man's Impact on Environment* (Collection of papers on all aspects of the natural environment)   McGraw-Hill   1971   Price F
Downs, R. & Stea, D. (eds.), *Image and Environment* (Relationship between behaviour and environment)   Arnold   1974   Price J
Dubos, R., *Man, Medicine and Environment*   Penguin   1970
Price C
Dubos, R., *So Human an Animal* (Dehumanising of man by the environmental conditions he is creating)   Hart-Davis   1970
Price F
Ehrlich, P. R. & A. H., *Population, Resources, Environment: Issues in Human Ecology*, 2nd edn.   Freeman   1972   Price F/H
Ehrlich, P. R., Holdren, J. P. & Holm, R. W. (eds.), *Man and the Ecosphere* (Readings from *Scientific American*)   Freeman   1971   Price F/J
Eisenberh, J. F. & Dillon, W. S. (eds.), *Man and Beast: Comparative Social Behaviour*   David & Charles   1971   Price H
Esser, A. H. (ed.), *Behaviour and Environment: The Use of Space by Animals and Man*   Plenum   1971   Price J
Eyre, S. R. & Jones, G. R. J., *Geography as Human Ecology, Methodology by Example*   Arnold   1966   Price F
F.O.E., *The Stockholm Conference: Only One Earth*   Earth Island   1972   Price D/F
Gates, D. M., *Man and his Environment: Climate*   Harper & Row   1972   Price E
Goin, G. J. & O. B., *Man and the Natural World. An Introduction to Life Science*   Collier-Macmillan   1971   Price F/J
Graham, M., *A Natural Ecology*   Manchester U.P.   1973   Price E/H
Grigson, G., *The Shell Country Alphabet* (An encyclopaedia on human history in Britain)   Joseph   1966   Price E
Grigson, G., *The Shell Country Book*, 2nd edn.   Dent   1962
Price E
Guggisberg, C. A. W., *Man and Wildlife*   Evans   1971   Price G
Hamilton, D., *Technology, Man and Environment*   Faber   1973
Price G
Hardin, G. (ed.), *Science, Conflict and Society* (Readings from *Scientific American*)   Freeman   1969   Price F
Hewitt, K. & Burton, I., *The Hazardousness of a Place: A Regional Ecology of Damaging Events*   O.U.P.   1972   Price F
Hillaby, J., *Nature and Man*   Phoenix House   1960   Price D
Holdren, J. P. & Ehrlich, P. R. (eds.), *Global Ecology: Readings towards a Rational Strategy for Man*   Harcourt Brace   1971   Price F

Hoskins, W. G., *The Making of the English Landscape,* 9th edn.
  Hodder & Stoughton   1970   Price **F**
  Penguin   1970   Price **D**
Hoyt, J. B., *Man and Earth,* 2nd edn.   Prentice-Hall   1967
  Price **G**
Jennings, B. H. & Murphey, J. E. (eds.), *Interactions of Man and his
  Environment*   Plenum   1965   Price **J**
Johnson, C. E. (ed.), *Eco-Crisis*   Wiley   1971   Price **E**
Johnson, H. (ed.), *No Deposit – No Return, Man and his Environment:
  A View towards Survival*   Addison-Wesley   1970   Price **E**
King, G. E. (ed.), *Conflict and Harmony. A Source-book of Man and
  his Environment* (Over 300 extracts)   Philip   1972
  Price **G**
Lauwerys, J. A., *Man's Impact on Nature* ('Interdependence in Nature'
  series)   Aldus   1969   Price **E**
Lee, D. H. K. & Minard, D., *Physiology, Environment and Man*
  Academic Press   1970   Price **J**
Majunda, S. K., *Drama of Man and Nature*   Prentice-Hall   1971
  Price **F**
Marx, W., *Man and his Environment: Waste*   Harper & Row   1971
  Price **E**
Matthews, W. H. *et al.* (eds.), *Man's Impact on the Climate*   M.I.T.
  1972   Price **J**
Matthews, W. H. *et al.* (eds.), *Man's Impact on Terrestrial and Oceanic
  Ecosystems*   M.I.T.   1971   Price **J**
Maunder, W. J., *The Value of the Weather*   Methuen   1970
  Price **F/H**
McHale, J., *World Facts and Trends* (Statistics on man and his
  environment)   Collier-Macmillan   1973   Price **D/F**
Michelson, W., *Man and his Urban Environment: A Sociological
  Approach*   Addison-Wesley   1970   Price **E**
Morris, D., *The Human Zoo*   Cape   1969   Price **E**
Moulton, R. & Macdonald, M. M., *Readings in Earth Science*   Van
  Nostrand Reinhold   1972   Price **E**
Murdoch, W. W. (ed.), *Environment: Resources, Pollution and Society*
  Sinauer   1971   Price **F**
Nicol, H., *The Limits of Man: An Enquiry into the Scientific Bases of
  Human Population*   Constable   1967   Price **E**
Owen, D. F., *Man's Environmental Predicament. An Introduction to
  Human Ecology in Tropical Africa*   O.U.P.   1973
  Price **D/G**
Pirages, D. C. & Ehrlich, P. R., *Ark II: Social Response to Environ-
  mental Imperatives*   Freeman   1974   Price **E**
Pringle, J. W. S. (ed.), *Biology and the Human Sciences* (Herbert
  Spencer lectures)   O.U.P.   1972   Price **E/F**
Rose, J. (ed.), *Technological Injury: The Effect of Technological
  Advances on Environment, Life and Society*   Gordon &
  Breach   1969   Price **J**

Russell, W. M. S., *Man, Nature and History*   Aldus   1967
    Price F
Saini, B. S., *Building Environment. An Illustrated Analysis of Problems
    in Hot Dry Lands* (A detailed study of ways in which man can
    come to terms with living in desert lands, including housing,
    solar power, desalination)   Angus & Robertson   1973
    Price J
Salter, C. L., *Cultural Landscape*   Prentice-Hall   1971   Price F
Scientific American, *The Biosphere*   Freeman   1970   Price E/G
Spencer, J. E. & Thomas, W. L., *Introducing Cultural Geography*
    Wiley   1969   Price J
Stamp, L. D., *Man and the Land* ('New Naturalist' series)   Collins
    1969   Price E
Stamp, L. D., *Applied Geography*   Penguin   1969   Price C
Stapleton, G., *Human Ecology*, 2nd edn. ('Classics of Human Ecology'
    series)   Knight   1972   Price F
S.C.E.P., *Man's Impact on the Global Environment: Assessment and
    Recommendations for Action*   M.I.T.   1971   Price E/J
Taylor, G. R., *The Doomsday Book*   Thames & Hudson   1970
    Price F
Wagner, K. A., *et al., Under Siege: Man, Men and Earth* (Compre-
    hensive study of the environment and man's battle against its
    abuse)   Intertext   1973   Price J
Wallace, B., *People, their Needs, Environment, Ecology*   Prentice-Hall
    1972   Price F/H
Ward, M. W., *Man and his Environment*   Pergamon   1970   Price J
Wegner, R., *Environments and Peoples*   Prentice-Hall   1972
    Price E/G

The Earth and Human Affairs   Harper & Row   1972   Price E
Human Habitat   G.L.C.   1971   Price E
Man and the Environment   Bowker   1972   Price J

BOOKS (SCHOOL)

Andrews, K., *Beneath the Oceans* ('Visual Books' series)   Macdonald
    Educational   1972   C.S.E.   Price D
Arthur, D. R., *Survival: Man and his Environment*   E.U.P.   1969
    17 years +   Price E
Baines, J. D., *The Environment*   Batsford   1974   Secondary
    Price E
Barrett, E. & Bailey, J., *Weather and Climate* ('Certificate Topics in
    Geography' series)   Collins   1971   Secondary   Price D
Bowood, R., *Our Land in the Making*
    Book 1: Earliest Times to Norman Conquest
    Book 2: Norman Conquest to Present Day
    Wills & Hepworth   1966   8–12 years   Price (each) B
Christian, G., *Tomorrow's Countryside: The Road to the Seventies*
    Murray   1966   17 years +   Price G

Clegg, E. J., *The Study of Man*   E.U.P.   1968   17 years +
Price **E**
Critchlow, K., *Into the Hidden Environment. Oceans: Lifestream
of our Planet*   Philip   1972   16 years+   Price **F**
Davis, A., *Inside the Earth* ('Visual Books' series)   Macdonald
Educational   1972   C.S.E.   Price **D**
Domnitz, M., *Studies of Human Environment*   Pergamon   1971
C.S.E.   Price **D**
Fairbrother, N., *Shelter: Environments and Human Needs* ('Connexions'
series)   Penguin   1974   Price **C**
Gordon, S., *World Problems* ('World Wide' series)   Batsford   1971
14 years +   Price **E**
Guest, A., *Man and Landscape: Practical Studies in Advanced Geography*
Heinemann   1972   17 years +   Price **F**
Harris, A., Harrison, C. & Smithson, P., *Man's Environment* ('Visual
Books' series)   Macdonald Educational   1972   C.S.E.
Price **D**
Jones, C. *et al.*, *The Land We Live On* ('Pollution' series)   Dent   1973
14 years +   Price **E**
Meade, F. & Zimmerman, A., *The Home and Neighbourhood* ('Inte-
grated Studies' series)   George Philip Alexander   1974
Primary   Price **D**
Mellersh, H. E. L., *The Wonders of Man and his Environment*   Burke
1964   10 years +   Price **E**
Morris, W. F. & Booker, R. W., *The Earth – Man's Heritage*   Harrap
1953   15–17 years   Price **D**
Perrott, E., *Man and his Environment* ('Biology: an Environmental
Approach' series)   Murray   1972   C.S.E./G.C.E.
Price **E/F**
Robson, R., *Man and his Environment* ('Nelson's Geography Studies'
series)   Nelson   1972   13–18 years   Price **C**
Sauvain, P., *Man and Environment* ('Practical Geography' series)
Hulton   1971   Price **E**
Savage, N. E. & Wood, R. S., *Man and his Environment* ('C.S.E.
General Science' series; 2 volumes)   Routledge   1971
C.S.E.   Price (each) **E**
Smith, J., *Write about your Environment* (6 topic books)   George
Philip Alexander   8 years +   Price (each) **C**
Wright, D. R., *Survival* ('Human Space' series)   Penguin   1974
10–13 years   Price **D**

FILMS

Conservation and the Balance of Nature
Concord   18 min., col.   Hire **F**
Earth and Mankind
1. *People by the Billions*
2. *Man and his Resources*

3. *To Each a Rightful Share*
4. *The Global Struggle for Food*
5. *Can the Earth Provide*
6. *Challenge to Mankind*
    Concord   Each 30 min., b/w.   Hire (each) **E**
Environment in the Balance
    S.P.N.R.   30 min., col.   Hire **G**
    Shell   Hire free
Evolution Today
    B.B.C.   20 min., b/w.   Hire **E**
House of Man – Our Crowded Environment
    N.A.V.A.L.   11 min., col.   Hire **E**
Making of the English Landscape, The
    B.B.C.   55 min., b/w.   Hire **H**
                 55 min., col.   Hire **J**
Oak Valley, U.S.A.
    N.A.V.A.L.   14 min., col.   Hire **E**
Shadow of Progress, The (1970)
    B.P.   27 min., col.   Hire free

FILMSTRIPS/SLIDES/FILMLOOPS/TRANSPARENCIES

Caring for the Countryside   15 years +
    1. *How Natural is our Countryside*
    2. *Man's Impact on the Countryside Environment*
    3. *Man and the Countryside: Conservation and Reclamation*
    E.P.   d/f., col.   Price (each) **F**
Looking at Things (Visual aspects of the environment)
    LAT 7 *Environment A*   LAT 8 *Environment B*
    Visual Publications   d/f., col.   Price (each) **F**
Men of the Rocks (1953) (Northern England)
    British Transport (BT 77)   54 f.   Hire free
Plants and Man
    S705 *Plants and Medicine*
    S706 *Plants and Folklore*
    S707 *Some Introduced Plants*
    S708 *Plants about the House*
    Slide Centre   12 slide folios   Price (each) **E**

WALLCHARTS/POSTERS

Man Takes Control
    P.C.E.T.   Secondary   Price **D**

GAMES/KITS/WORKCARDS

Man and his Environment (Role-playing game)
    Coca-Cola   1971   10–15 years   Price **J**

Man and his Environment: Uses and Abuses (Modular Learning
   Programme)
   C.I.A.V. (TSB-3)   14–18 years   Price **G**
You and Your Community (4 audio-visual filmstrips covering Homes,
   Travel, Work and Leisure)
   Coca-Cola   1974   8–13 years   Price **J**
You and Your Environment ('Viewfinder' kit on world poverty,
   population and pollution; includes case studies, viewcharts)
   Macmillan   Price **J**

ORGANIZATIONS

Association for Neighbourhood Councils
Conservation Society
Geographical Association (G.A.)
Landscape Research Group
Royal Geographical Society (R.G.S.)
Scottish Field Studies Association
Soil Association

JOURNALS/PERIODICALS

Ecologist, The
Geographical Magazine
Geography
National Geographic Magazine
New Scientist
New Society
Your Environment

ARTICLES

Boyden, S., 'Evolution and Health'   *Ecologist*   August 1973
Hardy, S., 'Man and the Landscape in Britain'   *Epoch*   Winter 1972/3
Brown, E. H., 'Man Shapes the Earth'   *Geographical Journal*
   March 1970
Chandler, T. J., 'Mankind's Impact on the Atmosphere'   *Geographical*
   Magazine   November 1970
McLean, B. J., 'Action for Tropical Africa: Man's Impact on Savanna
   Vegetation'   *Geographical Magazine*   February 1971
Wise, M., 'Prescription for Man's Habitat'   *Geographical Magazine*
   August 1972
Jones, D. K. C., 'Man Moulds the Landscape'   *Geographical Magazine*
   May 1973

6　FIELD STUDIES

See also Section 29 Environmental Education (*page* 168)

BOOKS (GENERAL)

Blit, B., *School in the Town* ('Evans Modern Teaching' series)　Evans
　1973　Teachers　　Price **E**
Briault, E. W. H. & Shave, D. W., *Geography in and out of School*
　Harrap　1973　Price **D**
Cotton, R. W. & Morgan, R. F., *Project Environment* (Schools Council)
　Learning from Trails　Price **E**
　The School Outdoor Resource Area　Price **E**
　Longman (in preparation)　8–18 years
Cross, M. F. & Daniel, P. A., *Field Work for Geography Classes*
　McGraw-Hill　1968　Price **D**
D. E. S., *Schools and the Countryside*　H.M.S.O.　1958　Price **D**
Devon Trust for Nature Conservation, *School Projects in Natural History*
　Heinemann　1972　Price **F**
Dilke, M. S. (ed.), *Field Studies for Schools: Volume 1 – The Purpose
　and Organization of Field Studies*　Rivingtons　1965　Price **D**
Dunning, G. R., *Local Sources for the Young Historian*　Muller
　1973　Price **E**
Jones, P. A., *Field Work in Geography*　Longman　1968　Price **F**
Knight, M., *Field Work for Young Naturalists*　Bell　1966　Price **E**
Knight, M., *The Young Field Naturalist's Guide*　Bell　1952　Price **D**
Martin, G. & Turner, E. (eds.), *Environmental Studies* ('Teachers'
　Handbooks' series)　Blond Educational　1972　Price **F**
Masterston, T. H., *Environmental Studies. A Concentric Approach*
　(Teachers' guide)　Oliver & Boyd　1969　Price **D**
McLean, R. C. & Ivimy Cook, W. R., *Practical Field Ecology* (Secondary
　teachers' guide)　Allen & Unwin　1969　Price **E**
Mills, D. G., *Field Excursions in the London Area*　Rivingtons　1973
　Price **F**
Perry, G. A., Jones, E. & Hammersley, A., *Handbook for Environmental
　Studies* (Teachers' guide to 'Approaches to Environmental
　Studies' series)　Blandford Press　1971　Price **E**
Pluckrose, H., *Let's Use the Locality: A Handbook for Teachers*
　Mills & Boon　1971　Price **F**
Proctor, E., *Natural Science: A Teachers' Handbook*　Black　1966
　Price **D**
Sankey, J., *A Guide to Field Biology*　Longman　1958　Price **D**
Ward, C. & Fyson, A., *Streetwork. The Exploding School* (Environmental
　education in towns)　Routledge　1973　Price **E/G**
Wheeler, K. S. (ed.) *Geography in the Field* ('Teachers' Handbooks'
　series)　Blond Educational　1970　Price **E**
Young, I. V., *Farm Studies in Schools* (Teaching methods handbook)
　Association for Agriculture　1968　Price **D**

Young, I. V., *Farm Visits* (Handbook for teachers)   Association for
    Agriculture   1972   Price **D**

Nature Trails in Britain (Guide to nearly 400 trails)   British Tourist
    Authority   1974   Price **B**

BOOKS (SCHOOL)

Bayliss, D. G. & Renwick, T. M., *Town Study through Photographs*
    ('Nelson's Geography Studies' series)   Nelson   1972
    13–18 years   Price **C**
Bell, S. & Williams, M., *Using the Urban Environment*   Heinemann
    1972   Primary   Price **D**
Bernard, R., *Looking at Landscape* ('Nelson's Geography Studies'
    series)   Nelson   1968   13–18 years   Price **C**
Bracey, H. E., 'Get to Know Series'
    Country Town Survey, 2nd edn. (1961)
    Village Survey, 2nd edn. (1957)
    Methuen   9 years +   Price (each) **C**
Bull, G. B. G., *A Rural Studies Companion*   Hulton   1972
    Secondary   Price **D**
Bull, G. B. G., *A Town Study Companion*   Hulton   1969
    Secondary   Price **D**
Dennis, E. (ed.), *Everyman's Nature Reserve. Ideas for Action* (Over
    40 practical projects in wildlife management)   David & Charles
    1972   Price **E**
Dodd, J. P., *Investigating Geography: Secondary School Field Studies*
    Heinemann   1969   Price **D**
Driscoll, K. J., *Town Study. A Sample Urban Geography*   Philip   1971
    C.S.E./G.C.E.   Price **E**
Evans, F., Searson, V. F. & Williams, G. H., *Local Studies for Schools*
    Philip   1972   9–16 years   Price **D**
Ford, V. E., *How to Begin your Fieldwork*
    1. *Woodlands*   2. *The Seashore*
    Murray   1959   C.S.E./G.C.E.   Price (each) **C**
Haddon, J., *Local Geography. Geographical Survey in Rural Areas*
    Philip   1964   16 years +   Price **C**
Haddon, J., *Local Geography in Towns*   Philip   1971   17 years +
    Price **D**
Hoy, K., *Looking into Water* ('Science and Your Surroundings' series)
    Ginn   1974   9–13 years   Price **C**
Kneeshaw, R., *Practical Urban Geography*   M. & E.   1972
    Price **C**
Lines, C. J. & Bolwell, L. H., *Discovering Your Environment*
    1. *Understanding Local Maps*
    2. *About the Weather*
    3. *People at Work*
    4. *Using Local Maps*
    5. *About Buildings and Scenery*

6. *People on the Move*
7. *History in a Village*
8. *History in Towns*
9. *History along Roads and Waterways*
10. *Crafts and Industries in the Past*
    Ginn   1968/71   9–13 years   Price (each) **C**
Miles, P. M. & H. B., *Biological Field Studies*
    Seashore Ecology
    Freshwater Ecology
    Town Ecology
    Woodland Ecology
    Chalkland and Moorland Ecology
    Hulton   1967/8   11 years +   Price (each) **D**
Millward, R. & Robinson, A., *Landscapes of Britain*
    The South Western Peninsula
    The West Midlands
    South Eastern England: Thameside and the Weald
    The Welsh Marches
    Cumbria
    South Eastern England: Channel Coastlands
    Macmillan   1970/1   11 years +   Price (each) **G**
Morgan, R. F., *Environmental Biology* (4 volumes)   Pergamon
    1963/6   C.S.E./G.C.E.   Price **C/D**
Proctor, E., *Looking at Nature*
1. *Nature Awake and Asleep*
2. *Nature at Home*
3. *Working with Nature*
4. *Looking at Life*
    Black   1961/71   Price (each) **D**
Sauvain, P., *Exploring at Home* ('Hulton's Environmental Studies'
    series)   Hulton   1966   Price **D**
Sauvain, P., *A Geographical Field Study Companion*   Hulton   1964
    Price **D**
Spoczynska, J., *Practical Fieldwork for the Young Naturalist*   Muller
    1973   Price **D**
Thurber, W. A., *Exploring Science* (4 volumes)   Burke   1962
    7–11 years   Price **C/D**
Titley, D. P., *Discovering Local History*   Mills & Boon   1972
    Price **D**
Walsh, J. W., *Environmental Studies Assignment Books*
1. *Weather*   4. *Timber*
2. *Farming*   5. *Simple Geology*
3. *Urban Studies*   6. *Transport*
    Schofield & Sims   1971   11–16 years   Price (each) **C**
Wigley, H. & Balding, J. W., *Beside the Sea* ('Science and Your
    Surroundings' series)   Ginn   1974   9–13 years   Price **C**
Wilson, R. W., *Nature in Your Town* (Teacher's book available)
    Humane Education Centre   1973   Price **B**

Wilson, R. W. & Wright, D. F., *A Field Approach to Biology*   Heinemann
    1972   Price **E**

'On Location' series (Each book takes a feature of the environment —
Rivers, Canals, Museums, etc. — and provides the pupil with the means
of understanding it)   Mills & Boon   1973   Secondary
    Price (each) **D**

FILMS
British Schools Exploring Society in Central Iceland
    Stewart   28 min., col.   Price **L**
Hidden World, The
    F.S.C.   19 min., col.   Hire free
World Outside, The (Neighbourhood field studies)
    Guild (900 4497-3)   19 min., col.   Hire **G**

FILMSTRIPS/SLIDES/FILMLOOPS/TRANSPARENCIES
Country Code, The
    Hulton (198)   f/s., b/w.   Price **E**
Field Study Series
    C 6236 *Malham Tarn Area*
    C 6224 *Langdale — The Lake District*
    C 6235 *The Mole Gap Area and Box Hill*
    C 6236 *The Helford River Estuary*
    C 6522 *The Garth Area*
    C 6484 *Slapton Ley Field Centre*
    C 6264 *Dale Fort*
    C 6497 *The Peak District (Castleton and Edale)*
    C 6594 *Preston Montford — the Shelve Hills*
    C 6724 *The Isle of Purbeck*
    E.P.   f/s., col.   Price (each) **E**

GAMES/KITS/WORKCARDS
Discovery Packs (Includes booklets, photographs, maps)
    1. *In Search of the Countryside*
    2. *In Search of Towns*
    3. *In Search of Roman Britain*
    A.C.E.   10–14 years   Price **E**
Enquiry Work in an Urban Setting (Discussion groups in teachers' centre;
    includes slides, tape, booklet) Schools Council
Piece of Land, A (Set of 32 cards)
    Blackwell   1971   9–12 years   Price **E**
Streetometer, The (Simple method of measuring quality of environ-
    ment)
    Priority   Price **C**
Urban Mapping (Modular Learning Programme)
    C.I.A.V. (UD 3)   13–18 years   Price **G**

ORGANIZATIONS

Council for Urban Studies Centres (C.U.S.C.)
Field Studies Council
Griffin & George Ltd.
National Association for Outdoor Education
Yorkshire Field Studies
Youth Hostels Association (Y.H.A.)
Youth Hostels Association of Scotland

JOURNALS/PERIODICALS

Bulletin of Environmental Education (BEE)
Field Studies

ARTICLES

Wheeler, K. & Waites, B., 'Town Trails Issue'   *BEE*   Aug./Sept. 1972
Buckhurst, E. A. J., 'School Grounds: A Resource for Teaching
    Environmental Studies'   *BEE*   March 1974
Boon, G., 'Instant Fieldwork; Making the Most of the School Locality'
    BEE   April 1974
Goodey, B., 'What about a Railtrail?'   *BEE*   May 1974
Hopkinson, M. F., 'Geography in the Built Environment – The Role
    of Urban Studies Centres'   *Geography*   April 1974

7 POPULATION GROWTH AND DISTRIBUTION

See also Section 8 Population Control (*page* 69)

BOOKS (GENERAL)

Allaby, M., *Who Will Eat?* Stacey 1972 Price F

Barham, R., *The Cancer of the Earth* C.A.L.L. 1972 Price E

Barraclough, O., *The Economic Costs of Population Growth* Conservation Society 1973 Price B

Benjamin, B., *Demographic Analysis* Allen & Unwin 1969 Price E

Benjamin, B. (ed.), *Population and the New Biology* (Symposium of Eugenics Society) Academic Press 1974 Price G

Benjamin, B., Cox, P. R. & Peel, J. (eds.), *Resources and Population* (Symposium of Eugenics Society) Academic Press 1973 Price F

Borgstrom, G., *The Hungry Planet,* rev. edn. Collier-Macmillan 1973 Price E

Borgstrom, G., *Too Many: An Ecological Over-view of the Earth's Limitations* Collier-Macmillan 1969 Price D/F

Borrie, W. D., *The Growth and Control of World Population* Weidenfeld & Nicolson 1970 Price H

Borrie, W. D., *Population, Environment and Society* (Sir Douglas Robb Lectures, 1972) Auckland U.P./O.U.P. 1973 Price E

Boughey, A. S., *Ecology of Populations* ('Current Concepts in Biology' series) Collier-Macmillan 1968 Price E

Brooks, E., *This Crowded Kingdom* (Growth and population control in Britain) Knight 1973 Price G

Chisholm, M. and Rodgers, B. (eds.), *Studies in Human Geography* Heinemann 1972 Price E/G

Cipolla, C. M., *The Economic History of World Population* Penguin 1970 Price C

Clark, C., *Population Growth and Land Use* Macmillan 1967 Price H

Clarke, J. I., *Population Geography,* 2nd edn. Pergamon 1972 Price E/F

Clarke, J. I., *Population Geography and Developing Countries* Pergamon 1971 Price E/F

Cox, P. R. & Peel, J. (eds.), *Population and Pollution* (Eugenics Society Symposium) Academic Press 1972 Price F

Ehrlich, P. R., *The Population Bomb* Pan/Ballantine 1972 Price C

Ehrlich, P. R., *The Population, Resources, Environment Crisis: Where Do We Stand Now?* Conservation Society 1972 Price B

Ehrlich, P. R. & A. H., *Population, Resources, Environment: Issues in Human Ecology,* 2nd edn. Freeman 1972 Price F/H

Flew, A. (ed.), *An Essay on the Principle of Population* (Malthus, 1798 and 1830)   Penguin   1970   Price **C**
Fremlin, J., *Be Fruitful and Multiply: Life at the Limits of Population* Hart-Davis   1972   Price **F**
Glass, D. V.˙& Eversley, D. E. C. (eds.), *Population in History. Essays in Human Demography*   Arnold   1964   Price **F/J**
Glass, D. V. & Revelle, R., *Population and Social Change*   Arnold 1972   Price **J**
Hardin, G. (ed.), *Population, Evolution and Birth Control: A Collage of Controversial Ideas*, 2nd edn.   Freeman   1969   Price **E/G**
Hardin, G. (ed.), *Science and Controversy: Population – A Case Study* Freeman   1969   Price **C**
Harrison, G. A. & Boyce, A. J. (eds.), *The Structure of Human Populations*   O.U.P.   1972   Price **G/J**
Hazen, W. E., *Readings in Population and Community Ecology*, 2nd edn.   Saunders   1970   Price **F**
Hodge, P. L. & Hauser, P. M., *The Challenge of America's Metropolitan Population Outlook 1960–1985*   Praeger   1969   Price **G**
Hopcroft, A., *Born to Hunger*   Pan/Ballantine   1968   Price **C**
Kammeyer, K. C., *An Introduction to Population*   Intertext   1972 Price **F**
Kelsall, R. K., *Population* ('Aspects of Modern Society' series) Longman   1967   Price **D/E**
Keyfitz, N. & Flieger, W., *Population, Facts and Methods of Demography* Freeman   1971   Price **J**
Laffin, J., *The Hunger to Come*   Abelard-Schuman   1966   Price **E**
Leach, G., *The Biocrats*   Penguin   1972   Price **D**
Llewellyn-Jones, D., *People Populating*   Faber   1974   Price **G**
Loraine, J. A., *Sex and the Population Crisis*   Kimpton   1970 Price **G**
Macarthur, R. H. & Connell, J. H., *The Biology of Populations*   Wiley 1966   Price **G**
McKenzie, A., *The Hungry World*   Faber   1969   Price **C**
Moraes, D., *A Matter of People*   Deutsch   1974   Price **E**
Morris, G., *Overpopulation. Everyone's Baby*   Priory Press   1973 Price **H**
Morris, L. N. (ed.), *Human Populations, Genetic Variations and Evolution*   Intertext   1972   Price **F**
Nicol, H., *The Limits of Man: An Enquiry into the Scientific Bases of Human Population*   Constable   1967   Price **E**
Osborn, F. (ed.), *Our Crowded Planet*   Allen & Unwin   1963 Price **E**
Parsons, J., *Population Versus Liberty*   Pemberton   1971 Price **E/G**
Petersen, W., *Readings in Population*   Collier-Macmillan   1972 Price **F**
Pohlman, E. (ed.), *Population: A Clash of Prophets*   Mentor Books 1973   Price **D**

Porter, E., *Pollution in Four Industrialized Estuaries: Studies in Relation to Changes in Population and Industrial Development* H.M.S.O. 1973 Price F

Pressat, R., *Demographic Analysis* Arnold 1972 Price J

Pressat, R., *Population* (Sociology) Penguin 1973 Price C

Pringle, J. W. S. (ed.), *Biology and the Human Sciences* (Herbert Spencer lectures) O.U.P. 1972 Price E/F

Russell, J., *World Population and World Food Supplies* Allen & Unwin 1954 Price F

Shelesnyak, M. C. (ed.), *Growth of Population: Consequences and Controls* Gordon & Breach 1972 Price J

Singer, S. F. (ed.), *Is There an Optimum Level of Population?* McGraw-Hill 1971 Price H

Stanford, Q. (ed.), *The World's Population: Problems of Growth* O.U.P. 1972 Price F

Taylor, L. R. (ed.), *The Optimum Population for Britain* Academic Press 1970 Price E

Trewartha, G. T., *A Geography of Population: World Patterns* Wiley 1969 Price E

Williams, R. M., *Britain's Population. Studies in the British Economy* Heinemann 1972 Price D

Williamson, M., *The Analysis of Biological Populations* Arnold 1972 Price F/H

Wilson, E. O. & Bossert, W. H., *A Primer of Population Biology* Freeman 1971 Price E

Young, L. B., *Population in Perspective* O.U.P. 1968 Price F

Oxfordshire. Too Many People? Conservation Society 1973 Price A

Population (Series of statistical charts) I.P.P.F. 1973 Price C

Population Growth in Oxfordshire Conservation Society 1973 Price C

Population of the U.K. Select Committee on Science and Technology H.M.S.O. 1971 Price F

Population of the U.K. Background Notes No. 3 W.E.A. 1973 Price B

A Population Policy for Britain Conservation Society 1972 Price B

Report of the Population Panel (Ross Report) H.M.S.O. 1973 Price D

BOOKS (SCHOOL)

Beaujeu-Garnier, J., *The Geography of Population* Longman 1966 17 years + Price G

Burton, J., *Population* ('Man and His World' series) Blackie 1974 12−16 years Price D/E

Cairns, J., *Population Dynamics* ('Patterns of Life' series) Murray 1969 15−18 years Price D

Garner, C. *et al.*, *The World and Britain* ('This is Your World' series)
    Holmes McDougall   1972   9–13 years   Price **D**
Hay, D., *Human Populations* ('Biology Topic Books' series)   Penguin
    1972   16 years +   Price **C**
Jones, C., *et al.*, *The Population Explosion* ('Pollution' series)   Dent
    1973   14 years +   Price **E**
Lowry, J. H., *World Population and Food Supply*   Arnold   1970
    17–18 years   Price **E**
McDougall, R., *The Human Multitude* ('Project Earth' series)
    Wayland   1974   13–16 years   Price **F**
Morgan, M., *Population and Food Supply* ('Certificate Topics in
    Geography' series)   Collins   1969   15–16 years   Price **D**
Osbaldiston, P. & Cooke, P., *A Matter of Life and Death* ('Social
    Biology' series)   Ginn   1975   C.S.E.   Price **E**
Palmer, M. D., *World Population* ('World Wide' series)   Batsford
    1974   Secondary   Price **E**
Park, C. W., *The Population Explosion*   Heinemann   1965
    17–18 years   Price **C**
Robinson, H., *Human Geography* ('Handbook' series)   M. & E.   1969
    17 years +   Price **D**
Robinson, T. K., *The Population of Britain* ('Key Discussion Books'
    series)   Longman   1968   17 years +   Price **C**
Solomon, M. E., *Population Dynamics* ('Studies in Biology' series)
    Arnold   1969   17 years +   Price **D/E**
Stamp, E., *The Hungry World*   E. J. Arnold   1967   14 years +
    Price **D**
Zelinsky, W. *et al.*, *Geography and a Crowded World: A Symposium
    on Population Pressures upon Physical and Social Resources in
    the Developing Lands*   O.U.P.   1971   17 years +   Price **H**

FILMS

Competition for Land
    B.B.C.   25 min., col.   Hire **J**
Day Before Tomorrow, The (1971) (Population in developing
    countries)
    Concord   30 min., col.   Hire **G**
Fable, A (1964) (Cartoon)
    B.F.I./Concord   3 min., col.   Hire **D**
Food – or Famine (rev. 1974)
    Shell   27 min., col.   Hire free
Great Problem, A
    Concord   10 min., col.   Hire **E**
India – Year of Crisis
    Concord   30 min., b/w.   Hire **D**
One Man's Hunger (1963)
    Concord   35 min., b/w.   Hire **E**
People by the Billions (1961)
    Concord   30 min., b/w.   Hire **D**

Population (1972) (Animated diagrams)
    Concord   5 min., col.   Hire **D**
Population and Pollution (North America)
    N.A.V.A.L./Concord   17 min., col.   Hire **E**
Population Dots (1972) (Population growth)
    Concord   5 min., col.   Hire **D**
Population Explosion (1960)
    Concord   60 min., b/w.   Hire **F**
Population Problem, The (1968)
    1. *Answer in the Orient* (Japan)
    2. *Brazil: the Gathering Millions*
    3. *The European Experience*
    4. *The Gift of Choice*
    5. *India: Writings in the Sand*
    6. *U.S.A.: Seeds of Change*
    Concord   Each 30 min., b/w.   Hire (each) **F**
Population Problem, The
    Guild (900 4465–0)   14 min., col.   Hire **G**
Save This One (Britain's population problem)
    Concord   25 min., col.   Hire **G**
Squeeze, The (1965)
    Concord   10 min., b/w.   Hire **E**
Tomorrow's Children (1971)
    Concord   17 min., col.   Hire **F**

FILMSTRIPS/SLIDES/FILMLOOPS/TRANPARENCIES
Population and Resources. Part 1 – Population
    D. Wyllie (DW–156)   37 f., col.   Price **F/G**
Population Explosion, The (1971)
    Encyclopaedia Britannica (30053)   Secondary   8 transp.,
    col.   Price **E**
Population Growth – Its Causes and Effects
    I.P.P.F.   17 slides   Price **F**
        1 flipchart   Price **D**

WALLCHARTS/POSTERS
Charting Poverty (1969)   Secondary
    Oxfam   4 charts   Price **D**
Food and Agriculture Organization Charts (World population growth)
    V.C.O.A.D.   4 charts   Price **B**
Food and Population   Secondary
    V.C.O.A.D.   4 charts   Price free
Population Growth (1971)
    V.C.O.A.D.   1 photo sheet   Price **A**
Population Growth – Its Causes and Effects
    I.P.P.F.   17 charts

Population Topics (1972)   Secondary
    I.P.P.F.   13 charts   Price **F**
Wallcharts on Population   Secondary
    Oxfam/F.A.O.   4 charts   Price **C**
War on Want (Population and food supply)
    W.O.W.   4 charts   Price **B**
World in Want, The (Population explosion)   Secondary
    P.C.E.T.   Price **D**

GAMES/KITS/WORKCARDS

Conservation (Social Education Kit; includes worksheets, filmstrips)
    Macmillan   14–15 years   Price **K**
Population (Modular Learning Programme)
    C.I.A.V. (SE 2)   13–17 years   Price **G**
                    Card pack   Price **C**
Population – A Delicate Balance (Seminar Cassette – 'Life on Earth'
    series)   Foulsham   (SS 109) 45 min.   Price **F**
Towards Tomorrow (Social Education study kit, includes tape,
    filmstrips, workcards)
    Macmillan   1973   15–16 years   Price **K**

ORGANIZATIONS

Conservation Society
Eugenics Society
International Planned Parenthood Federation (I.P.P.F.)
Population Stabilization
Survival
World Population Society

JOURNALS/PERIODICALS

Ecologist
Journal of Biosocial Science
New Scientist
Population Studies
Your Environment

ARTICLES

Harrison, G. A., 'Human Population Biology – Where Now?'
    Biologist   November 1973
Russell, W. M. S., 'Population and Inflation'   *Ecologist*   February
    1971
Mackay, B., 'Population: The Issues they Can't Talk Away'   *Ecologist*
    June 1972
Slesser, M., 'How Many Can We Feed?'   *Ecologist*   June 1973
Baldwin, G. B., 'Population Policy in Developed Countries'   *Finance and
    Development*   December 1973

Bowen, I., ' "Nature's Feast" today' *Finance and Development*
    December 1973
'Inquiry into People' series *Geographical Magazine* started February
    1974
Crosbie, A. J., 'One Nation for 550,000,000 People' *Geographical*
    Magazine March 1971
Hawthorn, G., 'Does Population Growth Threaten the Natural
    Environment?' *Nature in Focus* No. 16 1973
Stuyt, L. B. J., 'Adverse Effects of Population Development on the
    Dutch Environment' *Nature in Focus* No. 16 1973
Ehrlich, P. & Freedman, J., 'Population, Crowding and Human
    Behaviour' *New Scientist* 1 April 1971
Swanson, H., 'The Consequences of Overpopulation' *New Scientist*
    26 July 1973
Crowther, J. G., 'Malthus; The Founder of Population Theory' *New*
    Scientist 10 January 1974
'Can We Learn to Feed the World in Time?' *Plain Truth* June 1972
Johnson, S., 'The People Plague. People: the Ultimate Threat to
    Humanity' *Your Environment* Winter 1970
Johnson, S., 'The People Plague in Four Countries' *Your Environment*
    Winter 1970
Ross, D., 'A Policy for Population' *Your Environment* Summer
    1972

8　POPULATION CONTROL

See also Section 7 Population Growth and Distribution (*page* 62)

BOOKS (GENERAL)

Allison, A., *Population Control*　Penguin　1970　　Price **C**
Borrie, W. D., *The Growth and Control of World Population*
　Weidenfeld & Nicolson　1970　　Price **H**
Brooks, E., *This Crowded Kingdom* (Britain's population)　Knight
　1973　Price **G**
Draper, E., *Birth Control in the Modern World*　Penguin　1972
　Price **D**
Hardin, G. (ed.), *Population, Evolution and Birth Control: A Collage of
　Controversial Ideas*, 2nd edn.　Freeman　1969　　Price **E/G**
Havemann, E. *et al., Birth Control*　Time-Life　1967　　Price **D**
Johnson, S., *Life Without Birth: A Journey through the Third World in
　Search of the Population Explosion*　Heinemann　1970
　Price **F**
Medawar, J. & Pyke, D. (eds.), *Family Planning*　Penguin　1971
　Price **C**
National Academy of Sciences, *Rapid Population Control: Consequences
　and Policy Implications* (2 volumes)　Johns Hopkins　1971
　Price **J**
Potts, M. & Wood, C., *New Concepts in Contraception. A Guide to
　Developments in Family Planning*　M.T.P.　1972　　Price **H**
Stanford, Q. (ed.), *The World's Population: Problems of Growth*
　O.U.P.　1972　　Price **F**
Vaughan, P., *Family Planning. The F.P.A. Guide to Birth Control*
　F.P.A.　1969　　Price **B**

Family Planning in Five Continents (Statistical data)　I.P.P.F.
　1973　　Price **C**
A Population Policy for Britain　Conservation Society　1972
　Price **B**
Population Stabilization: A Policy for Britain　Population Stabiliza-
　tion　1972　　Price **C**
Report of the Population Panel (Ross Report)　H.M.S.O.　1973
　Price **D**

BOOKS (SCHOOL)

Kind, R. W. & Leedham, J., *Programmed Sex Information*
　1. *Babies and Families*
　2. *You Begin Life*
　3. *You Grow Up*
　4. *Sex and Your Responsibility*
　5. *Contraception*
　　Longman　1968/9　Secondary　　Price (each) **C**

Rhodes, P., *Birth Control* ('Oxford Biology Reader')   O.U.P.   1971
   17 years +   Price **B**

FILMS

Abortion (1965)
   Concord   30 min., col.   Hire **F**
About Abortion
   Concord   22 min., col.   Hire **D**
Beyond Conception (1968)   17 years +
   Concord   35 min., col.   Hire **F**
Bright Tomorrow, A (1968) (Family planning in Jamaica)
   Concord   30 min., col.   Hire **F**
Caught for a Baby (1970)
   Concord   25 min., b/w.   Hire **F**
Fair Chance, A (1964)
   Concord   15 min., col.   Hire **E**
Family Planning (1967)
   Concord   10 min., col.   Hire **D**
Human Reproduction, 2nd edn.
   McGraw-Hill   (647551)   20 min., b/w.   Hire **F**
                     (647550)   20 min., col.   Hire **J**
In Your Hands
   Concord   28 min., b/w.   Hire **E**
Margaret Sanger (1966)
   Concord   20 min., b/w.   Hire **E**
Physiology of Human Reproduction, The
   1. *How We Began*   14 min., b/w.
   2. *Biography Before Birth*   18 min., b/w.
   3. *Preparation for Parenthood*   17 min., b/w.
      Rank (20.4337/8/9)   11 years +   Hire (each) **E**
Planned Families
   Concord   20 min., col.   Hire **F**
To Plan Your Family (1967)   15 years +
   N.A.V.A.L. (67S D37)   9 min., col.   Hire **F**
Wait or Want (Family planning in Jamaica)
   Concord   20 min., b/w.   Hire **E**

FILMSTRIPS/SLIDES/FILMLOOPS/TRANSPARENCIES

Countdown (1972)
   F.P.A.   17 slides   Hire free
Family Planning (1966)
   Camera Talks   27 f., col.   Price **G**
Human Reproduction Series
   The Male Reproductive System
   The Female Reproductive System
   The Menstrual Cycle
   Fertilization

Development in Pregnancy
Labour and Birth
    McGraw-Hill (626100)   *c.* 32 f. each   Price (each) **H**

WALLCHARTS/POSTERS
Family Planning Instruction Charts
  1. *Caps*
  2. *Chemical contraceptives – using an applicator*
  3. *Foaming tablets*
  4. *Intrauterine Contraceptive Device – Lippes Loop*
     Adam, Rouilly   17 years +   Price **J**

GAMES/KITS/WORKCARDS
Population Control (Modular Learning Programme)
    C.I.A.V. (SE 5)   13–17 years   Price **G**

ORGANIZATIONS
Abortion Law Reform Society
Birth Control Campaign
Conservation Society
Family Planning Association (F.P.A.)
International Planned Parenthood Federation (I.P.P.F.)
Population Stabilization
World Population Society

JOURNALS/PERIODICALS
Family Planning
Population Studies

ARTICLES
Manning, A., 'No Standing Room'   *Ecologist*   July 1970
Shattock, F. M., 'The Effects of Wars, Natural Disasters and Disease
    on Population Control'   *Ecologist*   December 1973
Tinker, J., 'Whose Baby is Population Control?'   *New Scientist*
    28 February 1974
Tinker, J., 'Forward to Infanticide?'   *New Scientist*   7 March 1974

9   SETTLEMENT PATTERNS

See also Section 10 Urbanization (*page* 74)

BOOKS (GENERAL)

Blythe, R., *Akenfield* (Village life in England) Penguin 1972 Price **C**
Chisholm, M., *Rural Settlement and Land Use* ('Hutchinson University
Library' series), 2nd edn. Hutchinson 1970 Price **D/E**
Hoskins, W. G., *The Making of the English Landscape,* 9th edn..
    Hodder & Stoughton 1970 Price **F**
    Penguin 1970 Price **D**
Jennings, P., *The Living Village* Penguin 1972 Price **C**

BOOKS (SCHOOL)

Clout, H. D., *Rural Geography: An Introductory Survey* Pergamon
    1972 17 years + Price **E/G**
Crosher, G. R., *The Why of Our Towns and Villages* ('Just Why' series)
    Chatto & Windus 1972 7 years + Price **C**
Everson, J. A. & Fitzgerald, B. P., *Settlement Patterns* ('Concepts in
    Geography' series) Longman 1970 17−18 years Price **D**
Hudson, F. S., *Geography of Settlements* M. & E. 1970 17 years +
    Price **E**
Minshull, R., *Settlements from the Air* Macmillan 1971 17 years+
    Price **D**
Money, D. C., *Patterns of Settlement. Human Geography in Colour*
    Evans 1972 17−18 years Price **E/F**
Money, D. C., *Human Geography,* 6th edn.
    U.T.P. 1973 17 years + Price **E**
Wilson, T., *Settlement* ('Location and Links' series) Blackwell 1973
    11−16 years Price **D**
Young, E. W., *Settlement, Trade and Transport throughout the World*
    ('Basic Studies in Geography' series) Arnold 1972
    13−17 years Price **D**
Young, G., *This is Ours* ('National Trust Children's series') (Problems of
    conservation in a typical village) Dinosaur 1974 8 years +
    Price **C**

FILMS

Settlement
    Guild (900 4349−3) 20 min., b/w. Hire **E**

FILMSTRIPS/SLIDES/FILMLOOPS/TRANSPARENCIES

Habitation − Rural, Ancient and Strategic
    Aerofilms 24 slides Price **G**
    24 prints Price **G**
    24 transp. Price **J**

Habitation – Urban and Modern
    Aerofilms   24 slides   Price **G**
                     24 prints   Price **G**
                     24 transp.   Price **J**
Villages and Village Life ('Approaches to Environmental Studies' series)
    1. *Village Sites*
    2. *Some Typical Buildings in a Village*
    3. *Things Seen in a Village*
       Blandford Press   12 slides each   Price (each) **E**

GAMES/KITS/WORKCARDS
Settlement Part 1 – Villages/Towns/Cities (Topicards)
    Macmillan   13–17 years   Price **D**
*Settlement Part 2 – Character in Temperate Regions/Hot Regions/Cold
    Regions* (Topicards)
    Macmillan   13–17 years   Price **D**
Settlement and Villages (Modular Learning Programme)
    C.I.A.V. (PP 1)   Price **G**
    16 card pack   Price **C**
Study of a Village (A Schools Council Curriculum Discussion Kit,
    based on a Somerset village)
    Hart-Davis   56 slides, 2 tapes   Price **K**
                      20 teacher's charts   Price **D**

JOURNALS/PERIODICALS
Geographical Magazine

See also Sections 9 Settlement Patterns (*page* 72) and 12 Planning (*page* 86)

BOOKS (GENERAL)

Ash, M., *A Guide to the Structure of London*   Adams & Dart   1972
    Price **D/F**
Association of American Geographers, *Geography of Cities* ('Geography
    in an Urban Age' series; teachers' guide)   Collier-Macmillan
    1969   Price **D**
Banz, G., *et al.*, *Elements of Urban Form*   McGraw-Hill   1970
    Price **J**
Bell, G. & Tyrwhitt, J., *Human Identity in the Urban Environment*
    Penguin   1972   Price **E**
Bor, W., *The Making of Cities*   Hill   1972   Price **F/H**
Bourne, L. A., *Internal Structure of the City: Readings in Space and
    Environment*   O.U.P.   1971   Price **F**
Boyle, T. & Merritt, J. D., *The Urban Adventurers*   McGraw-Hill
    1972   Price **F**
Burke, G., *Towns in the Making* (Britain and Western Europe)   Arnold
    1971   Price **G**
Canty, D., *The New City: A Program for National Urbanization Strategy*
    (U.S.A.)   Pall Mall   1969   Price **J**
Carter, H., *The Study of Urban Geography*   Arnold   1972   Price **F/H**
Carver, H., *Cities in the Suburbs*   O.U.P.   1962   Price **E/G**
C.O.I., *Housing in Britain*   H.M.S.O.   1970   Price **C**
Chartrand, R. L., *Hope for the Cities*   Macmillan   1971   Price **J**
Cherry, G. E., *Urban Change and Planning: A History of Urban Develop-
    ment in Britain since 1750*   Intertext   1972   Price **H**
Chisholm, M. & Rodgers, B. (eds.), *Studies in Human Geography*
    H.E.B. Paperback   1973   Price **E/G**
Clarke, W. M., *The City in World Economy*   Penguin   1967
    Price **C**
Crowe, S., *Tomorrow's Landscape*   Architectural Press   1956
    Price **E**
Cullen, G., *Concise Townscape*, new edn.   Architectural Press   1971
    Price **E**
Curl, J. S., *European Cities and Society*   Hill   1970   Price **G**
Dwyer, D. J., *Asian Urbanization*   Hong Kong U.P.   1971
    Price **J**
Dwyer, D. J. (ed.) *The City in the Third World* ('Geographical Readings'
    series)   Macmillan   1974   Price **F/H**
Edel, M. & Rothenberg, J., *Readings in Urban Economics*   Collier-
    Macmillan   1972   Price **F**
Elkins, T. H., *The Urban Explosion* ('Studies in Contemporary Europe'
    series)   Macmillan   1973   Price **D**

Entwhistle, F., *Rape or Marriage* (Town and country)   Oriel Press
    1970   Price **C**
Geddes, P., *City Development*   Irish U.P.   1973   Price **J**
Germani, G. (ed.), *Modernization, Urbanization and the Urban Crisis*
    Eurospan   1973   Price **G**
Goodall, R., *Economics of Urban Areas*   Pergamon   1972
    Price **G**
Gottman, J. & Harper, R. A. (eds.), *Metropolis on the Move: Geo-
    graphers Look at Urban Sprawl*   Wiley   1967   Price **F**
Greenbank, A., *Survival in the City*   Wolfe   1972   Price **F**
Hall, P., *London 2000*, 2nd edn.   Faber   1969   Price **E/H**
Healy, S., *Town Life*   Batsford   1968   Price **D**
Herbert, D., *Urban Geography. A Social Perspective*   David &
    Charles   1972   Price **G**
Holliday, J. (ed.), *City Centre Development*   Knight   1972
    Price **J**
Hosken, F. P., *The Function of Cities* (Practical problems of cities)
    Eurospan   1973   Price **H**
Jackson, J. N., *The Urban Future*   Allen & Unwin   1972   Price **J**
Jacobs, J., *The Death and Life of Great American Cities*   Penguin
    1972   Price **D**
Jacobs, J., *The Economy of Cities*   Penguin   1969   Price **C**
Jensen, R., *High Density Living*   Hill   1966   Price **J**
Johnson, J. H. (ed.), *Suburban Growth: Geographical Processes at the
    Edge of the Western City*   Wiley   1974   Price **H**
Johnston, R. J., *Urban Residential Patterns*   Bell   1971   Price **G**
Jones, E. (ed.), *Life in the City*   Pergamon   1968   Price **C**
Jones, R. (ed.), *Essays on World Urbanization*   Philip   1974
    Price **G/H**
Leahy, W. H. *et al.*, *Urban Economics: Theory, Development and
    Planning*   Collier-Macmillan   1970   Price **F/G**
Lithwick, M. H. & Paquet, G., *Urban Studies: A Canadian Perspective*
    Methuen   1969   Price **F**
Lomas, G. M. (ed.), *Social Aspects of Urban Development*   N.C.S.S.
    1966   Price **D**
McGee, T. G., *The Urbanization Process in the Third World: Explora-
    tions in Search of a Theory*   Bell   1971   Price **F**
Meadows, P. & Mizruchi, E. H., *Urbanism, Urbanization and Change:
    Comparative Perspectives*   Addison-Wesley   1969   Price **H**
Michelson, W., *Man and his Urban Environment: A Sociological App-
    roach*   Addison-Wesley   1970   Price **E**
Miles, S. R., *Metropolitan Problems: International Perspectives*
    Methuen   1971   Price **J**
Moholy-Magy, S., *Matrix of Man: An Illustrated History of Urban
    Environment*   Pall Mall   1969   Price **H**
Morgan, D. R. & Kirkpatrick, S. (eds.), *Urban Political Analysis: A
    Systems Approach*   Collier-Macmillan   1972   Price **H**
Mumford, L., *The City in History*   Penguin   1966   Price **E**

Murphy, R. E., *The Central Business District. A Study in Urban Geography* Longman 1973 Price **E**

Nottridge, H. E., *The Sociology of Urban Living* Routledge 1972 Price **D/E**

Osborn, F. J. & Whittick, A., *The New Towns: an answer to Megalopolis* Hill 1969 Price **J**

Pahl, R., *Patterns of Urban Life* ('Aspects of Modern Sociology' series) Longman 1970 Price **D/E**

Putnam, R., Kettle, P. & Taylor, F. (eds.), *A Geography of Urban Places* Methuen 1971 Price **G**

Read, B., *Healthy Cities: A Study of Urban Hygiene* Blackie 1970 Price **D/E**

Rose, H., *The Housing Problem* Heinemann 1968 Price **C/D**

Rosing, K. E. & Wood, P. A., *Character of a Conurbation. A Computer Atlas of Birmingham and the Black Country* University of London Press 1971 Price **G**

Schnore, L. F., *The Urban Scene. Readings in Human Ecology and Demography* Collier-Macmillan 1965 Price **H**

Scientific American, *Cities: Their Origin, Growth and Human Impact* Freeman 1973 Price **H**

Sharp, T., *Town and Townscape* (A source book) Murray 1968 Price **F**

Smailes, A. E., *The Geography of Towns* ('Hutchinson University Library' series) Hutchinson 1966 Price **D/E**

T. & C. P. A., *London Under Stress* Knight 1971 Price **D**

Ward, C. & Fyson, A., *Streetwork. The Exploding School* (Environmental education in towns) Routledge 1973 Price **E/G**

Williams, W. M. & Morris, R. N., *Urban Sociology* Allen & Unwin 1968 Price **E**

Worskett, R., *Character of Towns* Architectural Press 1969 Price **H**

Yeates, M. H. & Garner, B. J., *The North American City* Harper & Row 1972 Price **J**

The Built Environment Open University 1973 Price **F**

The Process of Urbanization Open University 1973 Price **F**

The Spread of Cities Open University 1973 Price **F**

BOOKS (SCHOOL)

Aylmer, U., *A Town Grows Up* (York) O.U.P. 1971 8–11 years Price **E**

Bayliss, D. G. & Renwick, T. M., *Town Study Through Photographs* ('Nelson's Geography Studies' series) Nelson 1972 13–18 years Price **C**

Beaujeu-Garnier, J., *Urban Geography* Longman 1967 17 years + Price **H**

Boon, G. (ed.), *Townlook*
1. *Observing and Recording*

76

2. *What it Looks Like*
   Pergamon   1969   Secondary   Price (each) **D**
Bull, G. B. G., *A Town Study Companion*   Hulton   1969
   Secondary   Price **D**
Crockett, M., *Towns*
   Blackwell   1972   8–10 years   Price **D**
Crosher, G. R., *The Why of Our Towns and Villages* ('Just Why' series)
   Chatto & Windus   1972   7 years +   Price **C**
Dancer, W. S. & Hardy, A. V., *Greater London*   C.U.P.   1969
   13–18 years   Price **D**
Davies, R. L., *The Nature of Cities*   Pergamon   1972   13 years +
   Price **D**
Driscoll, K. J., *Town Study. A Sample Urban Geography*   Philip
   1971   C.S.E./G.C.E.   Price **E**
Everson, J. A. & Fitzgerald, B. P., *Inside the City* ('Concepts in
   Geography' series)   Longman   1971   17 years +
   Price **F**
Hall, P., *The World Cities*   W.U.L.   1968   17 years +   Price **D**
Hammersley, A., *Towns and Town Life* ('Approaches to Environmental
   Studies' series)   Blandford Press   1969   9–13 years
   Price **D**
Hardy, G. B., *Urban Land Use* ('Environment Through Photographs'
   series)   Cassell   1972   C.S.E.   Price **D**
Hebden, R. & Wilkinson, K., *Life in the Town* ('The World We Live In'
   series)   Muller   1971   Secondary   Price **D**
Hull, O., *London* ('Topics in Geography' series)   Macmillan   1971
   C.S.E./G.C.E.   Price **D**
Johns, E., *British Townscapes*   Arnold   1965   17 years +
   Price **F**
Johnson, J. H., *Urban Geography: An Introductory Analysis*
   Pergamon   1972   17 years +   Price **E/F**
Jones, E., *Towns and Cities*   O.U.P.   1966   17 years +   Price **C**
Kinsey, G., *The Growth of London* ('Past-into-Present' series)
   Batsford   1974   Secondary   Price **E**
Kneeshaw, R., *Practical Urban Geography*   M. & E.   1972
   Secondary   Price **C**
Mack, D., *Shelter* ('Today's World' series)   Holmes McDougall   1972
   10–13 years   Price **D**
May, J., *Living in Cities*   Longman   1966   17 years +   Price **D**
Palmer, M., *Cities* ('World Wide' series)   Batsford   1971   14 years +
   Price **E**
Robinson, H., *Human Geography*   M. & E.   1969   17 years +
   Price **D**
Robson, R., *The Development of Towns and Communications*
   ('Nelson's Geography Studies' series)   Nelson   1969
   13–18 years   Price **C**
Storm, M., *Urban Growth in Britain* ('The Changing World' series)
   O.U.P.   1965   Secondary   Price **C**

Szczelkun, S., *Survival Scrapbook 1: Shelter* (Low-technology housing)
Unicorn   1973   Price **E**
Turner, P. M., *Towns* ('Topics in Geography' series)   Macmillan
1974   C.S.E./G.C.E.   Price **D**
Unstead, R. J., *Houses*   Black   1958   13–15 years   Price **E**
Walker, E. A., *Location and Links. Book 1* (Includes mapwork, towns,
shopping, countryside)   Blackwell   1972   11–16 years Price **D**
Walsh, J. W., *Urban Studies* ('Environmental Studies Assignment' series)
Schofield & Sims   1971   Secondary   Price **C**
Ward, R , *People and Towns* ('Exploring Your World' series)   Holmes
McDougall   1972   9–10 years   Price **C/D**
Woolner, A. H., *Competition for Land in Britain* ('Oxford Social
Geography' series)   O.U.P.   1972   C.S.E.   Price **E**

Living in Towns   B.B.C.   1966   Price **C**
This is your City
   1. *Glasgow and Clyde*
   2. *London*
   3. *Manchester*
   4. *Cardiff*
   Holmes McDougall   1970/3   9–13 years   Price (each) **D**

FILMS

Decent Place to Live with Hot and Cold, A (Slums in the Midlands)
Concord   25 mins   Hire **F**
Everybody's London
Guild (300 2947-7)   24 min., col.   Hire **E**
G.L.C.   Hire free
For Your Pleasure (1970) (Cartoon on the advance of the concrete
jungle)
Concord   5 min., col.   Hire **E**
Growing Town, The
   1. *The Medieval Town*
   2. *The Georgian Town*
   3. *The Industrial Town*
   4. *The Contemporary Town*
   5. *A Look at the Future*
   B.F.I.   28 min., b/w.   Hire (each) **E**
Growth of London, The   11 years +
Rank (20.4575)   23 min., b/w.   Hire **E**
House is not a Home, A (1967) (New housing estates)
Concord   30 min., b/w.   Hire **F**
India: Urban Conditions
McGraw-Hill (633433)   19 min., col.
Lewis Mumford on the City (1963)
   1. *The City – Heaven and Hell*
   2. *The City – Cars or People*
   3. *The City and its Region*

4. *The Heart of the City*
5. *The City as Man's Home*
6. *The City and the Future*
    Concord   Each 28 min., b/w.   Hire (each) **F**
London, The Unique City (Urban sprawl)
    Concord   30 min., b/w.   Hire **F**
Megalopolis — Cradle of the Future (North-eastern U.S.A.)
    N.A.V.A.L.   22 min., col.   Hire **F**
Places for People
    A New Town in England: Runcorn
    A New Town in Germany: Wulfen
    London's Lambeth
    Aslfeld, Germany
    Tinbjerg, Copenhagen, Denmark
    An Expanding Town in Sweden: Gothenburg
    An Expanding Town in France: Toulouse-Le Mirail
    The North East: England
    Germany: Playgrounds for the Ruhr
    England: Time off in Towns
    B.B.C.   Each 25 min., b/w.   Hire (each) **H**
Rise of the American City, The
    N.A.V.A.L.   32 min., col.   Hire **G**
Somewhere Decent to Live (London's housing problems)
    G.L.C.   Col.   Hire free
Suburban Living: Six Solutions (1960)
    Concord   58 min., b/w.   Hire **G**

FILMSTRIPS/SLIDES/FILMLOOPS/TRANSPARENCIES

City Community, The ('The American Way of Life' series)
    7801 *Here is the City*
    7802 *Business in the City*
    7803 *Living in the City*
    7804 *Problems of the City*
    7805 *Working in the City*
    7806 *Keeping the City Alive*
    Encyclopaedia Britannica   s/f., col.   Price (each) **F**
Esso Geography Studies
    A15 *Sheffield — Steel City*
    A18 *Bognor Regis — Seaside Resort*
    A19 *Crawley New Town*
    A20 *London: Its Growth and Function*
    A21 *Nottingham — Regional Capital*
    A22 *Southampton — Port and City*
    Longman   6 slide folios   Price (each) **D**
Habitation — Urban and Modern
    Aerofilms   24 slides   Price **G**
        24 prints   Price **G**
        24 transp.   Price **J**

Let's Tour Megalopolis
    Milliken   12 transp./6 masters   Price **G**
Living in Cities
    S429 *Victorian London*
    S430 *Children Playing in the Street*
    S431 *Old Industrial Towns*
    S432 *Transition to Modern Planning*
    S433 *Contemporary Street Scenes*
    Slide Centre   12 slide folios   Price (each) **E**
Shanty Towns (1971) (Guayaquil, Lusaka, Manila)
    V.C.O.A.D.   12 slides, b/w.   Price **E**
Towns and Town Life ('Approaches to Environmental Studies' series)
    9–13 years
    1. *Building Types and Materials up to the Industrial Revolution*
    2. *Building Types and Materials from Industrial Revolution to Present Day*
    3. *The Development of Towns*
    Blandford Press   Each 12 slides   Price (each) **E**

WALLCHARTS/POSTERS

Housing
    Shelter   5 posters   Price **D**

GAMES/KITS/WORKCARDS

City, The (Geography Workcards series)
    Heinemann   1972   32 cards   14–16 years   Price **D**
Geography – Let's Tour Megalopolis
    Milliken (4C GO3)   12 transp./6 masters   Price **G**
Homes, Housing and Environment (1973) (Workcards, filmstrip)
    E.P.   Price **D**
Housing and Houses (A.C.E. study kit)
    E.S.A.   Price **E**
Housing and You (Includes worksheets, posters, simulation)
    Shelter   Price **J**
Man and Towns ('Jackdaw' series)
    Cape   Price **D**
Megalopolis (Modular Learning Programme)
    C.I.A.V. (AD 1)   Price **G**
    16 card pack   Price **C**
Settlement Part 1 – Villages/Towns/Cities ('Topicards')
    Macmillan   C.S.E./G.C.E.   Price **D**
Simulation Games in Geography
    Macmillan   Price **D**
Studying the City
    Heinemann (1972)   32 workcards   Price **E**
                               Teachers' book   Price **C**

Tenement (A simulation)
   Shelter   Price **D**
Town Growth (Modular Learning Programme)
   C.I.A.V. (UD 2)   14–17 years   Price **G**
Towns (A.C.E. study kit)
   E.S.A.   Price **E**
Towns and their Environment (Modular Learning Programme)
   C.I.A.V. (UD 4)   14–17 years   Price **G**
Urban Civilization (Audio-visual history of the modern city)
   E.A.V. (2TF 461)   Price **K**
Urbanization ('Beaver Unit')
   Philip (in preparation)   Price **K**
You and Your Community (4 audio-visual filmstrips covering Homes,
   Travel, Work and Leisure)
   Coca-Cola   1974   8–13 years   Price **J**

ORGANIZATIONS

Association of Metropolitan Authorities
Civic Trust
Homes Before Roads
Housing Centre Trust
London Boroughs Association
London Society
Men of the Stones
National Housing and Town Planning Association
Scottish Civic Trust
Scottish National Housing and Town Planning Association
Shelter
Young Liberals (Fight the Urban Crisis)

JOURNALS/PERIODICALS

Bulletin of Environmental Education (BEE)
Geographical Magazine
Journal of Urban Analysis
New Society

ARTICLES

'Urbanization'   *BEE*   May 1971
'Study Sheet 1: Urban Problems in Britain'   *BEE*   May 1971
Boon, G. S., 'Urban Studies and the Young School Leaver'   *BEE*
   March 1972
Goodson, I, 'Urban Studies at Countesthorpe College'   *BEE*
   December 1972
Ward, C. & Fyson, A., 'The Case for Urban Study Centres'   *BEE*
   February 1973
Higson, J., 'Introducing CUSC – The Council for Urban Studies Centres'
   BEE   February 1973

Boon, G., 'Language in Towns' *BEE* February 1973

'Urban Studies at the Epping Forest Centre' *BEE* February 1973

Fyson, A., 'In the Jungle of the Cities' *BEE* March 1973

Cottle, R. W., 'The Experience of the Cities in the Improvement of the Pedestrian Environment' *BEE* April 1973

MacLaren, R., 'The Urban Crisis: Housing the Inner City' *BEE* April 1973

Darbourne, J., 'High Density Housing need not Mean Tower Blocks' *BEE* April 1973

Dubos, R., 'Will Man Adapt to Megalopolis?' *Ecologist* October 1970

Watt, K. E., 'The Costs of Urbanization' *Ecologist* February 1972

Taitz, L., 'The Urban Crisis' *Ecologist* January 1974

Sadove, R., 'Urban policy in Developed Countries' *Finance and Development* June 1973

Milner, D., 'Calcutta: A City in Despair' *Geographical Magazine* October 1968

O'Connor, A. M., 'Expanding Cities in a Rural Continent' *Geographical Magazine* December 1971

Best, R., 'March of the Concrete Jungle' *Geographical Magazine* October 1972

Best, R., 'Caracas Develops Upwards' *Geographical Magazine* April 1973

Hall, J., 'Better Future for London' *Geographical Magazine* April 1973

Wilkinson, R. K. & Sigsworth, E. M., 'Slum Dwellers of Leeds' *New Society* 4 April 1963

Pahl, R. E., 'Whose City?' *New Society* 23 January 1969

11   LAND USE

See also Sections 12 Planning (*page* 86), 13 Food Production (*page* 92)
and 24 Reclamation and Irrigation (*page* 142)

BOOKS (GENERAL)

Andrews, R. B., *Urban Land Use Policy: The Central Policy*   Collier-
Macmillan   1972   Price **G**
Beresford, J. T., *et al.*, *Land and People*   Hill   1967   Price **E**
Best, R. H. & Coppock, J. T., *The Changing Use of Land in Britain*
Faber   1962   Price **F**
Best, R. H. & Rogers, A. W., *The Urban Countryside*   Faber   1973
Price **G**
Blunden, W. R., *The Land Use/Transport System*   Pergamon   1971
Price **G**
Bracey, H. E., *People and the Countryside*   Routledge   1970
Price **G**
Chisholm, M., *Rural Settlement and Land Use* ('Hutchinson University
Library' series), 2nd edn.   Hutchinson   1970   Price **D/E**
Clark, C., *Population Growth and Land Use*   Macmillan   1967
Price **H**
Clawson, M., *America's Land and Its Uses*   Johns Hopkins Press
1972   Price **E/G**
Clout, H. D., *Rural Geography. An Introductory Survey*   Pergamon
1972   Price **E/F**
Denman, D. R. & Prodano, S., *Land Use*   Allen & Unwin   1972
Price **H**
Fairbrother, N., *New Lives, New Landscapes*
Architectural Press   1971   Price **G**
Penguin   1972   Price **E**
Found, W. C., *A Theoretical Approach to Rural Land-Use Patterns*
Arnold   1971   Price **E/F**
Howard, J. A., *Aerial Photo-Ecology*   Faber   1971   Price **J**
Lovejoy, D. (ed.), *Land Use and Landscape Planning*
Intertext   1973   Price **K**
Patmore, J. A., *Land and Leisure* (in England and Wales)
David & Charles   1970   Price **H**
Penguin   1972   Price **C**
Stamp, L. D , *Applied Geography*   Penguin   1969   Price **C**
Stamp, L. D., *The Land of Britain   Its Use and Misuse*   Longman
1963   Price **J**
Thomas, M. F. & Whittington, G. W. (eds.), *Environment and Land Use
in Africa*   Methuen   1969   Price **F/H**
Weller, J., *Modern Agriculture and Rural Planning*   Architectural
Press   1968   Price **J**

Land and People (Cambridge University Summer Conference 1966)
Hill   1967   Price **E**

BOOKS (SCHOOL)

Hardy, G. B., *Urban Land Use* ('Environment through Photographs' series)   Cassell   1972   C.S.E.   Price **D**

Knights, M. J., *Farming in the British Isles* ('Nelson's Geography Studies' series)   Nelson   1971   13–18 years   Price **C**

Morris, M. C., *Britain's Changing Countryside* ('The Changing World' series)   O.U.P.   1971   13–18 years   Price **D**

Thomas, W. S. G., *Land: Use and Misuse* ('Topics in Geography' series)   Macmillan   1971   13–18 years   Price **D**

Woolner, A. H., *Competition for Land in Britain* ('Oxford Social Geography' series)   O.U.P.   1972   C.S.E.   Price **E**

FILMS

Competition for Land, The
B.B.C.   25 min., col.   Hire **J**

FILMSTRIPS/SLIDES/FILMLOOPS/TRANSPARENCIES

Cultivation
Aerofilms	24 slides	Price **G**
	24 prints	Price **G**
	24 transp.	Price **J**

Land Use and Misuse
Aerofilms	24 slides	Price **G**
	24 prints	Price **G**
	24 transp.	Price **J**

GAMES/KITS/WORKCARDS

Community Land Use Game (Simulation game)
Collier-Macmillan   1972   Price **F**

Rural Land Use (Modular Learning Programme)
C.I.A.V. (PP 4)   Price **G**

ORGANIZATIONS

Countryside Planning: Economic Forestry Group
Dartmoor Preservation Society
Forestry Commission
Institute of Landscape Architects
Royal Institute of Chartered Surveyors
Town and Country Planning Association

JOURNALS/PERIODICALS

Journal of Forestry
Journal of Urban Analysis
Scottish Forestry
Town and Country Planning

ARTICLES

Armstrong, P. H., 'Changes in the Land Use of the Suffolk Sandlings:
A Study of the Disintegration of an Ecosystem'   *Geography*
January 1973
Tidswell, W. V., 'Agricultural Land Use and the Local Environment'
Geography   November 1973

See also Sections 10 Urbanization (*page* 74), 11 Land Use (*page* 83) and 18 Transport (*page* 115)

BOOKS (GENERAL)

Allsopp, B., *Towards a Humane Architecture* (Housing for people) Muller   1974   Price **F**

Ardill, J., *Citizen's Guide to Town and Country Planning*   Knight 1973   Price **D/F**

Ash, M., *Regions of Tomorrow*   Adams & Dart   1969   Price **E**

Bell, C. & Bell, R., *City Fathers: The Early History of Town Planning in Britain*   Penguin   1972   Price **D**

Bell, C. & Newby, H., *Community Studies*   Allen & Unwin   1972   Price **E/G**

Benevolo, L., *The Origins of Modern Town Planning*   Routledge 1967   Price **E**

Best, R. H., *Land for New Towns*   T. & C. P. A.   1964   Price **D**

Blunden, W. R., *The Land Use/Transport System*   Pergamon   1971 Price **G**

Booth, R. G., *Living Space*   Intertext   1968   Price **D**

Bourne, L. A., *Internal Structure of the City: Readings on Space and Environment*   O.U.P.   1971   Price **F**

Buchanan, C., *The State of Britain*   Faber   1972   Price **E**

Burton, T. L. & Cherry, D. E., *Social Research Techniques for Planners* Allen & Unwin   1971   Price **F**

Carver, H., *Cities in the Suburbs*   O.U.P.   1962   Price **E/G**

C.O.I., *New Towns of Britain*   H.M.S.O.   1969   Price **C**

Chadwick, G., *A Systems View of Planning*   Pergamon   1971 Price **H**

Chadwick, G. F., *The Park and the Town* (The history of public parks) Architectural Press   1966   Price **H**

Cherry, G. E., *Town Planning in its Social Context*   Hill   1970 Price **E**

Chisholm, M. (ed.) *et al., Regional Forecasting* (Colston Papers No. 22) Butterworth   1971   Price **J**

Cowling, T. M. & Steeley, G. C., *Sub-Regional Planning Studies. An Evaluation*   Pergamon   1973   Price **G**

Crosby, T., *How to Play the Environment Game*   Penguin   1973 Price **D**

Cullingworth, J. B., *Town and Country Planning in Britain,* 4th edn. ('The New Town and County Hall' series)   Allen & Unwin 1972   Price **F**

Curl, J. S., *European Cities and Society*   Hill   1970   Price **G**

Dennis, N., *People and Planning* (Sociology of housing in Scotland) Faber   1970   Price **H**

Department of Environment, *People and Planning* (Skeffington Report)
H.M.S.O.   1969   Price **D**
de Wolfe, I., *Civilia* (Urban design)   Architectural Press   1971   Price **J**
Elkin, S. L., *Politics and Land Use Planning. The London Experience*
C.U.P.   1974   Price **H**
Evans, H., *New Towns. The British Experience*   Knight   1972
Price **F/H**
Falundi, A., *A Reader in Planning Theory*   Pergamon   1973
Price **F/H**
Freeman, T. W., *Geography and Planning*, 3rd edn. ('Hutchinson
University Library' series)   Hutchinson   1968   Price **D/E**
Gans, H. J., *People and Plans: Essays on Urban Problems and Solutions*
Penguin   1972   Price **D**
Gibberd, F., *Town Design*, 6th edn.   Architectural Press   1970
Price **J**
Goodey, B., *Perception of the Environment: An Introduction to the
Literature*   Birmingham U.P.   1971   Price **E**
Goodman, R., *After the Planners*   Penguin   1972   Price **D**
Green, R. J., *Country Planning: The Future of Rural Regions*
Manchester U.P.   1971   Price **F**
Gregory, R., *The Price of Amenity* (Five studies in conservation and
government)   Macmillan   1971   Price **J**
Hackett, B., *Landscape Planning: An Introduction to Theory and
Practice*   Oriel Press   1971   Price **H**
Hall, E. T., *The Hidden Dimension: Man's Use of Space in Public and
Private*   Bodley Head   1966   Price **F**
Hall, P., *London 2000*, 2nd edn.   Faber   1969   Price **E/H**
Hall, P., *Theory and Practice of Regional Planning*   Pemberton   1970
Price **D/E**
Hillman, J. (ed.), *Planning for London*   Penguin   1971   Price **C**
Jackson, J. N., *Surveys for Town and Country* ('Hutchinson University
Library' series)   Hutchinson   1963   Price **D/E**
Jenson, R., *High Density Living*   Hill   1966   Price **J**
Kaitz, E. M. & Hyman, H. H., *Urban Planning for Social Welfare:
Experience in the Model Cities Programme* (New York City)
Praeger   1970   Price **J**
Kulp, E. M., *Rural Development Planning: Systems Analysis and Working
Method*   Praeger   1970   Price **J**
Leibbrand, H. K., *Transportation and Town Planning*   Hill   1970
Price **J**
Lovejoy, D. (ed.), *Land Use and Landscape Planning Techniques*
Intertext   1973   Price **J**
McCrone, G., *Regional Policy in Britain*   Allen & Unwin   1969
Price **F**
McLoughlin, J. B., *Urban and Regional Planning: A Systems Approach*
Faber   1969   Price **E/G**
Merlin, P., *New Towns* (Examines new towns in various countries)
Methuen   1971   Price **J**

Orr, S. C. & Cullingworth, J. B., *Regional and Urban Studies* Allen & Unwin 1969 Price **G**
Osborn, F. J., *Green Belt Cities,* 2nd edn. Adams & Dart 1969 Price **E**
Peters, P. (ed.), *Design and Planning Series*
  1. *Factories*
  2. *Libraries for Schools and Universities*
  3. *Centres for Storage and Distribution*
  4. *The New Schools*
     Van Nostrand Reinhold 1972 Price **F/J**
Reekie, R. F., *Design in the Built Environment* Arnold 1972 Price **E/G**
Saini, B. S., *Building Environment. An Illustrated Analysis of Problems in Hot Dry Lands* (A detailed study of ways in which man can come to terms with living in desert lands, including housing, solar power, desalination) Angus & Robertson 1973 Price **J**
Tetlow, J. & Goss, A., *Homes, Towns and Traffic,* 2nd edn. Faber 1968 Price **E/G**
Thomas, D., *London's Green Belt* Faber 1970 Price **G**
T. & C. P. A., *Papers on Regional Planning* T. & C. P. A. 1968 Price **D**
T. & C. P. A., *London Under Stress* T. & C. P. A. 1970 Price **D**
T. & C. P. A., *Region in Crisis* Knight 1972 Price **D**
T. & C. P. A., *The New Citizen's Guide to Town and Country Planning* Knight 1974 Price **E/G**
Van Cleef, E., *Cities in Action* (Urban planning) Pergamon 1970 Price **G**
Weddle, A. E. (ed.), *Techniques in Landscape Architecture* Heinemann 1967 Price **H**
Whitaker, B. & Browne, K., *Parks for People* Seeley, Service & Cooper 1971 Price **F**
Whitby, M. C., *et al.*, *Rural Resource Development* (Includes land use, recreation, population, settlements, transport, etc.) Methuen 1974 Price **F**
Wilson, A. G., *Urban and Regional Models in Geography and Planning* Wiley 1974 Price **J**

The Future City Open University 1973 Price **F**
Peterborough New Town H.M.S.O. 1969 Price **E**
Planners versus People? Pemberton 1970 Price **C**
Planning and the City Open University 1973 Price **F**
The Planning of the Coastline H.M.S.O. 1970 Price **D**
The Strategic Plan for the South East of England H.M.S.O. 1970 Price **F**
Tomorrow's London G.L.C. 1969 Price **E**
Traffic in Towns (Buchanan Report)
  H.M.S.O. 1963 Price **F**
  Penguin 1964 (Shortened version) Price **D**

BOOKS (SCHOOL)

Calder, N., *Living Tomorrow. Planning for the Future* ('Connexions' series)   Penguin   1970   Secondary   Price **C**

Christian, G., *Tomorrow's Countryside: The Road to the Seventies*
    Murray   1966   17–18 years   Price **G**

Edwards, R. P. A., *The Changing Scene*

The Airport	*The Motorway*
The Branch Line	*The New School*
The By-Pass	*The New Town*
The Estate	*The Tower Block*

    Burke Books   1969/70   8–13 years   Price (each) **D/E**

Edynbry, D., *New Towns* ('Get to Know' series)   Methuen   1971
    9–13 years   Price **C**

Lee, D., *Regional Planning and Location of Industry*   H.E.B.
    1972   17 years +   Price **C**

Thomson, R. & Stuart, J. E., *Design and the Environment*   Holmes
    McDougall   1973   Secondary   Price **D**

Williams, M., *New Towns* ('Contemporary Scotland' series)
    Heinemann   1969   14–16 years   Price **C**

People in Towns   B.B.C.   1968   Secondary   Price **D**

FILMS

Experiment in Towns, An (1958)
    C.F.L. (UK 1564)   22 min., col.   Hire **D**

Face of Harlow
    Guild   30 min., col.   Hire **E**

Land for Leisure
    B.B.C.   25 min., col.   Hire **J**

Looking at Britain: National Parks (1961)
    C.F.L. (UK 1662)   15 min.   Hire **D**

Look to the Future (Town planning schemes)   17 years +
    N.A.V.A.L.   27 min., col.   Hire **E**

New Town (1948) (Cartoon)
    C.F.L. (UK 890)   9 min., col.   Hire **D**

Thamesmead '70
    G.L.C.   col.   Hire free

Washington – The First Seven Years (Washington New Town)
    C.F.L. (UK 2702)   17 min., col.   Hire free

FILMSTRIPS/SLIDES/FILMLOOPS/TRANSPARENCIES

Architecture: Man-Made World

1. *Environment*	36 f., col.
2. *Man and Machine*	37 f., col.
3. *Who Cares?*	37 f., col.
4. *Change is Normal*	37 f., col.

    D. Wyllie   Price (each) **F/G**

Esso Geography Studies
   A19 *Crawley − New Town*
   A20 *London: Its Growth and Functions*
      Longman   6 slide folios   Price (each) **D**
New Towns, The
      Looking & Seeing (D 2)   36 f., col.   Price **F**
Towards 2000
      Looking & Seeing (D 4)   36 f., col.   Price **F**

GAMES/KITS/WALLCHARTS

Living in New Towns: Who Likes New Towns ('Activity Factsheets'
   series)   C.S.E.
   Nelson   1973   Packs of 10   Price **E**
Need for New Towns, The: Building for a Better Future ('Activity
   Factsheets' series)   C.S.E.
   Nelson   1973   Packs of 10   Price **E**
New Steel Site − But Where? (Role-playing game)
   C.S.V. (SA 155)   Price **C**
Spring Green Motorway, The (Role-playing game)
   C.S.V. (7144)   Price **C**
Streets Ahead (Board game)
   Midwinter   Price **F**

ORGANIZATIONS

Central Committee for the Architectural Advisory Panels
Commission for the New Towns
Council for the Protection of Rural England (C.P.R.E.)
Council for the Protection of Rural Wales
Countryside Commission
Countryside Planning: Economic Forestry Group
Department of Environment
Homes Before Roads
Institute of Landscape Architects
London Boroughs Association
Ministry of Finance, Government of Northern Ireland: Works Division
National Housing and Town Planning Council
New Towns Association
Royal Institute of Chartered Surveyors (R.I.C.S.)
Scottish National Housing and Town Planning Council
Town and Country Planning Association (T. & C.P.A.)

JOURNALS/PERIODICALS

Architectural Journal
Bulletin of Environmental Education (BEE)
Design
Environment

Geographical Magazine
New Society
Outlook
Planning Bulletin
Planning Outlook
Town and Country Planning

ARTICLES

Squire, G., 'Rural Planning in Devon and Cornwall: Some Recent
Developments'   *BEE*   June 1972

Gemmell, R. P. & Doubleday, G. P., 'Biologists in Planning'   *Biologist*
November 1973

'Resources for Britain's Future' series   *Geographical Magazine*   June
1969-June 1970

Brown, E. H. & Salt, J., 'New City in the Oxford Clay'   *Geographical
Magazine*   August 1969

Robinson, K. W., 'Three Nations in Search of Utopia'   *Geographical
Magazine*   November 1971

Macfie, C., 'Geographers and Landscape Planning'   *Geographical
Magazine*   May 1973

Grimshaw, P. N. & Briggs, K., 'Geography and Citizenship: Pupil
Participation in Town and Country Planning'   *Geography*
July 1970

Hetherington, A. C., 'Green Belts in the United Kingdom'   *Nature
in Focus*   Spring 1970

Heraud, B. J., 'New Towns: The End of a Planner's Dream'   *New
Society*   11 July 1968

Cowan, P., 'Milton Keynes: The Creation of a City'   *New Society*
13 February 1969

'Planning New Towns' series   *Pictorial Education*   May-September
1970

13 FOOD PRODUCTION AND NUTRITION

See also Sections 11 Land Use (*page* 83) and 24 Reclamation and Irrigation (*page* 142)

BOOKS (GENERAL)

Allaby, M., *Who Will Eat?* Stacey 1972 Price **G**

Allaby, M., *et al., Losing Ground: U.K. Food Prospects* F.O.E. 1974 Price **D**

Association of American Geographers, *Manufacture and Agriculture* 'Geography in an Urban Age' series; teachers' guide) Collier-Macmillan 1970 Price **D**

Borgstrom, G., *The Hungry Planet,* rev. edn. Collier-Macmillan 1973 Price **E**

Borgstrom, G., *World Food Resources* Intertext 1973 Price **E**

Boserup, E., *Conditions of Agricultural Growth* Allen & Unwin 1965 Price **E**

Brown, L. R., *Seeds of Change: The Green Revolution and Development in the 1970's* Pall Mall 1970 Price **E**

C.O.I., *Agriculture in Britain* H.M.S.O. 1969 Price **C**

Clout, H. D., *Agriculture* ('Studies in Contemporary Europe' series) Macmillan 1973 Price **D**

Coppock, J. T., *An Agricultural Geography of Great Britain* Bell 1971 Price **F**

Crawford, M. & S. *What We Eat Today* (Food and environment) Spearman 1972 Price **F**

Dawson, O. L., *Communist China's Agriculture: Its Development and Future Potential* Praeger 1970 Price **J**

Donaldson, J. G. S. & F., *Farming in Britain Today* Penguin 1972 Price **D**

Dumont, R., *Types of Rural Economy: Studies in World Agriculture* Methuen 1957 Price **D/G**

F.A.O., *The State of Food and Agriculture 1971* F.A.O. 1971 Price **H**

F.A.O./W.H.O./U.N.I.C.E.F., *Lives in Peril* (Protein and children) V.C.O.A.D. Price **C**

Fream, W., *Elements of Agriculture,* 15th edn. Murray 1972 Price **G**

Gilchrist-Shirlaw, D. W., *An Agricultural Geography of Great Britain* Pergamon 1971 Price **E**

Grant, D., *Your Daily Food* Faber 1973 Price **F**

Gray, W. D., *The Use of Fungi as Food and in Food Processing* Butterworth 1971 Price **J**

Grigg, D., *The Harsh Lands: A Study in Agricultural Development* Macmillan 1970 Price **E**

Hauschka, R., *Nutrition* Stuart & Watkins 1967 Price **G**

Hickling, C. F., *Fish Culture* Faber 1962 Price **J**

Hills, L. D., *Growing your own Fruit and Vegetables* Faber 1973
Price F

Hutchinson, J., *Farming and Food Supply: The Interdependence of Countryside and Town* C.U.P. 1972 Price G

Jamick, J. et al., *Plant Agriculture* (Readings from *Scientific American*) Freeman 1970 Price F/H

Jenkins, A. C., *The Silver Haul* ('The World We are Making' series; Fishing) Methuen 1967 Price E

Johnson, D., *World Agriculture in Disarray* Macmillan 1973 Price G Fontana 1973 Price E

Johnson, S., *The Green Revolution* Hamilton 1972 Price F

Lappe, F. M., *Diet for a Small Planet* F.O.E./Ballantine 1971 Price D

Lawrie, R. A. (ed.), *Proteins as Human Food* Butterworth 1970 Price J

Mabey, R., *Food for Free* (Natural foods from the countryside) Collins 1972 Price F

Morgan, W. B. & Munton, R. J. C., *Agricultural Geography* Methuen 1971 Price F

Mount, L., *The Nation's Food and Health* Knight 1973 Price G

Palmer, I., *How Revolutionary is the Green Revolution?* V.C.O.A.D. 1972 Price B

Pirie, N. W., *Food Resources – Conventional and Novel* Penguin 1969 Price C

Rodale, R. & Furner, B. (eds.), *The Basic Book of Organic Gardening*, rev. edn. Pan/Ballantine 1972 Price C

Sebrell, W. H. & Haggerty, J. J., *Food and Nutrition* ('Life Science Library' series), rev. edn. Time-Life 1973 Price G

Selly, C., *Ill fares the Land* (British farming) Deutsch 1972 Price F

Seymour, J. & S., *Self Sufficiency. The Science and Art of Producing and Preserving your own Food* Faber 1973 Price F

Sinclair, H. E. & Hollingsworth, D. (eds.), *Hutchinson's Food and the Principles of Nutrition* Arnold 1968 Price J

Stamp, L. D. & Buchanan, K., *Types of Farming in Britain* (Handbook and map) Association for Agriculture 1967 Price D

Symons, L., *Agricultural Geography* Bell 1967 Price E

Szczelkun, S., *Survival Scrapbook 2: Food* Unicorn 1973 Price E

Walters, A. H., *Ecology, Food and Civilization: An Ecological History of Human Society* Knight 1973 Price F

Wolf, W. J. & Cowan, J. C., *Soybeans as a Food Source* Butterworth 1971 Price J

Young, I. V., *Farm Studies in Schools* (Teaching methods handbook) Association for Agriculture 1968 Price D

Young, I. V., *Farm Visits* (Handbook for teachers) Association for Agriculture 1972 Price D

The Death of the Green Revolution V.C.O.A.D. 1973 Price **B**
Red Alert! Bread (T.A.C.C. Report No. 1) Earth Island 1973
Price **D**

BOOKS (SCHOOL)

Alnwick, H. (rev. Rees, H.), *A Geography of Commodities* Harrap
1969 15 years + Price **E**
Critchlow, K., *Into the Hidden Environment. Oceans: Lifestream of our Planet* Philip 1972 16 years + Price **F**
Davies, R. M., *Food* ('Today's World' series) Holmes McDougall 1973
10–13 years Price **D**
Fyson, N. L., *World Food* ('World Wide' series) Batsford 1972
14 years + Price **E**
Glen, A., *Farming* ('Contemporary Scotland' series), 2nd edn.
Heinemann 1973 14–16 years Price **C**
Goaman, M., *Food* ('Through the Ages' series) Wills & Hepworth
1968 8–10 years Price **B**
Huggett, F. E., *A Short History of Farming* Macmillan 1971
C.S.E. Price **D**
Johnson, R., *Farms in Britain* (Series of farm studies) Macmillan
1971 11–18 years Price **D**
Jones, C. *et al., The Food We Eat* ('Pollution' series) Dent 1973
14 years + Price **E**
Knights, M. J., *Farming in the British Isles* ('Nelson's Geography Studies' series) Nelson 1971 13–18 years Price **C**
Lowry, J. H., *World Population and Food Supply* Arnold 1970
17 years + Price **E**
Mabey, R., *Food. The Impact of Food Technology on Everyday Life* ('Connexions' series) Penguin 1970 Secondary Price **C**
Mackintosh, R. D. *et al., Farming in Britain and the World* ('Living Geography' series) Holmes McDougall 1967 12–15 years
Price **D**
Morgan, M., *Population and Food Supply* ('Certificate Topics in Geography' series) Collins 1969 15–16 years Price **D**
Noel, S., *Fish and the Sea* ('Junior Reference Books' series) Black
1972 10 years + Price **D**
Rice, P., *Farming* ('National Trust Children's series') Dinosaur 1974
8 years + Price **C**
Riley, D., *World Agriculture* ('Nelson's Geography Studies' series)
Nelson 1971 13–18 years Price **C**
Shannon, T., *About Food and Where it Comes from* ('Look, Read and Learn' series) Muller 1967 8–12 years Price **D**
Stevens, L. W., *Food, Clothing and Shelter* ('Topics in Geography' series)
Macmillan 1971 C.S.E./G.C.E. Price **D**
Tappenden, B. M., *Man's Planet* Philip 1969 8–16 years Price **D**
Voysey, A. & Hawkes, J., *The Why of our Farms* ('Just Why' series)
Chatto & Windus 1972 7 years + Price **C**

Waites, B., Wheeler, K. S. & Giggs, J. A., *Patterns and Problems of
World Agriculture*   Blond Educational   1971   17 years +
Price **E**
Walker, M. J., *Farming* ('Location and Links' series)   Blackwell
1973   11–16 years   Price **D**
Walsh, J. W., *Farming* ('Environmental Studies Assignment Books'
series)   Schofield & Sims   1971   11–16 years   Price **C**
Whitlock, R., *Feast or Famine* ('Project Earth' series)   Wayland
1974   13–16 years   Price **F**
Young, E. W., *Farming, Fishing and Forestry throughout the World*
('Basic Studies in Geography' series)   Arnold   1971
C.S.E./G.C.E.   Price **D**

FILMS

Anatomy of a Disaster (1963)
    Concord   15 min., b/w.   Hire **D**
Bihar (1967)
    Concord   25 min., b/w.   Hire **D**
Bread from Wheat   11–15 years
    Guild (330 0348–3)   15 min., col.   Hire free
Calories and Proteins
    Guild (323 1140–6)   10 min., col.   Hire free
Children, The
    Concord   10 min., b/w.   Hire **D**
China: Feeding One Fourth of the Human Race   12 years +
    McGraw-Hill (401432)   16 min., col.   Price **L**
Developing Man, A (1968)
    Concord   30 min., col.   Hire **D**
Earth and Mankind, The (6 films)
    Concord   6 X 30 min., b/w.   Hire (each) **E**
Famine (1967)
    Concord   40 min., b/w.   Hire **D**
Food for Tomorrow
    Concord   10 min., b/w.   Hire **D**
Food – or Famine (rev. 1974)
    Shell   27 min., col.   Hire free
Generous Earth
    Concord   51 min., col.   Hire **H**
Green Revolution, The (1971)
    C.F.L. (US 565)   13 min., col.   Hire **D**
High Cost of Cheap Food, The
    B.B.C.   25 min., col.   Hire **J**
Hungry Ones, The (1964)
    Concord   15 min., col.   Hire **E**
India: The Struggle for Food   8 years +
    McGraw-Hill (633444)   18 min., col.   Price **L**
Insect War, The
    B.B.C.   25 min., col.   Hire **J**

Introduction to Nutrition, An
    Guild (323 1139–6)   10 min., col.   Hire free
Land Must Provide, The (1968)
    Shell   24 min., col.   Hire free
Locusts in Retreat
    C.F.L. (UK 3097)   29 min., col.   Hire F
Look to the Land (1968) (British agriculture)   11–15 years
    Rank/Guild (320 0348–3)   15 min., col.   Hire free
Man and his Resources
    Concord   30 min., col.   Hire E
Menu (1967) (Nutritional value of food in a balanced diet)
    Canada House   22 min., col.   Hire free
Mineral Elements and Vitamins
    Guild (323 1141–3)   10 min., col.   Hire free
One Man's Hunger (1963)
    Concord   35 min., b/w.   Hire E
Our Daily Bread
    Concord   30 min., col.   Hire F
Pesticides in Focus (1971)
    Shell   25 min., col.   Hire free
Red Sky at Night (Year's work on a Scottish hill sheep farm)
    I.C.I.   52 min., col.   Hire free
Revolution in Agriculture (Chemical farming)
    I.C.I.   23 min., col.   Hire free
Rice   8 years +
    McGraw-Hill (642150)   26 min., col.   Hire J
Rival World, The (1955) (Insects)
    Shell   26 min., col.   Hire free
Secret Hunger, The (1963)
    C.F.L. (V 683)   29 min.   Hire E
Tale of Four Shepherds, A (Problems of hill sheep farming in Britain)
    I.C.I.   45 min., col.   Hire free
Talk About Food (Principles of nutrition)
    Guild (323 2645–3)   21 min., col.   Hire free
Ten Thousand to One (Food and pests)
    Guild (300 2604–7)   17 min., col.   Hire free
Today and Tomorrow (1971)
    Concord   25 min., col.   Hire D
U.N.I.C.E.F's Children
    Guild (300 2090–2)   9 min.   Hire D
Vicious Spiral, The (1969)
    Concord   25 min., col.   Hire D
Walking Revolution (Agriculture and industry in India)
    Concord   40 min.   Hire G
Wheat (1972)
    Canada House   15 min., col.   Hire free
When a Man Hungers (1966/7 drought in Bihar)
    Guild (300 2911–6)   28 min., col.   Hire E

World is Rich, The
Concord   36 min., b/w.   Hire **E**

FILMSTRIPS/SLIDES/FILMLOOPS/TRANSPARENCIES
Cultivation
Aerofilms   24 slides   Price **G**
24 prints   Price **G**
24 transp.   Price **J**
Esso Geography Studies (6-slide folios)
A5   *An Arable Farm in East Anglia*
A6   *A Dairy Farm in Somerset*
A7   *A Fruit and Hop Farm in Kent*
A8   *A Sheep Farm in the Lake District*
A11   *Fishing* (Grimsby)
Longman   All ages   Price (each) **D**
Farming, Forestry and Fishing Industries (1970) (3 filmstrips and
tapes)   11 years +
Student Recordings (AVC/4)   Price **J**
Food
Marian Ray   f/s., col.   Price **F**
Patterns in Farming (1973)
C.G.   f/s., col.   Price **F**

WALLCHARTS/POSTERS
Farming – The Changing Pattern in Britain
P.C.E.T.   Secondary   Price **D**
Food and Agriculture
V.C.O.A.D.   1971   Price **A**
Food and Population   Secondary
V.C.O.A.D.   4 charts   Price free
Food from the Sea
C.O.I.   Secondary   Price **A**
Food Loss and Waste   Secondary
F.A.O.   4 charts   Price free
Hunger – Causes and Solutions
Oxfam   12 photos.   Price **A**
Indian Agriculture
P.C.E.T.   Secondary   Price **D**
Indicative World Plan for Agricultural Development
V.C.O.A.D./F.A.O.   Secondary   Price free
New Farming Techniques
Shell   1971   Price free
Two Typical Diets
Oxfam   Secondary   Price **A**
War On Want (Population and food supply)
W.O.W.   4 charts   Price **B**

GAMES/KITS/WORKCARDS

Agriculture Part 1 ('Topicards')
The Physical Environment
The Character of Farming
Farming in Britain
    Macmillan   C.S.E./G.C.E.   Price **D**
Agriculture Part 2 ('Topicards')
Tropical Agriculture
Temperate Crops
Mountain Areas
    Macmillan   C.S.E./G.C.E.   Price **D**
Coffee Game
    V.C.O.A.D.   Price **D**
Farm Study Schemes
  1. *An Intensive Fruit Farm on the Kent/Sussex Border*
  2. *An Upland Farm on the Welsh Border*
  3. *An Arable and Stock Farm in the Scottish Borders*
  4. *A Dairy Farm in Somerset*, rev. edn.
  5. *A Farm in the Yorkshire Dales*
  7. *An Arable Farm in North Norfolk*
  8. *A Hill Sheep Farm in the Western Highlands*, rev. edn.
  9. *A Landed Estate in North East Scotland*
 10. *A Dairy Farm in North Island* (New Zealand)
 12. *A Typical Farm in the Annapolis Valley of Nova Scotia* (Canada)
 13. *A Dairy Farm in French Canada*
 14. *A Mixed Farm in Southern Ontario*
 15. *A Grain Farm on the Portage Plains of Manitoba*, rev. edn.
 16. *A Sheep-Wheat Farm in New South Wales* (Australia)
    Association of Agriculture   1968/72   Price (each) **E**
Food and Eating ('Activity Factsheets' series)   C.S.E.
    Nelson   1973   Packs of 10   Price **E**
Science – Foods and your Health
    Milliken (4C 918)   12 transp./4 masters   Price **G**

ORGANIZATIONS

Association of Agriculture
Compassion in World Farming
Crofters Commission
Farm and Food Society
Farmers Union of Wales
Freedom From Hunger Campaign (F.F.H.)
Good Gardeners' Association
Henry Doubleday Research Association
Institute of Rural Life at Home and Overseas
McCarrison Society
Ministry of Agriculture, Fisheries and Food

National Farmers Union
Oxfam
Pye Research Centre
Royal Agricultural Society of England
Vegetarian Society (U.K.) Ltd.

JOURNALS/PERIODICALS

Agriculture
Association of Agriculture Journal
Ceres
Ecologist, The
Ecology of Food and Nutrition
Epoch
Geographical Magazine
Vegetarian, The
Seed
World Hunger

ARTICLES

Allaby, M., 'One Jump ahead of Malthus'   *Ecologist*   July 1970
Allaby, M., 'Green Revolution: Social Boomerang'   *Ecologist*
    September 1970
'Green Revolution: Genetic Backlash'   *Ecologist*   October 1970
Allaby, M., 'Miracle Rice and Miracle Locusts'   *Ecologist*   May 1973
Baker, R., 'Famine: The Cost of Development?'   *Ecologist*   June 1974
Tan, K., 'Staple Products: Soya Beans'   *Geographical Magazine*
    February 1969
Harley, C. W. S., 'Staple Products: Oil Palm'   *Geographical Magazine*
    May 1969
Coppock, J. T., 'Resources for Britain's Future: Farming for an Urban
    Nation'   *Geographical Magazine*   February 1970
Sinclair, D. J., 'Harvest of Wheat'   *Geographical Magazine*   February
    1970
Coppock, J. T., 'Farming in an Industrial Age'   *Geographical Magazine*
    April 1971
Johnson, B. L. C., 'Recent Developments in Rice Breeding and some
    Implications for Tropical Africa'   *Geography*   November 1972
Reubens, E., 'Food Shortage – But Why?'   *New Society*   9 May 1974
Jackson, D., 'Third World Food Crisis'   *New Society*   16 May 1974

14 RAW MATERIALS

See also Sections 15 Water Supply (*page* 104), 16 Energy and Power
Supplies (*page* 107) and 23 Waste Disposal (*page* 139)

BOOKS (GENERAL)

Allen, S. W. & Leonard, J. W., *Conserving Natural Resources,* 3rd edn.
McGraw-Hill   1966   Price **H**
Association of American Geographers, *Habitat and Resources*
('Geography in an Urban Age' series; teachers' guide)   Collier-
Macmillan   1970   Price **D**
Coghill, I., *Australia's Mineral Wealth*   Longman   1972   Price **H**
Ehrlich, P. R. & A. H., *Population, Resources, Environment: Issues in
Human Ecology,* 2nd edn.   Freeman   1972   Price **F/H**
Horsfield, B. & Stone, P. B., *The Great Ocean Business*   Hodder &
Stoughton   1972   Price **G**
Jackson, N. & Penn, P., *Dictionary of Natural Resources and their
Principle Uses*   Pergamon   1969   Price **D/E**
Jenkins, A. C., *A Wealth of Trees* ('The World we are Making' series)
Methuen   1969   Price **E**
Loftas, A., *The Last Resource: Man's Exploitation of the Oceans*
Hamilton   1969   Price **F**
Penguin   1973   Price **D**
Lovins, A., *Red Alert! Openpit Mining*   Earth Island   1973   Price **D**
Meadows, D. H., *et al.*, *The Limits to Growth: a Report for the Club of
Rome's Project on the Predicament of Mankind*   Earth Island
1972   Price **E**
Murdoch, W. W. (ed.), *Environment: Resources, Pollution and Society*
Sinauer   1971   Price **F**
National Academy of Sciences, *Resources and Man: A Study and
Recommendations by the National Academy of Sciences*
Freeman   1969   Price **E/F**
Newbold, P. J., *Methods for Estimating the Primary Production of
Forests*   Blackwell Scientific   1967   Price **D**
Osmaston, F. C., *The Management of Forests*   Allen & Unwin   1968
Price **F**
Owen, O., *Natural Resource Conservation: An Ecological Approach*
Collier-Macmillan   1971   Price **J**
Packard, V., *The Waste Makers*   Penguin   1963   Price **C**
Parson, R. L., *Conserving American Resources,* 3rd edn.   Prentice-
Hall   1972   Price **J**
Royle, G., *Forest Service: The First 45 Years of the Forestry
Commission of Great Britain*   David & Charles   1972
Price **E/G**
Tanks, R. W., *Focus on Environmental Geology: A Collection of Case
Histories and Readings from Original Sources*   O.U.P.   1973
Price **F**

100

Warren, K., *Mineral Resources*
  David & Charles   1973   Price **G**
  Penguin   1973   Price **D**

BOOKS (SCHOOL)

Alnwick, H. (rev. Rees, H.), *A Geography of Commodities*   Harrap
  1969   15 years +   Price **E**
Burton, J., *Resources* ('Man and His World' series)   Blackie   1974
  12–16 years   Price **D/E**
Critchlow, K., *Into the Hidden Environment. Oceans: Lifestream of
  our Planet*   Philip   1972   16 years +   Price **F**
Davies, E. N. & Northedge, G. A., *Mining and Minerals*   Pergamon
  1968   13–18 years   Price **D/E**
Johnson, R., *Mines and Quarries in Britain* ('Sample Study' series)
  Macmillan   1971   C.S.E./G.C.E.   Price **D**
Morris, J. H., *Minerals and Power* ('Nelson's Geography Studies' series)
  Nelson   1971   13–18 years   Price **C**
Paterson, J. H., *Land, Work and Resources*   Arnold   1972
  17 years +   Price **E/G**
Perry, G. A., *Minerals, Mines and Mining* ('Approaches to Environmental
  Studies' series)   Blandford Press   1970   8–13 years
  Price **D**
Simmons, G. E., *The Why of Our Trees* ('Just Why' series)   Chatto
  & Windus   1972   7 years +   Price **C**
Tappenden, B. M., *Man's Planet*   Philip   1969   8–16 years
  Price **D**
Young, E. W., *Farming, Fishing and Forestry throughout the World*
  ('Basic Studies in Geography' series)   Arnold   1971
  C.S.E./G.C.E.   Price **D**

FILMS

Eternal Forest, The (1970) (Forestry in U.S.A.)
  C.F.L. (US 557)   20 min., col.   Hire **E**
Forest Heritage (New Forest)
  C.F.L. (UK 1360)   23 min., b/w.   Hire free
Iron and Steel Supply of the World, The (1949)   Secondary
  Rank   12 min., b/w.   Hire **D**
Iron Ore in Britain (Includes land reclamation)
  Guild (171 2933–8)   31 min.   Hire free
Problems of Conservation – Minerals
  N.A.V.A.L.   16 min., col.   Hire **F**
Problems of Conservation – Our Natural Resources
  N.A.V.A.L.   11 min., col.   Hire **E**
Tomorrow's Timber (Timber in Australia)
  A.N.I.B.   17 min., col.   Hire **D**
Treasure Trove (Britain's minerals)
  I.C.I.   19 min., b/w.   Hire free

Treasures of the Earth (1962)   Secondary
  Boulton-Hawker   10 min., col.   Hire **E**

FILMSTRIPS/SLIDES/FILMLOOPS/TRANSPARENCIES

Extraction, Conservation and Pollution
  Aerofilms   24 slides   Price **G**
                 24 prints   Price **G**
                 24 transp.   Price **J**
Natural Resources and You   8 years +
  9151 *What We Need*
  9152 *Where We Find It*
  9153 *How To Get It*
    Encyclopaedia Britannica   34 f., col.   Price (each) **F**
Population and Resources. Part 2 — Renewable and Non-Renewable Resources
  D. Wyllie   37 f., col.   Price **F/G**
Timber (1968)   8 years +
  C.G.   38 f., b/w.   Price **E**
Useful Minerals   Secondary
    Visual Information (350 Gl)   49 f., b/w   Price **D**

WALLCHARTS/POSTERS

Earth's Resources
  P.C.E.T.   Secondary   Price **D**
Wealth from the Forests   Secondary
  P.C.E.T.   4 charts   Price **D**

ORGANIZATIONS

British Scrap Federation
Countryside Planning: Economic Forestry Group
Forestry Commission
Ministry of Agriculture, Government of Northern Ireland: Forestry Division
National Industrial Materials Recovery Association
Scottish Woodlands Owners' Association

JOURNALS/PERIODICALS

Ecologist, The
Geographical Magazine
Journal of Forestry
Reclamation Industries International
Scottish Forestry

ARTICLES

Lucas, C. E., 'Marine Resources and the Law of the Sea Conference'
    Biologist   November 1973

Cloud, P., 'Mined Out!'   *Ecologist*   August 1970
F.O.E., 'Rock Bottom: Nearing the Limits of Metal Mining in Britain'
    Ecologist   May 1972
Freyman, A. J., 'Mineral Resources and Economic Growth'   *Finance
    and Development*   March 1974
Lord Energlyn, 'Retapping Britain's Minerals'   *Geography Magazine*
    December 1971
Mott, P. G., 'The World Surveyed in 18 Days'   *Geographical Magazine*
    January 1973
Ridgway, R. B. & Hardy, J. R., 'Skylark over Woomera'   *Geographical
    Magazine*   January 1973
Ashwell, I., 'Remote View of Snow and Water'   *Geographical
    Magazine*   March 1973
Blunden, J. R., 'The Renaissance of the Cornish Tin Industry'
    Geography   July 1970
Putman, J. J., 'Timber. How Much is Enough?'   *National Geographic
    Magazine*   April 1974
Dunham, K., 'How Long Will our Minerals Last?'   *New Scientist*
    17 January 1974
Staines, A., 'Digesting the Raw Materials Threat'   *New Scientist*
    7 March 1974
Calkins, J., 'Resource War Ahead?'   *Plain Truth*   June/July 1974

15 WATER SUPPLY

See also Sections 20 Water/Sea Pollution (*page* 129) and 24 Reclamation and Irrigation (*page* 142)

BOOKS (GENERAL)

Addison, H., *Land, Water and Food* Chapman & Hall 1966 Price E
American Waterworks Association, *Water Quality and Treatment: A Handbook of Public Water Supplies,* 3rd edn. McGraw-Hill 1970 Price J
Association of American Geographers, *Habitat and Resources* (Unit 5, 'Geography in an Urban Age' series; teacher's guide) Collier-Macmillan 1970 Price D
Clawson, M. & Landsberg, H. H., *Desalting Seawater* Gordon & Breach 1972 Price J
Field, D. R., Barron, J. C. & Long, B. F. (eds.), *Water and Community Developments: Social and Economic Perspectives* Wiley 1974 Price J
Furon, R., *The Problem of Water. A World Study* Faber 1967 Price F
Kuiper, E., *Water Resources Project Economics* Butterworth 1971 Price J
Linsley, R. K. & Franzini, J. B., *Water-Resources Engineering,* 2nd edn. McGraw-Hill 1972 Price J
Smith, K., *Water in Britain: A Study in Applied Hydrology and Resource Geography* Macmillan 1972 Price F
Sporn, P., *Fresh Water from Saline Waters* Pergamon 1966 Price E
Twort, A. C., *et al., Water Supply,* 2nd edn. Arnold 1974 Price J/K
Vallentine, H. R., *Water in the Service of Man* Penguin 1967 Price C
Wiener, A., *The Role of Water in Development* McGraw-Hill 1972 Price J
Wisdom, A. S., *The Laws of Rivers and Watercourses,* 2nd edn. Shaw 1970 Price H
Wollman, M. & Borem, G. W., *The Outlook for Water: Quality, Quantity and National Growth* (U.S.A.) Johns Hopkins Press 1971 Price J

Must it be Reservoirs? Ramblers' Association 1971 Price B
Water ('Life Science Library' series), rev. edn. Time-Life 1972 Library Price G

BOOKS (SCHOOL)

Aston, O., *Water* ('Evans Integrated Themes' series) Evans 1972 8–16 years Price D

Baxter, E., *The Study Book of Water Supply*   Bodley Head   1959
    7 years +   Price **D**
Davies, R. M., *Water* ('Today's World' series)   Holmes McDougall
    1971   10–13 years   Price **D**
Havenhand, I. & J., *Water Supply* ('The Public Services' series)   Wills
    & Hepworth   1969   7–10 years   Price **B**
Jones, E., *The World of Water* ('Approaches to Environmental Studies'
    series)   Blandford Press   1969   9–13 years   Price **D**
More, R. J., *Water and Man* ('Certificate Topics in Geography' series)
    Collins   1972   15–16 years   Price **D**
Read, B., *The Water We Used*   World's Work   1972   13–15 years
    Price **E**
Tomalin, M., *Water Supply* ('Get to Know' series)   Methuen   1943
    9 years +   Price **C**
Webster, J., *Water* ('Ladybird Leader' series)   Wills & Hepworth
    1973   6 years +   Price **B**

FILMS

Count-down Under, The (1965) (Exploration of the oceans)
    C.F.L. (V 692)   43 min., b/w.   Hire **E**
Element Three
    Concord   45 min., col.   Hire **H**
Every Drop to Drink (1948) (London's water supply)
    C.F.L. (UK 2643)   20 min.   Hire **D**
London's Water Supply
    Metropolitan Water Board   27 min., col.   Hire **C**
Towards Purity
    I.W.P.C.   36 min., col.   Hire **G**
Water (Properties and chemical aspects of water)
    I.C.I.   22 min., col.   Hire free
Water (1962)
    C.F.L. (V 608)   14 min., col.   Hire **E**
Water – A First Film   Primary
    N.A.V.A.L. (316 D5)   10 min., col.   Hire **E**
Water Cycle, The
    Guild (900 4342–4)   16 min., col.   Hire **E**
Water for Life (Desalinisation)
    C.F.L. (UK 2643)   14 min., col.   Hire free
Water, Water Everywhere
    B.B.C.   25 min., col.   Hire **J**
Ways of Water, The (1960) (Hydraulic Research Station, Wallingford)
    C.F.L. (UK 1636)   31 min., col.   Hire **F**

FILMSTRIPS/SLIDES/FILMLOOPS/TRANSPARENCIES
Problems of Water in the Third World (1973)
    V.C.O.A.D.   12 slides, col.   Price **E**

WALLCHARTS/POSTERS

Ocean Resources   Secondary
      P.C.E.T.   5 charts   Price **D**
Water   All ages
      E.P.   6 charts   Price **E**
World of Water, The   Secondary
      P.C.E.T.   Price **D**

GAMES/KITS/WORKCARDS

Water ('Beaver Unit')
      Philip   in preparation   Price **K**
Water in the U.K. (Study kit)
      E.P.   Price **D**
Waters of the World (Seminar Cassettes — 'Life on Earth' series)
      Foulsham   (SS110)   58 min.   Price **F**

ORGANIZATIONS

Central Council for Rivers Protection
Central Water Planning Unit
Freshwater Biological Association
Inland Waterways Association Ltd.
Institution of Water Engineers
National Anti-Fluoridation Campaign
National Water Council
Pure Rivers Society
Water Research Association

JOURNALS/PERIODICALS

Geographical Magazine
Water and Waste Treatment
Water Research

ARTICLES

Steele, F. N., 'Nor any Drop to Drink'   *Ecologist*   July 1971
Rees, J. A., 'The Demand for Water in South East England'   *Geographical Journal*   February 1973
Rees, J., 'Resources for Britain's Future: Thirsty Land with a Temperate Climate'   *Geographical Magazine*   November 1969
Harrison-Church, R. J., 'Vital Water for West African Dry Zone'   *Geographical Magazine*   April 1970
Sinclair, D. J., 'Water Supply and Demand in Europe'   *Geographical Magazine*   November 1970

16   ENERGY AND POWER SUPPLIES

BOOKS (GENERAL)

Avebury, Lord, *The Energy Crisis: Growth, Stability or Collapse?*
(Conservation Society Presidential Address)   Conservation
Society   1974   Price **B**

Brinkworth, B. J., *Solar Energy for Man*   Compton Press   1972
Price **G**

Callow, C., *Power from the Sea. The Search for North Sea Oil and Gas*
Gollancz   1973   Price **G**

Garvey, G., *Energy, Ecology, Economy* (Effects of growing energy use
on environment)   Macmillan   1974   Price **F**

Gofman, J. W. & Tamplin, A. R., *Poisoned Power: The Case against
Nuclear Power Plants*   Chatto & Windus   1971   Price **F**

Hinde, P., *Fortune in the North Sea*   Foulis   1966   Price **G**

Hottel, H. C. & Howard, J. B., *New Energy Technology: Some Facts and
Assessments*   M.I.T.   1973   Price **E/H**

Illich, I. D., *Energy and Equity*   Calder & Boyars   1974
Price **D/E**

Jones, D., *Communications and Energy in Changing Urban Environments* (Colston Papers No. 21)   Butterworth   1970   Price **J**

Lovins, A. B., *World Energy Strategies: Facts, Issues and Options*
F.O.E.   1973   Price **E**

MacKillop, A., (ed.), *Hydropower*   Wadebridge Ecological Centre
1974   Price **E**

Manners, G., *The Geography of Energy*   ('Hutchinson University
Library' series)   Hutchinson   1966   Price **D/E**

Masters, G. M., *Introduction to Environmental Science and Technology*
(Gives special attention to the energy crisis and alternative sources
of energy)   Wiley   1974   Price **J**

Nicol, H., *Courtiers of Canute* (Use and depletion of fossil fuels)
Knight   1973   Price **G**

Odell, P. R., *Oil and World Power: A Geographical Interpretation*
Penguin   1972   Price **D**

Odum, H. T., *Environment, Power and Society*   Wiley-Interscience
1971   Price **F**

Patterson, W. C., *Red Alert! Nuclear Reactors*   Earth Island   1973
Price **D**

Pole, N., *Oil and the Future of Personal Mobility*   Eco-Publications
1973   Price **D**

Posner, M. V., *Fuel Policy: A Study in Applied Economics*   Macmillan
1973   Price **J**

Roberts, W. G., *The Quest for Oil* ('The World We Are Making' series)
Methuen   1970   Price **G**

Sampson, S. & MacKillop, A. (eds.), *Methane*   Wadebridge Ecological
Centre   1974   Price **E**

Scientific American, *Energy and Power*   Freeman   1973   Price **E/F**

Street, H. & Frame, F. R., *Law Relating to Nuclear Energy*   Butterworth   1966   Price J

Szczelkun, S., *Survival Scrapbook 5: Energy* (Includes solar power, wind, bio-gas, water power, etc.)   Unicorn   1973   Price E

Wilson, M., *Energy* ('Life Science Library' series), rev. edn.   Time-Life   1973   Price G

Energy Sources for Scottish Transport   Transport 2000   1973   Price free

Energy and the Environment (Report of a Working Party set up jointly by CoEnCo, R.S.A. and Institute of Fuel)   R.S.A.   1974   Price G

Methane, Fuel of the Future   Singer   1973   Price F

BOOKS (SCHOOL)

Burton, J., *Resources* ('Man and His World' series)   Blackie   1974   12–16 years   Price D/E

Davies, E. N. & Johnson, S. A., *Fuels and Power*   Pergamon   1969   13–16 years   Price E

Hennessey, R. A. S., *Power* ('Past-into-Present' series)   Batsford   1972   Secondary   Price E

Jones, C. *et al.*, *The Dangerous Atom* ('Pollution' series)   Dent   1973   14 years +   Price E

MacKillop, A., *Running out of Fuel* ('Project Earth' series)   Wayland   1974   13–16 years   Price F

Morris, J. H., *Minerals and Power* ('Nelson's Geography Studies' series)   Nelson   1971   13–18 years   Price C

Rees, H., *The Industries of Britain: A Geography of Manufacturing and Power, together with Farming, Forestry and Fishing*   Harrap   1970   17 years +   Price F

Siddle, W. D., *The Story of Oil* ('Ladybird Achievements' series)   Wills & Hepworth   1968   8 years +   Price B

Simpson, E. S., *Coal and Power Industries in Post-War Britain*   Longman   1966   17 years +   Price D

Warburton, C., *The Study Book of Power*   Bodley Head   1959   7 years +   Price D

Young, E. W., *Power, Mining and Manufacturing throughout the World* ('Basic Studies in Geography' series)   Arnold   1967   C.S.E./G.C.E.   Price D

Matter and Energy ('C.S.E. General Science' series)   Routledge   1971   C.S.E.   Price E

FILMS

As Old as the Hills (1949) (Cartoon on oil formation)   B.P.   10 min., col.   Hire free

Britain's Wealth from Coal (1959)   11 years +
        N.C.B. (315X)   22 min., b/w.   Hire free
Drilling through Time (North Sea gas)
        Guild (180 2402–9)   15 min., col.   Hire free
Electricity and the Environment
        C.E.G.B.   22 min., col.   Hire free
Energy and Man   9–13 years
        McGraw-Hill (682802)   10 min., col.   Price L
Energy in Store (1972) (Storing oil)
        Shell   18 min., col.   Hire free
Lonely Places, The (Power stations and the environment)
        C.E.G.B.   23 min., col.   Hire free
Oil (1971) (Formation, distribution, search, transport and refining
        oil)
        Shell   18 min., col.   Hire free
Origins of Coal, The (1953)   11 years +
        N.C.B. (322X)   25 min., b/w.   Hire free
September Spring (1964) (Snowy River Project)
        B.P.   20 min., col.   Hire free
Water Power
        Guild (900 4347–9)   20 min., b/w.   Hire E

FILMSTRIPS/SLIDES/FILMLOOPS/TRANSPARENCIES

Energy and Man
        S1 *Movement, Force and Energy*
        S2 *Mechanical Energy*
        S3 *Heat Energy I*
        S4 *Heat Energy II*
        S5 *Heat Energy III*
        S6 *Heat Energy IV*
        S7 *Chemical Energy I*
        S8 *Chemical Energy II*
        S9 *Chemical Energy III*
        Visual Publications   s/f., col.   Price (each) E
Esso Geography Studies (6 slide folios)
        A9 *Coal Mining* (in Britain)   A14 *Oil* (Fawley)
        Longman   All ages   Price (each) D

WALLCHARTS/POSTERS

Conservation of Energy
        P.C.E.T.   C.S.E./G.C.E.   Price D
Energy Resources/Energy Conversion/Energy Forms   Secondary
        Esso   3 charts   Price free
Fuel and Power in Britain
        P.C.E.T.   Secondary   Price D
Hydro-Electric Power
        P.C.E.T.   Secondary   Price D

GAMES/KITS/WORKCARDS

Oil: A World Crisis (Seminar Cassettes – 'International Report' series)
Foulsham   (IR 101)   30 min.   Price **F**
Petrol and Pollution (Seminar Cassettes – 'International Report' series)
Foulsham   (IR 105)   30 min.   Price **F**

ORGANIZATIONS

Central Electricity Generating Board (C.E.G.B.)
Conservation Society
Electricity Council
Intermediate Technology Development Group Ltd.
National Coal Board (N.C.B.)
North of Scotland Hydro-Electricity Board

JOURNALS/PERIODICALS

Appropriate Technology
Ecologist, The
Energy Policy
Geographical Magazine
Towards Survival

ARTICLES

Holliman, N., 'Some Costs of Nuclear Power Stations to Man and his Environment' *BEE*   January 1974
Bunyard, P., 'The Power Crisis'   *Ecologist*   October 1970
Manis, G., 'Canada and the United States Energy Crisis'   *Ecologist* May 1973
Patterson, W., 'Nuclear Power'   *Ecologist*   July 1973
MacKillop, A., 'Living off the Sun'   *Ecologist*   July 1973
MacKillop, A., 'Unravel the Grid!'   *Ecologist*   November 1973
Bunyard, P., 'Energy, Crisis or Crunch?'   *Ecologist*   December 1973
Slesser, M., 'The Energy Ration'   *Ecologist*   May 1974
Warman, H. R., 'The Future of Oil'   *Geographical Journal*   September 1972
Odell, P., 'Europe Sits on its own Energy'   *Geographical Magazine* March 1974
Odell, P., 'World Energy in the Balance'   *Geographical Magazine* May 1974
Grove, N., 'The Dwindling Treasure' (oil)   *National Geographic Magazine*   June 1974
de la Calle, P. A. F., 'Europe's Problematic Energy Outlook and the Protection of the Environment'   *Nature in Focus*   No. 18 1974
Hohfeld, T., 'Energy and the Environment. A Conflict of Interests for the Consumer?'   *Nature in Focus*   No. 18 1974
Odell, P. R., 'North Western Europe's Energy Revolution'   *Geographical Magazine*   June 1969

Manners, G., 'Resources for Britain's Future: 1970's Power Game'
    Geographical Magazine   March 1970
Falcon, N., 'Oil in its True Perspective'   *Geographical Magazine*
    December 1972
Howles, L., 'Earth's Dwindling Stock of Fossil Fuel'   *New Scientist*
    5 August 1971
Hudson, K., 'Nuclear Fusion and its Prospects'   *Towards Survival*
    November 1973
Croker, F. P. U., 'Wind as a Source of Power'   *Towards Survival*
    December 1973
Hetherington, T. F. S., 'Scottish Peat'   *Towards Survival*   December
    1973
Gentry, J., 'A New Look at the Energy Crisis'   *Plain Truth*   July-
    August 1973
Dahlberg, K. A., 'Towards a Policy of Zero Energy Growth'   *Ecologist,*
    September 1973
Turner, L., 'Energy in the Year 2001'   *New Society*   13 December
    1973
Henahan, J., 'Full Steam Ahead for Geothermal Energy'   *New
    Scientist*   4 January 1973
Chedd, G., 'Brighter Outlook for Solar Power'   *New Scientist*
    5 April 1973
Kenward, M., 'Here Comes the Sun'   *New Scientist*   12 July 1973
Bruckner, A., 'Taking Power off the Wind'   *New Scientist*   28 March
    1974
Khene, A., 'Energy Crisis: The World Oil Supply'   *Resurgence*
    Jan./Feb. 1974

17   INDUSTRIALIZATION

See also Section 16 Energy and Power Supplies (*page* 107)

BOOKS (GENERAL)

Association of American Geographers, *Manufacturing and Agriculture* ('Geography in an Urban Age' series; teachers' guide)   Collier-Macmillan   1970   Price **D**

Bracey, H. E., Collin, A. & Rees, A. M., *Industry and the Countryside: the Impact of Industry on Amenities in the Countryside*   Faber 1963   Price **E**

Calder, N., *Technopolis*   Panther   1970   Price **D**

Colvin, B., *Land and Landscape: Evolution, Design and Control,* 2nd edn.   Murray   1970   Price **H**

Dickson, D., *Alternative Technology and the Politics of Technical Change*   Fontana   1974   Price **D**

Estall, R. C. & Buchanan, R. O., *Industrial Activity and Economic Geography,* 2nd. edn.   Hutchinson   1972   Price **D**

Fischer, R. B., *Science, Man and Society*   Saunders   1971   Price **E**

Forbes, R. J., *The Conquest of Nature: Technology and its Consequences*
Pall Mall   1968   Price **E**
Penguin   1971   Price **C**

Goodman, G. T. *et al., Ecology and the Industrial Society*   Blackwell 1965   Price **G**

Martin, J. E., *Greater London: An Industrial Geography*   Bell   1966 Price **F**

Milton, J. P. & Farvar, T. (eds.), *The Careless Technology: Ecology and International Development*   Stacey   1973   Price **K**

Porter, E., *Pollution in Four Industrialized Estuaries: Studies in Relation to Changes in Population and Industrial Development* H.M.S.O.   1973   Price **F**

Riley, R. C., *Industrial Geography* (Location of factories)   Chatto & Windus   1973   Price **G**

Rose, J. (ed.), *Technological Injury: The Effect of Technological Advances on Environment, Life and Society*   Gordon & Breach 1969   Price **J**

West, R., *River of Tears* (Rise of the Rio Tinto Zinc Corporation) Earth Island   1972   Price **E**

BOOKS (SCHOOL)

Lee, D., *Regional Planning and Location of Industry*   H.E.B.   1972 17 years+   Price **C**

Rees, H., *The Industries of Britain: A Geography of Manufacturing and Power, together with Farming, Forestry and Fishing*   Harrap 1970   17 years +   Price **F**

Wilson, T., *Industry and Communications* ('Location and Links' series)
    Blackwell   1973   11–16 years   Price **D**
Woolner, A. H., *Modern Industry in Britain* ('The Changing World'
    series)   O.U.P.   1968   13–18 years   Price **C/D**
Young, E. W., *Power, Mining and Manufacturing throughout the
    World* ('Basic Studies in Geography' series)   Arnold   1967
    C.S.E./G.C.E.   Price **D**

Man and Industry (Discussion book)   Shell   Secondary
    Price free

FILMS

Brave New World (Industrialization and pollution in Hungary)
    Concord   12 min., col.   Hire **F**
New Neighbour, The (Location of a new steel plant at Newport)
    Guild (180 1641–9)   24 min., col.   Hire free
Shadow of Progress, The (1970)
    B.P.   27 min., col.   Hire free
Walking Revolution (Industry and agriculture in India)
    Concord   40 min.   Hire **G**
Your Move Next (Advantages of moving industry to an expanding
    town)
    G.L.C.   col.   Hire free

FILMSTRIPS/SLIDES/FILMLOOPS/TRANSPARENCIES

Esso Geography Studies (6 slide folios)
    A10   *The Cotton Industry* (Rochdale)
    A12   *The Iron and Steel Industry at Scunthorpe*
    A13   *The Motor Vehicle Industry* (Longbridge)
    A14   *Oil* (Fawley)
    A15   *Sheffield – Steel City*
    A16   *Shipbuilding on the Clyde*
    A17   *Industrial South Wales*
    A23   *The North East*
    Longman   All ages   Price (each) **D**
Industry and Utilities
    Aerofilms   24 slides   Price **G**
            24 prints   Price **G**
            24 transp.   Price **J**
Location of Industry in Great Britain, The (1963)
    Economics Association (297 G5)   30 f., b/w.   Price **E**
Manufacturing Industries (1970) (Filmstrips and tapes)
    AVC/5   *Large Scale Industry*
    AVC/6   *Medium Scale Industry*
    AVC/7   *Small Scale Industry*
    Student Recordings   Price (each) **J**

Patterns in Industry (1973)
C.G.   f/s., col.   Price F

WALLCHARTS/POSTERS

Britain's Early Industries   Secondary
  1. *Wool*   2. *Cotton*   3. *Iron*
  P.C.E.T.   3 charts   Price D
Industrialization (1971)
  V.C.O.A.D.   Price A
Industrial Revolution, The — Technology
  P.C.E.T.   Secondary   Price D
Industrial Revolution, The — Textiles
  P.C.E.T.   Secondary   Price D
Locational Analysis of the Steel Industry
  P.C.E.T.   Secondary   Price D
Technology — Exciting or Frightening
  P.C.E.T.   Price D

GAMES/KITS/WORKCARDS

Information Kit on I.T.D.G.
  I.T.D.G.   Price D
New Steel Site, But Where? (Role-playing game)
  C.S.V.   (SA 148)   Price C
Pollution and Industry (Seminar Cassettes — 'International Report' series)
  Foulsham   (IR 102)   30 min.   Price F
Technology: The Two-Edged Sword (Seminar Cassettes — 'Life on Earth' series)
  Foulsham   (SS 112)   53 min.   Price F

ORGANIZATIONS

Council for Small Industries in Rural Areas
Intermediate Technology Development Group Ltd.
Small Industries Council for Rural Areas of Scotland

JOURNALS/PERIODICALS

Appropriate Technology
Environment and Industry
Geographical Magazine
New Scientist

ARTICLES

Warren, K., 'The Location of British Heavy Industry — Problems and Policies' *Geographical Journal* February 1973
Keeble, D., 'Resources for Britain's Future: The Proper Place for Industry' *Geographical Magazine* August 1969

See also Sections 12 Planning (*page* 86), 21 Air Pollution (*page* 133) and 22 Noise (*page* 137)

BOOKS (GENERAL)

Aird, A., *The Automotive Nightmare*   Hutchinson   1972   Price **G**

Antoniou, J., *Environmental Management: Planning for Traffic* McGraw-Hill   1971   Price **J**

Ayres, R. U. & McKenna, P., *Alternatives to the Internal Combustion Engine*   Johns Hopkins   1972   Price **J**

Bagwell, P. S., *The Transport Revolution from 1770*   Batsford   1974 Price **G/J**

Beesley, M. E., *Urban Transport: Studies in Economic Policy* Butterworth   1973   Price **K**

Blunden, W. R., *The Land Use/Transport System*   Pergamon   1971 Price **G**

Blunden, W. R., *Motorways* (Britain's motorway system)   Faber 1969   Price **H**

Brierley, J., *Car Parking and the Environment*   I.M.E.   1971 Price **C**

Bruton, M. J., *Introduction to Transportation Planning*   Hutchinson 1970   Price **F**

Buchanan, C. D., *Mixed Blessing: the Motor in Britain*   Hill   1958 Price **F**

Capelin, M. A., *Adjusting Traffic to the Environment*   I.M.E. Price **C**

Cohen, L. B., *Work Staggering for Traffic Relief: An Analysis of Manhattan's Central Business District*   Praeger   1968 Price **J**

Dept. of Environment, *Roads for the Future*   H.M.S.O.   1970 Price **B**

Dept. of Environment, *Cars for Cities*   H.M.S.O.   1967   Price **E**

Dyos, H. J. & Aldcroft, D. H., *British Transport: An Economic Survey from the Seventeenth Century to the Twentieth*   Penguin 1974   Price **E**

Gumston, B., *Transport Technology*   Chapman   1972   Price **D**

Gumston, B., *Transport: Problems and Prospects*   Thames & Hudson 1972   Price **E/F**

Hay, A., *Transport for the Space-Economy: A Geographical Study* Macmillan   1973   Price **F/H**

Hibbs, J., *Transport Studies: An Introduction*   Baker   1970 Price **E**

Hoyle, B. S. (ed.), *Transport and Development*   Macmillan   1973 Price **E**

Jones, D., *Communications and Energy in Changing Urban Environments* Butterworth   1970   Price **J**

Lane, R. *et al.*, *Analytical Transport Planning* Duckworth 1971
Price **G**
Leibbrand, H. K., *Transportation and Town Planning* Hill 1970
Price **J**
Lundberg, B., *The Supersonic – and Hypersonic – Challenge* Earth
Island 1972 Price **F**
Mann, R., *Rivers in the City* David & Charles 1973 Price **J**
Miles, J. C. C., *The Goyt Valley Traffic Experiment* Countryside
Commission 1972 Price **D**
Perman, D., *Cublington. A Blueprint for Resistance* Bodley Head
1973 Price **F**
Plowden, S. P. C., *Towns against Traffic* Deutsch 1972 Price **F**
Plowden, W., *The Motor Car and Politics 1896–1970* Bodley Head
1971 Price **J**
Pole, N., *Oil and the Future of Personal Mobility* Eco-Publications
1973 Price **D**
Pole, N., *Recreation Traffic in National Parks: Beyond the Car* Eco-
Publications 1973 Price **C**
Ritter, P., *Planning for Man and Motor* Pergamon 1964 Price **J**
Rivers, P., *The Restless Generation. A Crisis in Mobility* Davis-
Poynter 1972 Price **G**
Rolt, L. T. C., *Transport and Communications* ('The World We are
Making' series) Methuen 1967 Price **E**
Roth, G., *Paying for Roads: The Economics of Traffic Congestion*
Penguin 1967 Price **C**
Rubinstein, D. & Speakman, C., *Leisure, Transport and the Country-
side* Fabian Society 1969 Price **B**
Savage, C. I., *An Economic History of Transport* Hutchinson 1966
Price **D/E**
Stone, T. R., *Beyond the Automobile: Reshaping the Transportation
Environment* Prentice-Hall 1971 Price **E**
Storer, J. D., *Aviation* ('The World We are Making' series) Methuen
1968 Price **E**
Tetlow, J. & Goss, A., *Homes, Towns and Traffic*, 2nd edn. Faber
1968 Price **E/G**
Thomas, R., *The Economics of Traffic Congestion* Open University
1972 Price **E**
Thomson, J. M., *Motorways in London: Report of a Working Party*
Duckworth 1969 Price **F**
Walford, R., *Games in Geography* ('Education Today' series) Longman
1969 Price **E**
Wiggs, R., *Concorde: The Case Against Supersonic Transport* Pan/
Ballantine 1971 Price **C**
Williams-Ellis, C., *Roads in the Landscape* H.M.S.O. 1967 Price **B**

A Case for the Railways Conservation Society 1972 Price **B**
*Changing Directions: A Report from the Independent Commission on
Transport* Coronet 1974 Price **D**

The Channel Tunnel with Reference to Maplin Airport   Conservation
Society   1973   Price **B**
Energy Sources for Scottish Transport   Transport 2000   1973
Price free
Heavy Lorries: Memorandum to the Minister of Transport   Civic
Trust   1970   Price **D**
Red Alert! Foulness   Earth Island   1973   Price **D**
Rural Transport in Crisis   Ramblers' Association   1973   Price **B**
Traffic in Towns
H.M.S.O.   1964   Price **F**
Penguin   1964   Price **D**
Transport: Co-ordination or Chaos?   C.P.R.E.   1974   Price **B**

BOOKS (SCHOOL)

Farnworth, W., *Canals* ('On Location' series)   Mills & Boon   1973
Secondary   Price **D**
Goaman, M., *Transport* ('Through the Ages' series)   Wills & Hepworth
1970   7–10 years   Price **B**
Hammersley, A., *Roads and Road Transport* ('Approaches to Environ-
mental Studies' series)   Blandford Press   1969   9–13 years
Price **D**
Hammersley, A. & Perry, G. A., *Railways and Rail Transport* ('Approa-
ches to Environmental Studies' series)   Blandford Press   1969
9–13 years   Price **D**
Howlett, A. H., *The Why of our Roads, Railways and Waterways* ('Just
Why' series)   Chatto & Windus   1972   7 years +   Price **C**
Hull, O., *Transport* ('Topics in Geography' series)   Macmillan   1971
C.S.E./G.C.E.   Price **D**
McArthur, R. W., *Transport,* 2nd edn. ('Contemporary Scotland' series)
Heinemann   1973   14–16 years   Price **C**
McCullagh, P., *Transport in Modern Britain* ('The Changing World'
series)   O.U.P.   1971   13–18 years   Price **D/E**
Robson, R., *The Development of Towns and Communications*
('Nelson's Geography Studies' series)   Nelson   1969
13–18 years   Price **C**
Tappenden, R. M., *Man's Planet*   Philip   1969   8–16 years   Price **D**
Turner, W. A., *Transport* ('Today's World' series)   Holmes McDougall
10–13 years   Price **D**
Vialls, C., *Crossing the River* ('Industrial Archaeology' series)   Black
1971   9–12 years   Price **C**
Vince, J., *Rivers and Canal Transport* ('Approaches to Environmental
Studies' series)   Blandford Press   1970   8–13 years
Price **D**
Walsh, J. W., *Environmental Studies Assignment Book 6: Transport*
Schofield & Sims   1971   11–16 years   Price **C**
Wilson, T., *Industry and Communications* ('Location and Links' series)
Blackwell   1973   11–16 years   Price **D**

Woolner, A. H., *Competition for Land in Britain* ('Oxford Social Geography' series)   O.U.P.   1972   C.S.E.   Price E
Young, E. W., *Settlement, Trade and Transport throughout the World* ('Basic Studies in Geography' series)   Arnold   1972   C.S.E./G.C.E.   Price D

FILMS

Bart – Vision to Reality (1970) (San Francisco's Bay Area Rapid Transport system)   C.F.L. (US 588)   19 min., col.   Hire E
Development of the Major Railway Trunk Routes, The (1965) (Beeching Report)   17 years +
  British Transport (BT 776)   17 min., b/w.   Hire E
Flight Plan (1971) (Problems of growth of air transport)   B.P.   28 min., col.   Hire free
Holloway Road
  Concord   20 min., b/w.   Hire E
'I tried cotton wool but it made my ears go funny' (Harmful effects of motorway on the environment)
  Morris Documentary Films   24 min., col.   Hire H
Living with a Motor Car
  B.F.I.   45 min., b/w.   Hire G
London on the Move (1970)
  British Transport (BT 796)   15 min., col.   Hire E
Routes and Transport (Water transport)
  Guild (900 4348–6)   20 min., b/w   Hire E
Solutions? (1972) (Rail v. road, and their effects on the environment)
  British Transport (BT 1089)   7 min., col.   Hire E
Third Age of Transport, The (1971) (Road transport in Britain)
  Shell/Guild (292 2677–9)   35 min., col.   Hire free
Tide of Traffic, The (1972)
  B.P.   28 min., col.   Hire free
Town that nearly Died – of Traffic, The (1971) (High Wycombe)
  Shell   30 min., col.   Hire free
Traffic in Towns (1963) (Buchanan Report)
  C.F.L. (UK 1743)   33 min., col.   Hire F
Traffic Island (Deterioration of the environment caused by motor traffic)
  B.F.I.   17 min., b/w.   Hire F
Transport through the Ages
  Guild (294 1854–9)   9 min., col.   Hire free
What on Earth? (1966) (Cartoon on traffic congestion)
  Concord   10 min., col.   Hire E
World of the Waterways, The (1970)   11 years +
  British Transport (BT 1003)   30 min., col.   Hire E
You Can Choose (Hove)
  Civic Trust   20 min., b/w.   Hire E

18   TRANSPORT

FILMSTRIPS/SLIDES/FILMLOOPS/TRANSPARENCIES
Communications
    Aerofilms   24 slides   Price **G**
               24 prints   Price **G**
               24 transp.   Price **J**
Ports, Docks and Harbours (1970) (Filmstrip and tape)
    Student Recordings (AVC/9)   Price **J**
Roads and Road Transport ('Approaches to Environmental Studies' series)   9–13 years
1. *Before the Motor Car*
2. *The Advent of the Motor Car*
3. *Roads and Road Making*
    Blandford Press   12 slides   Price (each) **E**
Transport Systems and Communications (1970) (Filmstrip and tape)
    11 years +
    Student Recordings (AVC/10)   Price **J**

WALLCHARTS/POSTERS
Containerization
    C.O.I.   All ages   Price **B**

GAMES/KITS/WORKCARDS
Air Transport Study Kit (1969) (Includes filmstrip, workcards)
    E.P. (K 468)   All ages   Price **D**
Auto Suggestions (Work kit on the car as an urban problem)
1. *The Development of the Motor Car*
2. *Owning a Motor Car*
3. *Travel in a Motor Car*
4. *Safety in the Motor Car*
5. *The Significance of the Motor Car*
    Priority   9–13 years   Price **G**
Communications Part 1 ('Topicards')
    The Story of a Bookcase
    Simple Transport
    Modern Transport
    Macmillan   C.S.E./G.C.E.   Price **D**
Communications Part 2 ('Topicards')
    The 'Flying Scotsman' Route
    The Trans-Siberian Railway
    The Canadian Pacific Railway
    Macmillan   C.S.E./G.C.E.   Price **D**
Communications by Land (Modular Learning Programme)
    C.I.A.V. (UD 1)   14–17 years   Price **G**
               16 card pack   Price **C**
New Transport Revolution, The (Multi-media kit)
    Encyclopaedia Britannica   16 years +   Price **J**

119

North American Railways (Simulation game)
    Longman   1972   Price **G**
Spring Green Motorway, The (Role-playing game)
    C.S.V. (7144)   Price **C**
Towards Tomorrow (Social Education study kit, includes tape, film-
    strips, wallcharts)
    Macmillan   1973   15—16 years   Price **K**
Transport and Communications (1971) (6 tape recordings)
    Student Recordings (RH/9—14)   Price (each) **G**
Transport Problems: Heading for Chaos? ('Activity Factsheets.')
    Nelson   1973   Packs of 10   Price **E**
Waterways (1972)
    E.P.   Price **E**
You and Your Community (4 audio-visual filmstrips, including one on
    Transport)
    Coca-Cola   1974   8—13 years   Price **J**

ORGANIZATIONS
All Change
Automobile Association (A.A.)
British Airports Authority
British Cycling Bureau
British Railways Board
British Road Federation
British Waterways Board
Chartered Institute of Transport
Commitment
Conservation Society Transport Working Party
Department of Environment
Federation Against Aircraft Nuisance
Inland Waterways Association Ltd.
Kennet and Avon Canal Trust Ltd.
Light Railway Transport League
Maritime Trust
National Council on Inland Transport
National Ports Council
Pedestrians' Association for Road Safety
Railway Invigoration Society
Royal Automobile Club (R.A.C.)
Traffic Trust
Transport 2000
Transport and Road Research Laboratory
Transport Reform Group
Transport Studies Society
Transport Trust
Transport Users' Consultative Committees
Welsh Railways Action Committee

JOURNALS/PERIODICALS
Arrive
Geographical Magazine
New Scientist
Transportation Planning and Technology

ARTICLES
'Transport Issue'   *BEE*   July 1972
Liedloff, J., 'The Supersonic Albatross'   *Ecologist*   September 1970
Coates, I., 'Railways: The Fight is on'   *Ecologist*   March 1973
'The Maplin Manifesto'   *Ecologist*   April 1973
Patmore, A., 'Resources for Britain's Future: New Directions for
      Transport'   *Geographical Magazine*   July 1969
Tolley, R. S., 'New Technology and Transport Geography: The Case
      of the Hovercraft'   *Geography*   July 1973
Breach, I., ' "The Automobile, Man and the Environment" – in that
      12 July 1973
'Channel Tunnel: Bore of the Century?'   *New Scientist*   11 October
      1973
Loveless, B. W., 'The Effects of Oil Shortages on Transport'   *Towards
      Survival*   November 1973
Breach, I., ' "The Automobile, Man and the Environment" – in that
      Order?'   *Your Environment*   Summer 1972

19   POLLUTION (GENERAL)

See also Sections 20 Water/Sea Pollution (*page* 129), 21 Air Pollution (*page* 133), 22 Noise (*page* 137) and 23 Waste Disposal (*page* 139)

BOOKS (GENERAL)

Adamson, R. G., *Pollution: An Ecological Approach*   Heinemann
    1972   Price E
Andrews, W. A. *et al.*, *Guide to the Study of Environmental Pollution*
    Prentice-Hall   1972   Price E
Ashby, E. (Chairman), *Royal Commission on Environmental Pollution*
    (Annual reports)   H.M.S.O.   1971/3   Price (each) C
Association of American Geographers, *Habitat and Resources* ('Geo-
    graphy in an Urban Age' series; teachers' guide)   Collier-
    Macmillan   1970   Price D
Auld, D. A. L. (ed.), *Economic Thinking and Pollution Problems*
    O.U.P.   1972   Price J
Barr, J., *The Assaults on Our Senses*
    Methuen   1970   Price F
    Sphere   1971   Price C
Baxter, R. & Burke, J. (eds.), *Tomorrow's World: 2nd Volume*   B.B.C.
    1971   Price F
Berkowitz, D. A. & Squires, A. M. (eds.), *Power Generation and
    Environmental Change*   M.I.T.   1971   Price J
Bockris, J. O'M. (ed.), *Electrochemistry of Cleaner Environments*
    Plenum   1972   Price K
Bourne, A., *Pollute and be Damned*   Dent   1972   Price F
Bugler, J., *Polluting Britain: A Report*   Penguin   1972   Price C
Carson, R., *Silent Spring*
    Hamish Hamilton   1963   Price F
    Penguin   1965   Price C
Clarke, R., *We All Fall Down: The Prospects of Biological and Chemical
    Warfare*   Penguin   1969   Price C
Commoner, B., *The Closing Circle: The Environmental Crisis and its
    Cure*   Cape   1972   Price F
Cox, P. R. & Peel, J. (ed.), *Population and Pollution* (Eugenics Society
    Symposium)   Academic Press   1972   Price F
Deju, R. A., *Environment and its Resources*   Gordon & Breach   1972
    Price J
Denney, R. C., *This Dirty World*   Nelson   1971   Price F
D.E.S., *Further Review of Certain Persistent Organochlorine Pesticides
    in Great Britain: Report 1969*   H.M.S.O.   1969   Price D
Dept. of Environment, *Pollution: Nuisance or Nemesis?*   H.M.S.O.
    1972   Price E
Dept. of Environment, *Progress Report of the Standing Technical
    Committee on Synthetic Detergents* (Annual surveys. 1959—1970)
    H.M.S.O.   Price (each) C

Dept. of Local Govt., *The Protection of the Environment: The Fight against Pollution*   H.M.S.O.   1970   Price **D**

Edwards, C. A., *Persistent Pesticides in the Environment*   Butterworth   1971   Price **J**

Epstein, S. & Legator, M. S., *The Mutagenicity of Pesticides: Concepts and Evaluations*   M.I.T.   1971   Price **J**

Finstein, M. S., *Pollution Microbiology: A Laboratory Manual*   Marcel Dekker   1972   Price **G**

Fish, B. R., *Surface Contamination*   Pergamon   1967   Price **J**

Goldman, M. I., *The Spoils of Progress: Environmental Pollution in the Soviet Union*   M.I.T.   1972   Price **G**

Graham, F., *Since Silent Spring*
Hamilton   1970   Price **F**
Pan/Ballantine   1972   Price **C**

Hamblin, L., *Pollution: The World Crisis*   Stacey   1970   Price **E**

Hartley, G. S. & West, T. F., *Chemicals for Pest Control*   Pergamon   1969   Price **E/F**

Hartmann, N. N. *et al.*, *Nature in the Balance*   Heinemann   1973   Price **E**

Hassal, K. A., *Pesticides*   Butterworth   1969   Price **J**

Hills, H. C., *Living Dangerously* (Pollution in the home)   Stacey   1973   Price **F**

Hutnik, R. J. & Davis, G., *Ecology of Devastated Land*   Gordon & Breach   1972   Price **L**

Kennet, W. Y., *Controlling our Environment*   Fabian Society   1970   Price **B**

Lund, H. F. (ed.), *Industrial Pollution Control Handbook*   McGraw-Hill   1971   Price **K**

McLoughlin, J., *The Law Relating to Pollution: An Introduction* ('Studies in Environmental Pollution' series)   Manchester U.P.   1972   Price **E**

Mellanby, K., *Pesticides and Pollution* ('New Naturalist' series), 2nd rev. edn.   Collins/Fontana   1970   Price **C/E**

Mellanby, K., *The Biology of Pollution* ('Studies in Biology' series)   Arnold   1972   Price **D/E**

Murdoch, W. W. (ed.), *Environment: Resources, Pollution and Society*   Sinauer   1971   Price **F**

Porter, E., *Pollution in Four Industrialized Estuaries: Studies in Relation to Changes in Population and Industrial Development*   H.M.S.O.   1973   Price **F**

Rogers, T. H., *Marine Corrosion*   Butterworth   1968   Price **H**

Rose, J. (ed.), *Technological Injury: The Effect of Technological Advances on Environment, Life and Society*   Gordon & Breach   1969   Price **J**

Rudd, R. L., *Pesticides and the Living Landscape*   Faber   1964   Price **F**

Smith, G. & Smyth, J. C. (eds.), *The Biology of Affluence*   Oliver & Boyd   1972   Price **E**

Sternglass, E. J., *Low Level Radiation* (A scientist calls attention to radiation damage to infants and the unborn)   Earth Island 1973   Price F
Stevens, R. W. (ed.), *Pesticides in the Environment*   Marcel Dekker 1971   Price J
Strobbe, M. A., *Understanding Environmental Pollution*   Kimpton 1971   Price F
S.C.E.P., *Man's Impact on the Global Environment: Assessment and Recommendations for Action*   M.I.T.   1971   Price E/J
Taylor, F. *et al.* (eds.), *Pollution: The Effluence of Affluence* Methuen   1971   Price G
Tucker, A., *The Toxic Metals*
  Earth Island   1972   Price F
  Pan/Ballantine   1972   Price D
Turk, A. *et al.*, *Ecology, Pollution, Environment*   Saunders   1972 Price E
Victor, P. A., *Pollution, Economy and Environment*   Allen & Unwin 1972   Price J
Walker, C., *Environmental Pollution by Chemicals*   Hutchinson Educational   1971   Price E
Wallis, H. F., *The New Battle of Britain*   Knight   1972   Price D/F
Ward, M. W., *Man and his Environment*   Pergamon   1970   Price J
White-Stevens, R., *Pesticides in the Environment* (2 volumes)   Marcel Dekker   1971   Price (each) K
Whittington, D., *The Effluent Society*   Nelson   1972   Price F
Wolozin, H. (ed.), *The Economics of Pollution*   Eurospan   1974 Price G
Yap, W. B. & Smith, M. I., *Production, Pollution, Protection*   Wykeham 1972   Price F

How You Can Protect Yourself against Pollution   Conservation Society   1973   Price B
Pollution   G.L.C.   1971   Price D
Pollution Engineering Techniques. (Collected papers of the Second Annual International Pollution Engineering Congress)   Wiley 1974   Price J
The Problems of Persistent Chemicals   O.E.C.D.   1972   Price D
Radio Active Waste Management in Western Europe   O.E.C.D. 1972   Price E
Third Report of the Research Committee on Toxic Chemicals (Agricultural Research Council)   H.M.S.O.   1970   Price C

BOOKS (SCHOOL)

Baker, R. E. & Bushel, J. A., *The Unclean Planet* ('Social Biology' series)   Ginn   1972   C.S.E.   Price E
Burton, J., *Pollution* ('Man and His World' series)   Blackie   1974 12–16 years   Price D/E

Edwards, R., *Pollution* ('Oxford Biology Reader' series)   O.U.P.
    1972   17 years +   Price **B**
Jackson, O., *Conservation and Pollution* ('World Wide' series)   Batsford
    1971   14 years +   Price **E**
Warner, M., *Your World – Your Survival*   Abelard-Schuman   1971
    10 years +   Price **E**
Wentworth, P. F. *et al., Pollution*   Blond Educational   1973
    10–13 years   Price **E**

FILMS

After the Torrey Canyon
    R.S.P.B.   13 min., col.   Hire **F**
And on the Eighth Day (1970) (4 films on misuse of chemicals)
    Concord   4 X 15 min., col.   Hire **J**
Black Spot to Beauty Spot (Stoke-on-Trent)
    C.F.L (UK 3091)   15 min., col.   Hire **E**
Brave New World (Industrialization and pollution in Hungary)
    Concord   12 min., col.   Hire **F**
Choice, The (Practical approach to the control of pollution)
    I.C.I.   29 min., col.   Hire free
Electricity and the Environment
    C.E.G.B.   22 min., col.   Hire free
Environment in the Balance (1970)
    Shell   30 min., col.   Hire free
Germs and Chemical Warfare
    Concord   30 min., b/w.   Hire **F**
Help Me (Effects of the Torrey Canyon disaster)
    R.S.P.C.A.   10 min., col.   Hire free
It Gets into Everything (Pesticides)
    B.B.C.   25 min., col.   Hire **J**
Matter of Attitudes, A (1968) (Pollution in Canada)
    Concord   30 min., b/w.   Hire **F**
Multiply and Subdue the Earth
    Concord   50 min., col.   Hire **J**
Persistent and Finagling (Pressure group on pollution)
    Concord   60 min., b/w.   Hire **H**
Poisons, Pests and People
    Concord   60 min., b/w.   Hire **G**
Population and Pollution
    Concord/N.A.V.A.L.   17 min., col.   Hire **F**
Teesside? We Only Live Here (1969) (Industrial pollution)
    Concord   27 min., col.   Hire **G**

FILMSTRIPS/SLIDES/FILMLOOPS/TRANSPARENCIES

Dangerous Litter (Litter and animals; includes tape recording)
    R.S.P.C.A. (ST 3)   24 slides, col.   Hire free

Don't Spoil our World (Paintings by children on pollution)
    Concord   f/s., col.   Price **G**
Extraction, Conservation and Pollution
    Aerofilms   24 slides   Price **G**
                  24 prints   Price **G**
                  24 transp.   Price **J**
Industrial Pollution ('The Environment' series)
    Griffin & George   f/s., col.   Price **G**
Introduction and Historic Background ('Pollution' series)
    Slide Centre (S716)   18 slides, col.   Price **F**
Pollution by Waste ('Pollution' series)
    Slide Centre (S758)   12 slides, col.   Price **E**
Us versus the Rest − Extinction ('Pollution' series)
    Slide Centre (S719)   12 slides, col.   Price **E**

WALLCHARTS/POSTERS

Pollution
    P.C.E.T.   10 photoposters   Price **D**

GAMES/KITS/WORKCARDS

Conservation ('Social Education Kit')
    Macmillan   14−15 years   Price **K**
Conservation and Pollution ('Beaver Unit')
    Philip   in preparation   Price **K**
Countryside, The (A.C.E. study set)
    E.S.A.   Price **E**
Local Pollution: The Air we Breathe, the Water we Drink
    ('Activity Factsheet' series)   C.S.E.
    Nelson   1973   Packs of 10   Price **E**
Petrol and Pollution (Seminar Cassettes − 'International Report' series)
    Foulsham (IR 105)   30 min.   Price **F**
Pollution (Modular Learning Programme)
    C.I.A.V. (SE 3)   13−16 years   Price **G**
Pollution Control (Modular Learning Programme)
    C.I.A.V. (SE 6)   13−17 years   Price **G**
Pollution and Industry (Seminar Cassettes − 'International Report' series)
    Foulsham (IR 102)   30 min.   Price **F**
Pollution Test Kit (material and instructions for 10 experiments)
    Griffin & George   Price **J**

ORGANIZATIONS

Anti-Concorde Project
Coastal Anti-Pollution League Ltd.
Conservation Society
Federation Against Aircraft Nuisance
Howey Foundation

Institute of Petroleum
Institution of Public Health Engineers
National Coal Board (N.C.B.)
Royal Commission on Environmental Pollution
Royal Society of Health
Survival

JOURNALS/PERIODICALS

Ecologist, The
Enviro-Bulletin
Environmental Pollution
Environmental Pollution Management
Epoch
Natural History
Naturopa
Pollution
Pollution Control
Pollution Monitor
Pollution Monthly
Pollution Technology International
Your Environment

ARTICLES

Waters, L. & Tansey, P., 'Environmental Pollution Simulation'   *BEE*
    May 1972
Holdgate, M. W., 'Action against Pollution'   *Biologist*   May 1972
Lawton, J. H. & McNeill, S., 'Primary Production and Pollution'
    Biologist   November 1973
Huddle, N. & Reich, M., 'The Octopus that Eats its own Legs'
    Ecologist   August 1973
Goldsmith, E., 'Pollution by Tourism'   *Ecologist*   January 1974
Bunyard, P., 'Is There a Peaceful Atom?'   *Ecologist*   July 1970
Hills, L. D., 'Fertility or Pollution?'   *Ecologist*   November 1970
Bridger, R., 'The Pesticide Fallacy'   *Ecologist*   February 1971
Goldsmith, E., 'The Cost of Pollution'   *Ecologist*   September 1971
Leff, D. N., 'Politics of Pollution'   *Ecologist*   September 1971
Lofroth, G., 'Who Cares about D.D.T.?'   *Ecologist*   November 1971
Allaby, M., 'Why not ban D.D.T.?'   *Ecologist*   April 1972
Davoll, J., 'Canute and the Pollutants'   *Ecologist*   January 1972
McLoughlin, J., 'Pollution and the Individual'   *Ecologist*   August
    1972
'Pollution Control – Legislation/Technology'   *Epoch*
Garnett, A., Sheffield Emerges from Smoke and Grime'   *Geographical*
    Magazine   November 1970
Steiner, S., 'Effluence of the Eternal City'   *Geographical Magazine*
    September 1971
'Healing the Scars of Progress'   *Geographical Magazine*   August 1972

Jamison, A., 'How Sweden Tackles Pollution'   *New Scientist*
    4 February 1971
Loftas, T., 'Mediterranean Pollution: Another Year of Neglect'   *New
    Scientist*   15 July 1971
Tinker, J., 'How to Measure Disgust'   *New Scientist*   20 September
    1973
Bugler, J., 'Our Polluted World'   *New Society*   3 July 1969
'Our Environment' series   *Pictorial Education*   October 1970–
    February 1971
Gott, L., 'Who's that Polluting my World?'   *Plain Truth*   January
    1973
Gentry, J., 'How One Town Solves Pollution and Saves Water'   *Plain
    Truth*   January 1973
'Public Safety: Mercury'   *Which?*   June 1974
Patterson, W. C., 'Odourless, Tasteless and Dangerous. Hazards of
    Radioactive Waste'   *Your Environment*   Summer 1970
Montague, K. & P., 'Don't Eat the Fish'   *Your Environment*   Winter
    1971
Tucker, A., 'The Toxic Cocktail'   *Your Environment*   Winter 1971
Price, B., 'The Paraquat Follies. Pesticides Legislation in Britain'
    Your Environment   Spring 1973

See also Section 19 Pollution (General), (*page* 122)

BOOKS (GENERAL)

Bennett, G. W., *Management of Lakes and Ponds*   Van Nostrand
    Reinhold   1971   Price **J**
Ciaccio, L., *Water and Water Pollution Handbook* (4 volumes)   Marcel
    Dekker   1971/2   Price (each) **K**
Dept. of Environment, *River Pollution Survey*   H.M.S.O.   1970
    Price **H**
Dept. of Environment, *Out of Sight, Out of Mind* (Effect of dumping
    in Liverpool Bay)   H.M.S.O.   1972   Price **E**
Dugan, P. R., *Biochemical Ecology of Water Pollution*   Plenum
    1972   Price **J**
Gill, C., Booker, F. & Soper, T., *The Wreck of the Torrey Canyon*
    David & Charles   1967   Price **E**
Goldberg, E. D., *A Guide to Marine Pollution*   Gordon & Breach
    1972   Price **H/J**
Hood, D. W. (ed.), *Impingement of Man on the Oceans*   Wiley   1971
    Price **K**
Hoult, D. P. (ed.), *Oil on the Sea*   Plenum   1969   Price **H**
Hynes, H. B. N., *The Biology of Polluted Waters*   Liverpool U.P.   1960
    Price **H**
Hynes, H. B. N., *The Ecology of Running Waters*   Liverpool U.P.
    1970   Price **E/J**
James, G. V., *Water Treatment*   Technical Press   1971   Price **H**
Jenkins, S. H., *Advances in Water Pollution Research*   Pergamon
    1971   Price **L**
Johnson, A. A. (ed.), *Water Pollution in the Greater New York Area*
    Gordon & Breach   1970   Price **J**
Jones, J. R. E., *Fish and River Pollution*   Butterworth   1964
    Price **F**
Klein, L., *River Pollution*
    Volume 1 Chemical Analysis   1959   Price **F**
    Volume 2 Causes and Effects   1962   Price **J**
    Volume 3 Control   1966   Price **J**
    Butterworth
Mancy, K. H., *Instrumental Analysis for Water Pollution Control*
    Wiley   1971   Price **J**
Marx, W., *The Frail Ocean*   Pan/Ballantine   1970   Price **C**
Moorcraft, C., *Must the Seas Die?*   Temple Smith   1972
    Price **E/F**
Muirhead-Thomson, R. C., *Pesticides and Freshwater Fauna*   Academic
    Press   1971   Price **G**
Nelson-Smith, A., *Oil Pollution and Marine Ecology*   Elek Science
    1972   Price **C**

Olson, T. A. & Burgess, F. J. (eds.), *Pollution and Marine Ecology*
Wiley 1967 Price **J**
Petrow, R., *The Black Tide: In the Wake of the Torrey Canyon*
Hodder & Stoughton 1968 Price **E**
Reed, L., *An Ocean of Waste: Some Proposals for Clearing the Seas
around Britain* Conservative Political Centre 1972 Price **D**
Robertson, L., *Pollution of Seas and Rivers* I.M.E. 1972 Price **C**
Shuval, H. I. (ed.), *Developments in Water Quality Research* Wiley
1970 Price **J**
Sibthorp, M. M., *Oceanic Pollution: A Survey and some Suggestions
for Control* David Davies 1970 Price **C**
Southgate, B. A., *Water: Pollution and Conservation* Thunderbird
Enterprises 1969 Price **F**
Tebbutt, T. H. Y., *Principles of Water Quality Control* Pergamon
1971 Price **E/F**
Warren, C. E., *Biology and Water Pollution Control* Saunders 1971
Price **H**
Wisdom, A. S., *The Law on the Pollution of Waters,* 2nd edn. Shaw
1966 Price **G**

Report of a River Pollution Survey of England and Wales H.M.S.O.
Volume 1 1971 Price **H**
Volume 2 1972 Price **J**
*Water Pollution as a World Problem: The Legal, Scientific and Political
Aspects* Europa Publications 1971 Price **G**
Water Pollution Control Engineering H.M.S.O. 1970 Price **D**

BOOKS (SCHOOL)

Jones, C. *et al., The Waters of the Earth* ('Pollution' series) Dent
1973 14 years + Price **E**
Mabey, R., *The Pollution Handbook* ('Extensions' series) Penguin
1974 8–13 years Price **D**

FILMS

After the Torrey Canyon
R.S.P.B. 13 min., col. Hire **F**
Ageing of Lakes, The
N.A.V.A.L. 14 min., col. Hire **E**
Deterioration of Water
Rank (21.1296) 19 min., col. Hire **G**
Operation Oil (1969)
Canada House 20 min., col. Hire free
Problems of Conservation – Water
N.A.V.A.L. 16 min., col. Hire **F**
River Must Live, The (1966)
Shell 21 min., col. Hire free

River with a Problem (1961) (Ottawa River)
 Concord 28 min., b/w. Hire **F**
Towards Purity
 I.W.P.C. 36 min., col. Hire **G**
Water, Water Everywhere . . .
 B.B.C. 25 min., col. Hire **J**

FILMSTRIPS/SLIDES/FILMLOOPS/TRANSPARENCIES

Marine Pollution ('The Environment' series)
 Griffin & George f/s., col. Price **G**
Pollution of the Sea ('Pollution' series)
 Slide Centre (S720) 12 slides, col. Price **E**
Ponds and Rivers ('Pollution' series)
 Slide Centre (S717) 12 slides, col. Price **E**
Water Pollution ('The Environment' series)
 Griffin & George f/s., col. Price **G**
Water Pollution
 DW147 *Sources and Effects of Inland Water Pollution*
 DW148 *The Effects of Marine Pollution/The Control of Water*
 Pollution
 D. Wyllie c.40 f., col. Price **F/G**
World of Water, The ('Approaches to Environmental Studies' series)
 9–13 years
 1. *Water and Living things*
 2. *Water and its Properties I*
 3. *Water and its Properties II*
 Blandford Press 12 slides Price (each) **E**

GAMES/KITS/WORKCARDS

Star River Project (Game, with sufficient material for up to 30 players)
 Esso/C.R.A.C. 1973 17 years + Price **J**
Water Pollution Kit (A.C.E. study kit)
 E.S.A. Price **D**
Waters of the World (Seminar Cassettes – 'Life on Earth' series)
 Foulsham (SS 110) 58 min. Price **F**

ORGANIZATIONS

Anglers' Co-operative Association
Central Council for Rivers Protection
Coastal Anti-Pollution League Ltd.
Freshwater Biological Association
Institute of Water Pollution Control (I.W.P.C.)
National Pure Water Association
National Water Council
Pure Rivers Society
Water Pollution Research Laboratory

JOURNALS/PERIODICALS

Effluent and Water Treatment Journal
Marine Pollution Review
Operculum
Pollution Control
Pollution Monitor
Water and Waste Treatment
Water Pollution Abstracts
Water Pollution Control
Water Pollution Research
Water Research

ARTICLES

George, J. D., 'Can the Seas Survive?'   *Ecologist*   March 1971
Pilpel, N., 'Oil Pollution of the Sea'   *Ecologist*   March 1972
'Pollution of the Sea'   *Nature in Focus*   Summer 1971
Pilpel, N., 'Sunshine on a Sea of Oil'   *New Scientist*   13 September 1973
Sandbrook, R., 'No Slick Solution to Oil Pollution'   *New Scientist* 6 December 1973
Loftas, T.,'The New Marine Poison'   *New Scientist*   29 July 1971
'Bathing, Sewage and Illness'   *Which?*   July 1973
Cowell, E. B., 'Biological Effects of Oil Pollution'   *Your Environment* Summer 1970
Heyerdahl, T., 'The Ocean is like a Boiling Pot'   *Your Environment* Autumn 1971

See also Section 19 Pollution (General) (*page* 122)

BOOKS (GENERAL)

Adler, I. & R., *Air* ('The Reason Why' series)   Dobson   1962
    Price D
Agricultural Research Council, *The Effects of Air Pollution on Plants
    and Soils*   H.M.S.O.   1967   Price C
Bach, W., *Atmospheric Pollution*   McGraw-Hill   1972   Price E/F
Brodine, V., *Air Pollution* ('Environmental Issues' series)   Harcourt
    Brace   1973   Price E
Cantuti, V. (ed.), *Air Pollution – Cortina 1969*   Butterworth   1971
    Price G
Crenson, M., *The Un-Politics of Air Pollution: A Study of Non-Decision-
    Making in the Cities*   Johns Hopkins   1971   Price H
Dept. of Trade & Industry, *National Survey of Air Pollution 1961–71:
    Volume 1: Introduction, U.K., South East, Greater London*
    H.M.S.O.   1972   Price G
Garner, J. F. & Crow, R. K., *Clean Air – Law and Practice,* 3rd edn.
    Shaw   1969   Price J
Gilpin, A., *Control of Air Pollution*   Butterworth   1963   Price J
Gregory, P., *Polluted Homes* (Air pollution in Billingham)   Bell
    1965   Price D
Hagevik, G. H., *Decision-Making in Air Pollution Control: A Review of
    Theory and Practice, with Emphasis on Selected Los Angeles and
    New York City Management Experiences*   Praeger   1970
    Price J
Isaac, P. C. G., *The Effects, Measurement and Control of Atmospheric
    Pollution due to Combustion*   Oriel Press   1954   Price B
Ledbetter, J. O., *Air Pollution* (2 volumes)   Marcel Dekker   1972
    Price J
Leithe, W., *The Analysis of Air Pollutants*   Wiley   1970   Price J
Mamantov, G. & Shults, W. D. (eds.), *Determination of Air Quality*
    Plenum   1972   Price J
Meethan, A. R., *Atmospheric Pollution,* 3rd edn.   Pergamon   1964
    Price F
Momhebel, G. (ed.), *Gas Purification Processes for Air Pollution Control,*
    2nd edn.   Butterworth   1972   Price K
Royal College of Physicians, *Air Pollution and Health,* 3rd edn.
    Pitman Medical   1971   Price E
Scorer, R. S., *Air Pollution*   Pergamon   1968   Price F/G
Starkman, E. S. (ed.), *Combustion-Generated Air Pollution*   Plenum
    1971   Price J
Stern, A. C. (ed.), *Air Pollution*
    1. *Air Pollution and its Effects*

2. *Analysis, Monitoring and Surveying*
3. *Sources of Air Pollution and their Control*
    Academic Press   1968/9   Price (each) **K**
Strauss, W., *Air Pollution Control*   Wiley   1971   Price **J**
Summer, W., *Odour Pollution of Air: Causes and Control*   Intertext
    1971   Price **J**

Air Pollution: Background Notes No. 1   W.E.A.   1973   Price **B**
Clean Air Yearbook   National Society for Clean Air   1969 onwards
    Price **E**
*Inadvertent Climate Modification: Report of the Study of Man's Impact
    on the Climate*   M.I.T.   1972   Price **E/J**

BOOKS (SCHOOL)

Jones, C. *et al.*, *The Air We Breathe* ('Pollution' series)   Dent   1973
    14 years +   Price **E**
O'Donnell, P. *et al.*, *Air Pollution* ('Environmental Pollution' series)
    Addison-Wesley   1971   13–16 years   Price **D**

FILMS

Air (Properties of air and production of gases)
    I.C.I.   14 min., col.   Hire free
Air – A First Film (1969)   Primary
    N.A.V.A.L. (315 D57)   10 min., col.   Hire **E**
Air, The – My Enemy
    Gas Council   25 min., col.   Hire free
Air Pollution: A Medical Investigation of One Aspect (1972)
    C.F.L. (UK 2686)   17 min., col.   Hire free
Fall Out
    Italian Institute   12 min., col.   Hire free
First Mile Up, The (1961)
    Concord   30 min., b/w.   Hire **E**
    Canada House   Hire free
Free as Air
    B.B.C.   25 min., col.   Hire **J**
Paradise Lost (1970) (Effect of air pollution on wildlife)
    Canada House   4 min., col.   Hire free
Something to Sing About (How I.C.I. tackle air pollution at Billingham)
    I.C.I.   12 min., col.   Hire free
We Call it Petrol (1972) (Includes research on exhausts and air pollution)
    Shell   24 min., col.   Hire free

FILMSTRIPS/SLIDES/FILMLOOPS/TRANSPARENCIES

Air Pollution
    DW145   *Local, Continental and National Pollution*
    DW147   *Industrial Pollution*
    D. Wyllie   f/s., col.   Price **F/G**

Air Pollution ('The Environment' series)
    Griffin & George   f/s., col.   Price **G**
Air We Need, The ('Approaches to Environmental Studies' series)
    9–13 years
    1. *Air and Air Pressure*
    2. *Winds and their Origins and Breathing Underwater*
    3. *Aerodynamics and Animals that Fly*
    4. *Photosynthesis and Ingredients of the Air*
    Blandford Press   12 slides   Price (each) **E**
Air You Breathe, The
    D. Wyllie (DW 159)   43 f., col.   Price **F/G**
Pollution of the Air ('Pollution' series)
    Slide Centre (S718)   12 slides, col.   Price **E**

WALLCHARTS/POSTERS

Air Pollution
    National Society for Clean Air
    5 posters   Price (each) **B**
    1 wallchart   Price **B**
    Notes   Price **C**
Clean Air
    E.P.   Secondary   Price **B**

GAMES/KITS/WORKCARDS

Air Pollution (Gas Council study kit; includes workcards, study prints
    data sheets)
    E.P.   Price **D**
Clean Air Research Kit (Pollution testing kit)
    A.C.E.   All ages   Price **D**

ORGANIZATIONS

Alkali and Clean Air Inspectorate
Clean Air Council for England and Wales
Clean Air Council for Scotland
National Society for Clean Air

JOURNALS/PERIODICALS

Atmospheric Environment
Clean Air
Pollution Control
Pollution Monitor
Smokeless Air

ARTICLES

Albone, E., 'The Ailing Air'   *Ecologist*   September 1970
Briggs, R. T., 'SO$_2$: Acid in the Sky'   *Ecologist*   November 1972

Bryson, R. A., 'Drought in Sahelia' *Ecologist* October 1973
Holt-Jensen, A., 'Acid Rains in Scandinavia' *Ecologist* October 1973
Blokker, P. C., 'Air Pollution Today' *Nature in Focus* Winter 1972
Bovay, E., 'The Effects of Air Pollution on Plants, Animals and Soils'
 Nature in Focus Winter 1972
Lob, M., 'Air Pollution and its Effects on Human Health' *Nature in
 Focus* Winter 1972
Ross, F., 'Sulphur Dioxide over Britain and Beyond' *New Scientist*
 13 April 1971
'Public Safety. Lead' *Which?* April 1973

BOOKS (GENERAL)

Attenborough, K., *Noise Abatement*   Open University   1972   Price **D**
Bell, A., *Noise: An Occupational Hazard and a Public Nuisance*   W.H.O.
    1966
Burns, W., *Noise and Man*   Murray   1968   Price **G**
Burns, W. & Robinson, D. W., *Hearing and Noise in Industry*   D.H.S.S.
    1970   Price **E**
Duerden, C., *Noise Abatement* (Technical handbook)   Butterworth
    1970   Price **J**
Kryter, K. D., *The Effects of Noise on Man*   Academic Press   1970
    Price **J**
McKennal, A. C. & Hunt, E. A., *Noise Annoyance in Central London*
    H.M.S.O.   1968   Price **D**
Rodda, M., *Noise and Society*   Oliver & Boyd   1967   Price **C**
Starkie, D. N. & Johnson, D. M., *The Economic Value of Peace and
    Quiet*   Saxon House   (1975-in preparation)
Taylor, R., *Noise*   Penguin   1970   Price **C**

Aircraft Noise: Flight Routing near Airports   H.M.S.O.   1971
    Price **C**
*Aircraft Noise: Second Survey of Aircraft Noise Annoyance around
    London Airport*   H.M.S.O.   1971   Price **F**
The Law on Noise   Noise Abatement Society   1969   Price **E**
Neighbourhood Noise (Report on Noise Abatement Act)   H.M.S.O.
    1971   Price **D**
Noise Pollution: Background Notes No. 2   W.E.A.   1973   Price **B**
Quieter Living   B.B.C.   1970   Price **C**
Traffic Noise: Vehicle Regulations and their Enforcement   H.M.S.O.
    1972   Price **D**
Urban Design Bulletin 1: Traffic Noise   G.L.C.   1970   Price **D**
Urban Design Bulletin 2: Industrial Noise   G.L.C.   1970   Price **C**

BOOKS (SCHOOL)

Jones, C. *et al.*, *The Noise We Hear* ('Pollution' series)   Dent   1973
    14 years +   Price **E**
O'Donnell, P., *et al.*, *Noise Pollution* ('Environmental Pollution' series)
    Addison-Wesley   1971   13–16 years   Price **D**

FILMS

Noise Invasion, The
    B.B.C.   50 min., b/w.   Hire **J**
Noise Pollution
    Rank (21.1295)   18 min., col.   Hire **G**

ORGANIZATIONS
British Association for the Control of Aircraft Noise
Federation Against Aircraft Nuisance
Local Authorities Aircraft Noise Council
Noise Abatement Society
Noise Advisory Council

JOURNALS/PERIODICALS
Noise and Vibration Bulletin
Noise Control and Vibration Reduction
Noise News Digest
Quiet Please
Which?

ARTICLES
'Prosecuting for Noise Abatement' *Ecologist* November 1972
Sibley, C. B., 'For Whom the Decibel Tolls' *Epoch* Autumn 1972
    and Winter 1972/3
Adams, J. G. U. & Haigh, N., 'Booming Discorde' *Geographical Magazine* July 1972
Bryan, N., 'Noise Laws don't Protect the Sensitive' *New Scientist*
    27 September 1973
'Traffic Noise: The 20,000 Worst Culprits' *Which?* January 1973
'Traffic Noise: What it Means to You' *Which?* April 1973

See also Sections 15 Water Supply (*page* 104), 19 Pollution (General) (*page* 122) and 20 Water/Sea Pollution (*page* 129)

BOOKS (GENERAL)

Amphlett, C. B., *Treatment and Disposal of Radio-Active Wastes*
    Pergamon   1961   Price **H**
Association of American Geographers, *Habitat and Resources* ('Geography in an Urban Age'; teachers' guide)   Collier-Macmillan
    1970   Price **D**
Bolton, R. L. & Klein, L., *Sewage Treatment: Basic Principles and Trends*   Butterworth   1971   Price **J**
Dept. of Environment, *Refuse Disposal: Report of the Working Party on Refuse Disposal*   H.M.S.O.   1971   Price **E**
Downing, P. B., *Economics of Urban Sewage Disposal*   Praeger
    1969   Price **J**
Escritt, L. B., *Public Health Engineering Practice*, 4th edn. (2 volumes)
    M. & E.   1972   Price (each) **J**
Escritt, L. B., *Sewers and Sewage Works*   Allen & Unwin   1971
    Price **G**
Goransson, B. (ed.), *Industrial Waste Water – Stockholm 1970*
    Butterworth   1972   Price **K**
Imhoff, K. *et al.*, *Disposal of Sewage and other Water-Borne Wastes*,
    2nd edn.   Butterworth   1971   Price **J**
Isaac, P. C. G., *Waste Treatment*   Pergamon   1960   Price **J**
Koziurowski, B. & Kucharski, J., *Industrial Waste Disposal*   Pergamon
    1972   Price **J**
Marx, W., *Man and his Environment: Waste*   Harper & Row   1971
    Price **E**
Ministry of Housing & Local Govt., *Disposal of Solid Toxic Wastes: Report of the Technical Committee on the Disposal of Solid Toxic Wastes*   H.M.S.O.   1970   Price **D**
Ministry of Housing & Local Govt., *Taken for Granted: Report of the Working Party on Sewage Disposal*   H.M.S.O.   1970
    Price **D**
Neal, A. W., *Industrial Waste: Its Handling, Disposal and Re-Use*
    Business Books   1971   Price **G**
Nemerow, M. L., *Liquid Waste of Industry: Theories, Practices and Treatment*   Addison-Wesley   1971   Price **K**
Packard, V., *The Waste Makers*   Penguin   1963   Price **C**
Patterson, W. & Searle, G., *Packaging in Britain. A Policy for Containment*   F.O.E.   1973   Price **D**
Skitt, J., *Disposal of Refuse and other Wastes*   Knight   1972   Price **J**
Small, W. E., *Third Pollution: The National Problem of Solid Waste Disposal*   Pall Mall   1971   Price **G**

Staudinger, J. J. P., *Disposal of Plastics Waste and Litter*   Society of
    Chemical Industry   1970   Price **F**
Stirrup, F. L., *Public Cleansing*   Pergamon   1965   Price **E/F**
Tchobamoglaus, G., *Waste Water Engineering* (rev.)   McGraw-Hill
    1972   Price **J**
Zajic, J. E., *Water Pollution: Disposal and Re-use* (2 volumes)   Marcel
    Dekker   1971   Price **J**

The Ecology of Refuse Tips   Heinemann   1970   Price **E**
Good Riddance to Good Rubbish (Recycling of waste material)
    Maybank   Price free
The Great Paper Chase. A Guide to Paper Salvage   F.O.E.   1974
    Price **C**
*Waste Not . . . A Report Prepared for Camden Council on the Feasi-
    bility of Recycling Waste Paper*   F.O.E.   1974   Price **D**
Waste Paper   British Waste Paper Assn.   1971   Price **F**

BOOKS (SCHOOL)

Holliman, J., *Waste Age Man* ('Project Earth' series)   Wayland   1974
    13–16 years   Price **F**

FILMS

Funny Thing Happened on the Way to the Garbage Dump, A (1972)
    Concord   51 min., b/w.   Hire **G**
Garbage Explosion, The
    N.A.V.A.L.   16 min., col.   Hire **F**
Litter
    C.P.R.E.   col.   Hire **F**
Refuse Disposal   11 years +
    Rank (20.4658)   11 min., b/w.   Hire **D**
    Guild (900 4502–0)   Hire **E**
Sewage Disposal   11 years +
    Rank (20.0946)   10 min., b/w.   Hire **D**
Taken for Granted (London's sewage disposal)
    C.F.L. (UK 1136)   20 min., col.   Hire **E**
Trade it in, Throw it away (Planned obsolescence)
    Concord   50 min., b/w.   Hire **G**

WALLCHARTS/POSTERS
Leave No Litter
    Countryside Commission   Price free

ORGANIZATIONS
British Scrap Federation
Institution of Public Health Engineers

Keep Britain Tidy Group
Maybank (J. & J.) Ltd. (*see page* 186)
National Industrial Materials Recovery Association

JOURNALS/PERIODICALS

Compost Science
Effluent and Water Treatment Journal
Industrial Recovery
Journal of the Institute of Public Health Engineers
Pollution Technical International
Public Cleansing
Reclamation Industries International
Your Environment

ARTICLES

Housden, R., 'Rubbish Dump Blues' *Ecologist* December 1972
Hardy, S., 'Going to Waste' *Epoch* Spring/Summer 1973
Jaag, O., 'The Present Problems of Waste Disposal and the Future of
Waste Management in Europe' *Nature in Focus* Winter 1972
'Rubbish' *Which?* May 1974
'The Household Environment – 2. Waste Paper' *Your Environment*
Summer 1971
'The Household Environment – 4. Non-Returnable Bottles' *Your
Environment* Winter 1971
'The Household Environment – 5. Packaging' *Your Environment*
Spring 1972

24   RECLAMATION AND IRRIGATION

See also Sections 23 Waste Disposal (*page* 139) and 25 Conservation (*page* 145)

BOOKS (GENERAL)

Arnon, I., *Crop Production in Dry Regions* (2 volumes)   Intertext   1972   Price (each) **J**
Barr, J., *Derelict Britain*, rev. edn.   Penguin   1970   Price **C**
Carson, R., *Silent Spring*
    Hamilton   1963   Price **F**
    Penguin   1965   Price **C**
Collins, W. G. (ed.), *Proceedings of the Derelict Land Symposium*
    Iliffe   1969   Price **G**
Graham, F., *Since Silent Spring*
    Hamilton   1970   Price **F**
    Pan/Ballantine   1972   Price **C**
Hart, R. A. de J., *The Inviolable Hills: the Ecology, Conservation and Regeneration of the British Uplands*   Stuart & Watkins   1968   Price **F**
Jenkins, A. C., *The Golden Band* ('The World we are Making' series; reclamation in the Netherlands)   Methuen   1967   Price **E**
Olivier, H., *Irrigation and Water Resources Engineering*   Arnold   1972   Price **J**
Oxenham, J. R., *Reclaiming Derelict Land*   Faber   1966   Price **F**
Pownall, E., *The Thirsty Land* ('The World we are Making' series; irrigation in Australia)   Methuen   1967   Price **E**

Derelict Land: A Study of Industrial Dereliction and how it may be Redeemed   Civic Trust   1964   Price **C**
Reclamation of Derelict Land   Civic Trust   1970   Price **C**
The Rhondda Valleys: Proposals for the Transformation of an Environment   Civic Trust   1965   Price **C**

BOOKS (SCHOOL)

Simons, M., *Deserts. The Problem of Water in Arid Lands* ('The Changing World' series)   O.U.P.   1967   13–18 years   Price **D**

FILMS

Arid Lands (1960)
    C.F.L. (V 723)   27 min., b/w.   Hire **E**
Black Spot to Beauty Spot (1972) (Reclamation in Stoke-on-Trent)
    C.F.L. (UK 3091)   15 min., col.   Hire **E**

Down to Earth (1966) (Reclamation of gravel workings)
     C.F.L. (UK 2652)   17 min., col.   Hire free
Generous Earth (1966) (Soil reclamation)
     C.F.L. (V 749)   51 min.   Hire **H**
Indus Waters (1967) (Irrigation)   11 years +
     Guild (900 4051–3)   25 min., col.   Hire **G**
Irrigation
     Guild (900 4346–2)   20 min., b/w.   Hire **E**
Land Reclamation (1959) (Modern techniques of reclamation)
     Shell   25 min., col.   Hire free
Price to Pay, The (Effects of open-cast mining)
     Concord   56 min., col.   Hire **J**
Seven Million Acres (1973) (History of land drainage in Britain)
     C.F.L. (UK 3189)   16 min.   Hire **E**
Trees on the Move
     Civic Trust   19 min., col.   Hire **E**
Valley of the Tennessee (1944)
     C.F.L. (UK 1632)   12 min., b/w.   Hire **C**

FILMSTRIPS/SLIDES/FILMLOOPS/TRANSPARENCIES

Irrigation on the River Nile
     Macmillan (IV/4013)   Filmloop   Price **H**
New Land from the Sea (Zuider Zee scheme)
     Hulton (480)   f/s., col.   Price **F**
Reclaiming the Desert
     Hulton (11)   f/s., b/w.   Price **E**
Tierras Muertas (1953) (Irrigation and soil conservation)
     E.F.V.A.   60 f., b/w.   Price **D**
Water in the Desert
     Hulton (13)   f/s., b/w.   Price **E**

WALLCHARTS/POSTERS

Changing Face of the Earth, The – 4. Deserts
     P.C.E.T.   Secondary   Price **D**
Lower Swansea Valley (Dereliction and recovery)
     P.C.E.T.   Price **D**

GAMES/KITS/WORKCARDS

Conservation (Social Education Kit)
     Macmillan   14–15 years   Price **K**

ORGANIZATIONS

National Coal Board (N.C.B.)

JOURNALS/PERIODICALS
Geographical Magazine

ARTICLES
Bunyard, P., 'Will the Desert Bloom?' *Ecologist* September 1973
Rodda, J. C., 'Controlling Flood and Drought' *Geographical Magazine*
  November 1970
Mountjoy, A. B., 'Egypt Cultivates her Deserts' *Geographical*
  Magazine January 1972
Smith, C. G., 'Water Resources and Irrigation Development in the
  Middle East' *Geography* November 1970
Hughes, D., 'Towards a Recycling Society' *New Scientist* 10 January
  1974
de Hart, R. A. J., 'Desert Reclamation for Middle East Peace' *Towards*
  Survival December 1973

25 CONSERVATION

See also Sections 3 Natural History (*page* 30) and 24 Reclamation and
Irrigation (*page* 142)

BOOKS (GENERAL)

Baron, W. M., *Nature Conservation*   Methuen Educational   1971
  Price D
Black, J. D., *Biological Conservation*   McGraw-Hill   1954
  Price G
Black, J. D., *Management and Conservation of Biological Resources*
  Blackwell Scientific   1969   Price G
Bracey, H. E., *People and the Countryside*   Routledge   1970
  Price G
Curry-Lindahl, K., *Conservation for Survival*   Gollancz   1972
  Price G
Dasmann, R. F., *Environmental Conservation*, 3rd edn.   Wiley
  1972   Price G/J
Denman, D. R., Roberts, R. A. & Smith, H. J. F., *Commons and
  Village Greens*   Hill   1967   Price J
Dennis, E. (ed.), *Everyman's Nature Reserve. Ideas for Action* (Over
  40 practical projects in wildlife management).
  David & Charles   1972   Price E
Dept. of Environment, *New Life in Old Towns*   H.M.S.O.   1972
  Price G
Duffey, E., *Conservation of Nature*   Collins   1970   Price E
Edwards, R. W. & Garrod, D. J. (eds.), *Conservation and Productivity
  of Natural Waters*   Academic Press   1972   Price J
Ehrenfeld, D. W., *Conserving Life on Earth*   O.U.P.   1973
  Price H
Fisher, J. *et al., The Red Book: Wildlife in Danger*   Collins   1969
  Price H
Geddes, P., *City Development*   Irish U.P.   1973   Price J
Graham, A., *The Gardeners of Eden*   Allen & Unwin   1973
  Price H
Gregory, R., *The Price of Amenity* (Five studies in conservation and
  government)   Macmillan   1971   Price J
Hart, R. A. de J., *The Inviolable Hills: The Ecology, Conservation and
  Regeneration of the British Uplands*   Stuart & Watkins   1968
  Price F
Harvey, J., *The Conservation of Buildings*   Baker   1972   Price H
Hoskins, W. G. & Stamp, L. D., *The Common Lands of England and
  Wales* ('New Naturalist' series)   Collins   1963   Price F
Hudson, N. W., *Soil Conservation*   Batsford   1971   Price H
Joffe, J., *Conservation* ('Interdependence in Nature' series)   Aldus
  1969   Price E

Johnson, W. A., *Public Parks on Private Land in England and Wales*
Johns Hopkins   1971   Price **G**
Kennet, W., *Preservation*   Temple Smith   1972   Price **F**
Laydet, F., *Time and the River Flowing: Grand Canyon*   Earth
Island   1972   Price **E**
Little, C. E., *Challenge of the Land*   Pergamon   1969   Price **F**
Lovins, A. & Evans, P., *Eryri, the Mountains of Longing* (Snowdonia
National Park)   Allen & Unwin   1972   Price **K**
Luther, H. & Rzoska, J., *Project Aqua: A Source Book of Inland
Waters proposed for Conservation*   Blackwell Scientific   1971
Price **F**
Moffat, G., *Survival Count*   Gollancz   1972   Price **F**
Mossman, A. S., *Towards Conservation* (Comprehensive survey of
world environmental problems)   Intertext   1974   Price **E**
Nicholson, E. M., *Handbook to the Conservation Section of the
International Biological Programme*   Blackwell Scientific
1968   Price **D**
Nicholson, M., *The Environmental Revolution. A Guide for the New
Masters of the Earth*
Hodder & Stoughton   1970   Price **H**
Penguin   1972   Price **D**
Owen, O., *Natural Resource Conservation: An Ecological Approach*
Collier-Macmillan   1971   Price **J**
Papegeorgiou, A., *Continuity and Change: Preservation in City
Planning*   Pall Mall   1971   Price **K**
Passmore, P., *Man's Responsibility for Nature*   Duckworth   1974
Price **F**
Pitts, J. N. & Metcalf, R. L. (eds.), *Advances in Environmental
Sciences*   Wiley   1969   Price **J**
Shirrefs, R, W., *Improvement Areas and Conservation Areas*   I.M.E.
1972   Price **C**
Shoman, J. J., *Open Land for Urban America: Acquisition, Safe-
keeping and Use*   Johns Hopkins   1971   Price **G**
Smith, G. H. (ed.), *Conservation of Natural Resources*, 4th edn.   Wiley
1971   Price **J**
Stamp, L. D., *Nature Conservation in Britain*   Collins   1969
Price **E**
Thomas, T. M., *Yellowstone: A Century of the Wilderness Idea*
Collier-Macmillan   1973   Price **J**
Usher, M. B., *Biological Management and Conservation*   Chapman &
Hall   1973   Price **J**
Ward, P. (ed.), *Conservation and Development in Historic Towns and
Cities*   Oriel Press   1968   Price **G**
Warren, A. & Goldsmith, F. B. (eds.), *Conservation in Practice*   Wiley
1974   Price **G/J**
Weiss, D. E. *et al., Nature in the Balance*   Heinemann   1972   Price **E**
Worskett, R., *Character of Towns*   Architectural Press   1969
Price **H**

The Coastal Heritage: A Conservation Policy for Coasts of High
    Quality Scenery   Countryside Commission   1970   Price **H**
Colne Valley Park: A New Prospect   G.L.C.   1972   Price **D**
Conservation Areas: Preserving the Architectural and Historic Scene
    Civic Trust   1967   Price **C**
Conservation in Action   Civic Trust   1972   Price **E**
Do You Care about Historic Buildings?   G.L.C.   1970   Price **D**
Financing the Preservation of Old Buildings   Civic Trust   1971
    Price **C**
G.L.C. Architecture 1965/70   G.L.C.   1970   Price **F**
Index of Conservation Areas 1967–71   Civic Trust   1972
    Price **C**
The Meldon Story
    Dartmoor Preservation Society   Price **C**
New Life for Old Buildings   H.M.S.O.   1972   Price **D**
The Preservation Policy Group Report   H.M.S.O.   1971   Price **C**
The Scientific Study of Plant and Animal Communities for Conserva-
    tion   Blackwell Scientific   1971   Price **H**
Special Study Report. Volume II: Nature Conservation of the Coast
    Countryside Commission   1970   Price **E**
Studies in Conservation
    Bath   1968   Price **G**
    Chester   1968   Price **J**
    Chichester   1968   Price **J**
    York   1970   Price **J**
    H.M.S.O.
Wild Country: National Asset or Barren Waste?
    C.P.R.E.   1972   Price **C**

BOOKS (SCHOOL)

Allsop, K., *Fit to Live In?* ('Connexions' series)   Penguin   1970
    Secondary   Price **C**
Bainbridge, J., *Conservation* ('Evans Integrated Themes' series)   Evans
    1972   9–14 years   Price **D**
Burton, J., *The Conservation of Wildlife* ('Man and His World' series)
    Blackie   1974   12–16 years   Price **D/E**
Goff, C., *Archaeology* ('Visual Books' series)   Macdonald Educational
    1973   C.S.E.   Price **E**
Hardy, G. B., *Conservation* ('Environment Through Photographs' series)
    Cassell   1973   C.S.E.   Price **D**
Jackson, O., *Conservation and Pollution* ('World Wide' series)
    Batsford   1971   14 years +   Price **E**
Mellanby, J., *Nature Detection and Conservation*   Carousel Books
    1972   Price **C**
Mellanby, J., *Wildlife in Danger* ('Project Earth' series)   Wayland
    1974   13–16 years   Price **F**
Morgan, M., *Soil Erosion and Conservation* ('Certificate Topics in
    Geography' series)   Collins   1969   15–16 years   Price **D**

Nebden, R. & Wilkinson, K., *The World We Live In*
1. *Life in Towns*
2. *The World of Today*
3. *The World of the Past*
    Muller   1973   13–16 years   Price (each) **D**
Whinray, J., *Conservation* ('Black's Picture Information Books' series)
    Black   1973   8–13 years   Price **D**
Young, G., *This is Ours* (National Trust Children's series) (Problems of
    preservation in a typical village)   Dinosaur   1974   8 years +
    Price **C**

FILMS

Atonement (1970) (Conservation of wildlife)
    Canada House   60 min., col.   Hire free
Beauty in Trust (1959) (National Trust)
    National Benzole   23 min., col.   Hire free
Beyond Conception (1968)
    Concord   35 min., col.   Hire **F**
Changing Forest, The (1967)
    National Benzole   27 min., col.   Hire free
Conservation and Balance in Nature (1966)   13 years +
    Concord/N.A.V.A.L. (600 D78)   18 min., col.   Hire **F**
Do you Dig National Parks? (1972) (Mining in Snowdonia)
    Concord   80 min., col.   Hire **J**
Facelift (Tyne-Tees)
    Civic Trust   25 min., b/w.   Hire **E**
Future for the Past, A (Conservation in urban areas)
    Civic Trust   37 min., col.   Hire **K**
Into your Hands (Wildlife and conservation in Australia)
    Concord   26 min., col.   Hire **H**
Life in Western Marshes (1945) (Canada)
    N.A.V.A.L. (606 D16)   14 min., col.   Hire **D**
                         14 min., b/w.   Hire **C**
Lonely Places, The (Conservation near power stations)
    C.E.G.B.   23 min., col.   Hire free
Looking at Britain – Forestry (1960) (Management and afforestation)
    C.F.L. (UK 1632)   12 min.   Hire **C**
Looking at Britain – National Parks (1961)
    C.F.L. (UK 1662)   15 min., b/w.   Hire **D**
National Trust
    Guild (233 2970–6)   25 min., col.   Hire free
Nature in Trust
    S.P.N.R./Lincs. Trust   35 min., col.   Hire **J**
Oak Valley, U.S.A.
    N.A.V.A.L.   14 min.   Hire **E**
Peak, The (National Park)
    B.B.C.   30 min., b/w.   Hire **G**

Place for Wildlife, A
    S.P.N.R./Scottish Trust   25 min., col.   Hire **G**
Problems of Conservation − Forest and Range
    N.A.V.A.L.   14 min., col.   Hire **E**
Problems of Conservation − Soil
    N.A.V.A.L.   14 min., col.   Hire **E**
Railways Conserve the Environment (1970)
    British Transport (BT 1032)   17 min., col.   Hire **E**
Secret Highway, The (Hedgerows in East Anglia)
    Soil Association/Guild (300 2577−0)   30 min., col.
    Hire **E**
Survival
    Cloud over Paradise (Ceylon)   25 min.
    Elephants have Right of Way (Uganda)   26 min.
    The First in the Game − 1 (South Africa)   22 min.
    The First in the Game − 2 (South Africa)   19 min.
    Last Stronghold (Southern Spain)   26 min.
    The New Ark (W.W.F. in Africa)   52 min.
    One that Came Back (Suffolk)   25 min.
    S.O.S. Rhino (Uganda)   25 min.
    Tomorrow may be too late (Operation Noah)   25 min.
    B.F.I.   b/w.   Hire (each) **F**
Today and Tomorrow
    S.P.N.R./Gloucs. Trust   30 min., col.   Hire **G**
Tree is Planted, A (1955) (Reafforestation in Scotland)
    C.F.L. (UK 1491)   8 min., b/w.   Hire **C**
Vanishing Coast, The (1965)
    National Benzole   29 min., col.   Hire free
Wildlife in Danger
    Guild (230 1383−0)   22 min., col.   Hire free
Wildlife in Trust
    S.P.N.R./B.B.O.N.T.   20 min., col.   Hire **F**

FILMSTRIPS/SLIDES/FILMLOOPS/TRANSPARENCIES

Conservation is Everybody's Business
    Saving the Soil
    People, our most Valuable Resource
    Using our Forests Wisely
    Nothing can Live without Water
    McGraw-Hill (137000)   4 x *c.* 52 f.   Price (each) **F**
Conserving our Natural Resources ('American Way of Life' series)
    Secondary
    9091 *What is Conservation*
    9092 *Saving our Soil*
    9093 *Enough Water for Everyone*
    9094 *Improving our Grasslands*
    9095 *Using our Forests Wisely*

9096 *Giving our Wildlife a Chance*
9097 *Using our Minerals Wisely*
    Encyclopaedia Britannica   f/s., col.   Price (each) **F**
Extraction, Conservation and Pollution
    Aerofilms   24 slides   Price **G**
                24 prints   Price **G**
                24 transp.   Price **J**
How Man Conserves the Soil   Secondary
    Encyclopaedia Britannica (7368)   60 f., b/w.   Price **E**
Nature Conservation in the British Isles
    D. Wyllie (DW 144)   40 f., col.   Price **F/G**
Walking in the Peak District (1966)
    British Transport (BT 810)   52 f., col.   Hire free

WALLCHARTS/POSTERS

Conservation
    Collins   2 charts   Price **D**
National Parks (One poster for each park)
    Countryside Commission   Price free
Posters Set
    1. *Upper Dart*
    2. *Longparish, Hampshire*
    3. *Guard the Countryside*
    4. *Montage of News Headlines*
    C.P.R.E.

GAMES/KITS/WORKCARDS

Conservation (Social Education study kit)
    Macmillan   14–15 years   Price **K**
Conservation Game (Bird protection)
    R.S.P.B.   Price **E**
Conservation and Pollution ('Beaver Unit')
    Philip   Price **K**
Free Yet Unspoilt? (Documents and notes on access to the countryside
    and coast)
    Pergamon   Price **G**
People and the Countryside (Conservation study kit; includes charts,
    workcards)   Secondary
    Peak Park Planning Board   Price **F**
Siting an Oil Terminal ('Decisions' series)
    School Government Publishers   17 years +   Price **K**
Why Save Animals? (Seminar Cassettes – 'Life on Earth' series)
    Foulsham (SS 111)   59 min.   Price **F**

ORGANIZATIONS

Ancient Monuments Society
Animals in Danger Corps

Association for the Preservation of Rural Scotland
Association for Studies in the Conservation of Historic Buildings
British Butterfly Conservation Society
British Trust for Conservation Volunteers
Chiltern Society
Civic Trust
Committee for Environmental Conservation (CoEnCo)
Commons, Open Spaces and Footpaths Preservation Society
Conservation Corps
Conservation Society
Conservation Youth Association
Council for British Archaeology
Council for Nature
Council for the Protection of Rural England (C.P.R.E.)
Council for the Protection of Rural Wales
Countryside Commission
Countryside Commission for Scotland
Cumberland Countryside Conference
Dartmoor Preservation Society
Eastern Federation of Amenity Societies
Exmoor Society
Fauna Preservation Society
Friends of the Lake District
Game Conservancy
Georgian Group
Green Survival Campaign
Howey Foundation, The
International Union for the Conservation of Nature (I.U.C.N.)
International Youth Federation for Environmental Studies and
        Conservation
Joint Committee for Conservation of British Insects
Keep Britain Tidy Group
London Society
Men of the Trees
Ministry of Development, Government of Northern Ireland: Conserva-
        tion Branch
Ministry of Finance, Government of Northern Ireland: Ancient
        Monuments Branch
National Association of Boys' Clubs
National Park Authorities
National Trust
National Trust for Scotland
Nature Conservancy
Offa's Dyke Association
Pilgrim Trust
Rescue
Salmon and Trout Association
Save the Village Pond Campaign

Scottish Civic Trust
Scottish Wildlife Trust
Snowdonia National Park Society
Society for the Protection of Ancient Buildings
Society of Antiquaries of London
Society of Sussex Downsmen
Survival International
Ulster Society for the Preservation of the Countryside
World Wildlife Fund (W.W.F.)

JOURNALS/PERIODICALS

Biological Conservation
Communus
Conservation News
Conservation Review
Ecologist
Journal of the Soil Association
Kingfisher
Naturopa
Outlook
Oryx
Span

ARTICLES

Syer, G. N., 'Ahead of their Time' *Ecologist* February 1971
'Conservation in Europe' issue *Geographical Magazine* January 1970
Evans, G., 'Sanctuaries for India's Wild Life' *Geographical Magazine* August 1970
Goodes, J., 'Conservation in a Desert Landscape' *Geographical Magazine* July 1971
Clayton, K. M., 'Reality in Conservation' *Geographical Magazine* November 1971
Thomas, D., 'Guardians of the Environment' *Geographical Magazine* May 1972
McKinlay, D., 'The Park between Cities' *Geographical Magazine* September 1972
Nelson, G., 'Centenary Conference of World National Parks' *Geographical Magazine* November 1972
Acland, C. H. D., 'Precious Spot of the North West' *Geographical Magazine* June 1973
Bell, M., 'Land Conservation for a Nation of Town Dwellers' *Geographical Magazine* October 1973
Escritt, E. A. & Gittins, J., 'Limits of a Nature Reserve' *Geographical Magazine* October 1973
Condry, W., 'Beneath the Skin of Snowdonian Beauty' *Geographical Magazine* October 1973

'Map of Cherished Land'   *Geographical Magazine*   October 1973

Burton, S. H., 'Elusive Exmoor'   *Geographical Magazine*   November 1973

Munch, W., 'Local Authorities and Nature Conservation'   *Nature in Focus*   Summer 1971

Steers, J. A., 'Conservation of Coasts'   *Nature in Focus*   Summer 1971

Budowski, G. & Standish, R. I., 'A World View of Conservation'   *Nature in Focus*   Summer 1971

Champigneulle, B., 'Nature and History: a Common Heritage for Conservation'   *Nature in Focus*   Winter 1971/2

Winge, E. N., 'Yellowstone Park — its First Century'   *Nature in Focus*   Summer 1972

Wagenaar Hummelinck, M. G., 'Putting a Pricetag on Nature'   *Nature in Focus*   No. 16 1973

Nebbia, G., 'Costs and Benefits of Environmental Protection'   *Nature in Focus*   No. 16 1973

Leodolter, I., 'Topical Problems of Environmental Protection'   *Nature in Focus*   No. 16 1973

26   ECONOMIC, SOCIAL AND POLITICAL ASPECTS

BOOKS (GENERAL)

Ackland, R., *The Next Step*   R. Ackland, P. O. Box 41, Exeter,
   EX4 6EQ   1974   Price **D**
Andrews, R. B., *An Introduction to Urban Land Economics*   Collier-
   Macmillan   1971   Price **F**
Auld, D. A. L. (ed.), *Economic Thinking and Pollution Problems*
   O.U.P.   1972   Price **J**
Balogh, T., *The Economics of Poverty*   Weidenfeld & Nicolson   1974
   Price **F/H**
Barkley, P. W. & Seckler, D., *Economic Growth and Environmental
   Decay: The Solution becomes the Problem*   Harcourt Brace
   1972   Price **E**
Barraclough, O., *The Economic Costs of Population Growth*   Conser-
   vation Society   1973   Price **B**
Bateson, G., *Steps to an Ecology of the Mind*   Paladin   1973
   Price **E**
Beesley, M. E., *Urban Transport: Studies in Economic Policy*
   Butterworth   1973   Price **K**
Bhagwati, J., *The Economics of Underdeveloped Countries*   W.U.L.
   1970   Price **D**
Bohm, P. & Kneese, A. V., *The Economics of Environment*
   Macmillan   1971   Price **G**
Caldwell, M., *Oil and Imperialism in East Asia*   Bertrand Russell
   Peace Foundation   1971   Price **C**
Chisholm, A., *Philosophers of the Earth. Conversations with Ecologists*
   Sidgwick & Jackson   1972   Price **F**
Cipolla, C. M., *The Economic History of World Population*   Penguin
   1970   Price **C**
Clarke, W. M., *The City in World Economy*, new edn.   Penguin   1967
   Price **C**
Culbertson, J. M., *Economic Development*   Knopf   1971   Price **H**
Cullingworth, J. B., *Housing and Local Government*   Allen &
   Unwin   1966   Price **F**
Dales, J. H., *Pollution, Property and Prices: An Essay on Policy-making
   and Economics*, new edn.   Toronto U.P.   1970   Price **E**
Daly, H. E., (ed.), *Towards a Steady State Economy*   Freeman   1973
   Price **E**
Dasmann, R. F. et al., *Ecological Principles for Economic Development*
   Wiley   1973   Price **F**
de Chardin, P. T., *The Future of Man* (Philosophy)   Collins   1969
   Price **C**
Dickson, D., *Alternative Technology and the Politics of Technical
   Change*   Fontana   1974   Price **D**
Edel, M. & Rothenberg, J., *Readings in Urban Economics*   Collier-
   Macmillan   1972   Price **F**

154

Elkin, S. L., *Politics and Land Use Planning. The London Experience*
C.U.P.   1974   Price **H**
Fox, C., *The Countryside and the Law*   David & Charles   1971
Price **F**
Freeman, T. W., *Geography and Regional Administration: England
and Wales 1830–1968*   Hutchinson   1968   Price **D/E**
Friend, J. K. & Jessop, W. N., *Local Government and Strategic Choice:
An Operational Research Approach to the Processes of Public
Planning*   Tavistock   1969   Price **F/H**
Galbraith, J. K., *The Affluent Society,* 2nd edn.   Penguin   1970
Price **C**
Goldsmith, E. *et al.,* *Blueprint for Survival* (Reprinted from *The Ecolo-
gist*)   Stacey   1972   Price **E**
Goodall, B., *The Economics of Urban Areas*   Pergamon   1972
Price **G**
Goreux, L. M. & Manne, A. S. (eds.),   *Multi-Level Planning: Case
Studies in Mexico*   North-Holland   1973   Price **K**
Hall, G., *Ecology: Can we Survive under Capitalism?*   International
1972   Price **D**
Hodson, H. V., *The Diseconomics of Growth*
Earth Island   1972   Price **F**
Pan/Ballantine   1972   Price **D**
Hopkins, H., *The Numbers Game* (Statistics and philosophy)   Secker
& Warburg   1973   Price **F**
Illich, I. D., *Celebration of Awareness*
Calder & Boyars   1971   Price **D**
Penguin   1973   Price **C**
Illich, I. D., *Energy or Equity*   Calder & Boyars   1974   Price **D/E**
Illich, I. D., *Tools for Conviviality*   Calder & Boyars   1973   Price **F**
Jacobs, J. (ed.), *The Economy of Cities*   Penguin   1972   Price **C**
Johnson, S. P., *The Politics of Environment. The British Experience*
Stacey   1973   Price **F**
Johnson, W. H. & Hardisty, J., *Economic Growth vs. the Environment*
Prentice-Hall   1972   Price **F**
Kneese, A. V. *et al., Economics and the Environment: A Materials
Balance Approach*   Johns Hopkins   1970   Price **E**
Kraus, G., *Homo Sapiens in Decline*   New Diffusionist Press   1973
Price **E**
Kuznets, S., *Population, Capital and Growth*   Heinemann   1974
Price **G**
McHale, J., *World Facts and Trends* (Statistics on man and his environ-
ment)   Collier-Macmillan   1973   Price **D/F**
Meadows, D. H. *et al., The Limits to Growth: A Report for the Club
of Rome's Project on the Predicament of Mankind*   Earth Island
1972   Price **E**
Meadows, D. L. (ed.), *Dynamics of Growth in a Finite World*   Wiley
1974   Price **K**
Mishan, E. J., *Growth: The Price we Pay*   Staples Press   1969   Price **F**

Mishan, E. J., *The Costs of Economic Growth*   Penguin   1971
Price **C**
Mishan, E. J., *21 Popular Economic Fallacies*   Penguin   1971
Price **C**
Morgan, D. R. & Kirkpatrick, S., (eds.), *Urban Political Analysis: A Systems Approach*   Collier-Macmillan   1972   Price **H**
Nicol, H., *Courtiers of Canute* (Use and depletion of fossil fuels)
Knight   1973   Price **G**
Noble, P., *Case Studies in Applied Economics*   O.U.P.   1972
Price **F**
Posner, M. V., *Fuel Policy: A Study in Applied Economics*
Macmillan   1973   Price **J**
Ramsay, W. & Anderson, C., *Managing the Environment: An Economic Primer*   Macmillan   1972   Price **G**
Robinson, E. A. G., *Problems in Economic Development*   Macmillan
1965   Price **H**
Roszak, T., *Making of a Counter Culture,* new edn.   Faber   1971
Price **E**
Roszak, T., *Where the Wasteland Ends*   Faber   1973   Price **G**
Schumacher, E. F., *Buddhist Economics*   Resurgence   1968   Price **A**
Schumacher, E. F., *Economics of Permanence*   Resurgence   1970
Price **A**
Schumacher, E. F., *Small is Beautiful: A Study of Economics as if People Mattered*   Blond & Briggs   1973   Price **G**
Schwab, M. (ed.), *Teach-in for Survival*   Robinson & Watkins   1972
Price **E/F**
Science Policy Research Unit of Sussex University, *Thinking about the Future. A Critique of 'The Limits to Growth'*   Chatto & Windus
1973   Price **E/G**
Self, P. & Storing, H. J., *The State and the Farmer*   Allen & Unwin
1962   Price **E**
Shanks, M., *The Quest for Growth* ('Studies in Contemporary Europe' series)   Macmillan   1973   Price **D**
Smith, V. L., *Economics of Natural and Environmental Resources*
Gordon & Breach   In preparation – due 1975
Taylor, G. R., *Rethink. A Paraprimitive Solution*   Secker & Warburg   1972   Price **F**
Thomas, R., *The Economics of Traffic Congestion*   Open University
1972   Price **E**
Toffler, A., *Future Shock* (The sociology of rapid change)   Pan   1972
Price **D**
Victor, P. A., *Pollution, Economy and Environment*   Allen & Unwin
1972   Price **J**
Waller, R., *Be Human or Die. A Study in Ecological Humanism*   Knight
1973   Price **H**
Whitby, M. C. et al., *Rural Resource Development* (The economics of rural land use, settlement and transport planning)   Methuen
1974   Price **F**

Wilkinson, R. G., *Poverty and Progress. An Ecological Model of
    Economic Development*   Methuen   1973   Price **E/F**
Williams, D., *To be or not to be. A Question of Survival*
    Davis-Poynter   1974   Price **F**

The City as an Economic System   Open University   1973
    Price **F**
*The Economics of Conservation. An Outline Plan for the United
    Kingdom*   Conservation Society   1973   Price **C**

BOOKS (SCHOOL)

Barr, J., *Standards of Living* ('Connexions' series)   Penguin   1969
    Price **C**
Power, J., *Development Economics*   Longman   1971   17 years +
    Price **D**
Shenov, S., *Underdevelopment and Economic Growth* ('Key Discussion
    Books' series)   Longman   1970   17 years +   Price **C**

FILMS

Co-operation is Our Business (O.E.C.D.)
    Concord   22 min., col.   Hire **E**
Limits to Growth, The (1972) (Club of Rome report)
    Concord   60 min., col.   Hire **J**

GAMES/KITS/WORKCARDS

Towards Tomorrow (Social Education studies kit, includes tape,
    filmstrips, workcards).
    Macmillan   1973   15–16 years   Price **K**

ORGANIZATIONS

Alternative Society
Association of County Councils
Association of County Councils in Scotland
Association of District Councils
Consumers' Association (C.A.)
Convention of Royal Burghs
Council for Small Industries in Rural Areas
District Councils Association of Scotland
Highlands and Islands Development Board
Local Government Information Service
National Association of Local Councils
National Industrial Materials Recovery Association
Political and Economic Planning
Research Institute for Consumer Affairs
Scottish Counties and Cities Association

JOURNALS/PERIODICALS
Ecologist, The
Energy Policy
New Society
Towards Survival

ARTICLES
Goldsmith, E., 'The Stable Society: Can we Achieve it?' *Ecologist* December 1970

Misham, E. J., 'The Economics of Hope' *Ecologist* January 1971

Gurstein, M., 'Environmental Politics in Britain' *Ecologist* April 1971

Brachi, P., 'Economics and Ecology' *Ecologist* November 1971

Daly, H. E., 'The Stationary-State Economy' *Ecologist* July 1972

Georgescu-Roegen, N., 'Economics and Entropy' *Ecologist* July 1972

Daly, H. E., 'How to Stabilize the Economy' *Ecologist* March 1973

Bunyard, P., 'How much Growth is Possible?' *Ecologist* March 1973

Lord Gladwyn, 'The Logic of Growth' *Ecologist* April 1973

'Limits to Growth?' *Ecologist* August 1973

Wilkinson, R. G., 'Progress to Poverty' *Ecologist* September 1973

Goldsmith, E., 'What of Britain's Future?' *Ecologist* November 1973

Coddington, A. & Victor, P., 'Ecology/Economy' *Your Environment* Spring 1972

Coddington, A., 'The Cheermongers, or How to Stop Worrying and Love Growth' *Your Environment* Autumn, 1972

27 DEVELOPING COUNTRIES

BOOKS (GENERAL)

Baver, P. T., *Dissent on Development. Studies and Debates on Development Economics* Weidenfeld & Nicolson 1972 Price **H**

Bhagwati, J., *The Economics of Underdeveloped Countries* W.U.L. 1970 Price **D**

Campbell, G., *Brazil Struggles for Development* Knight 1973 Price **G**

Clarke, J. R., *Population Geography and the Developing Countries* Pergamon 1971 Price **E/F**

Donaldson, P., *Worlds Apart: The Economic Gulf between Nations* B.B.C. 1971 Price **F**

Dwyer, D. J., *The City in the Third World* Macmillan ('Geographical Readings' series) 1974 Price **F/H**

Farvar, M. T. & Milton, J. P., *The Careless Technology: Ecology and International Development* (Technical development in the third world and its effects on ecology) Stacey 1973 Price **K**

Gordon, S., *World Problems* Batsford 1971 Price **E**

Helleiner, G. K., *International Trade and Economic Development* Penguin 1972 Price **D**

Herbert, J. D. & Van Huyck, H. P., *Urban Planning in the Developing Countries* Praeger 1968 Price **J**

Holliman, J., *The Ecology of World Development* V.C.O.A.D. 1972 Price **B**

McGee, T. G., *The Urbanization Process in the Third World: Explorations in Search of a Theory* Bell 1971 Price **F**

McQueen, M., *The Economics of Development. Problems and Policies* Weidenfeld & Nicolson 1973 Price **E/F**

Mountjoy, A. B., *Developing the Underdeveloped Countries* ('Geographical Readings' series) Macmillan 1971 Price **E/G**

Mountjoy, A. B., *Industrialization and Underdeveloped Countries* Hutchinson 1971 Price **D/E**

Myint, H., *The Economics of the Developing Countries* Hutchinson 1967 Price **D/E**

Myrdal, G., *The Challenge of World Poverty* Penguin 1970 Price **D**

Myrdal, G. & Kessle, G., *China: The Revolution Continued* Penguin 1971 Price **D**

O'Connor, A. M., *The Geography of Tropical African Development* Pergamon 1971 Price **E/G**

O'Kelly, E., *Aid and Self-Help* Knight 1973 Price **F**

Seers, D. & Joy, L. (eds.), *Development in a Divided World* Penguin 1971 Price **C**

Walford, R., *Games in Geography* ('Education Today' series) Longman 1969 Price **E**

Action for World Development   W.D.M.   Price **B**
The Death of the Green Revolution   V.C.O.A.D.   1973   Price **B**
Medical Care in Developing Countries   V.C.O.A.D.   1972
   Price **C**
Preferences: A Better Deal for the Poor World?   W.D.M.   Price **B**
UNCTAD 3: Make-or-break for Development   W.D.M.   Price **B**

BOOKS (SCHOOL)

Dalgleish, N., *The Developing Nations* ('In Focus Books' series)
   Nelson   1972   Secondary   Price **C**
Ferris, B. & Toyne, P., *World Problems*   Hulton   1970   14 years +
   Price **E**
Fyson, N. L., *The Development Puzzle*, new edn.   V.C.O.A.D.   1974
   Price **D**
Garner, C. *et al.*, *The World and Britain* ('This is Your World' series)
   Holmes McDougall   1972   9–13 years   Price **D**
Hanson, W. J., 'Longman Oxfam Series'
Set A   1. *Ecuador: Learning by radio*
         2. *Nigeria: A boy and leprosy*
         3. *Tibet: Refugees from the roof of the world*
Set B   4. *Botswana: This is a hungry year*
         5. *East Pakistan: In the wake of the cyclone*
         6. *Korea: The aftermath of war*
Set C   7 *India: The Mysore maize harvest*
         8. *Lesotho: A home in the mountains*
         9. *Hong Kong: The overcrowded room*
Set D   10. *Algeria: Building the peace*
         11. *Kenya: A school for Githae*
         12. *Eastern Caribbean: Poor island girl*
   Longman   1970   C.S.E.   Price (each) **D**
Henderson, P., *World Poverty* ('World Wide' series)   Batsford   1971
   14 years +   Price **E**
Long, M. & Roberson, B. S., *World Problems: A Topic Geography*
   E.U.P.   1969   C.S.E./G.C.E.   Price **D**
Merry, M. & Harvey, D., *People, Poverty and Wealth* ('Certificate
   Topics in Geography' series)   Collins   1972   15–16 years
   Price **D**
Power, J., *Development Economics*   Longman   1971   17 years +
   Price **D**
Shenov, S., *Underdevelopment and Economic Growth* ('Key Discussion
   Books' series)   Longman   1970   17 years +   Price **C**
Simons, M., *Poverty and Wealth in Cities and Villages* ('Oxford Social
   Geographies' series)   O.U.P.   1972   C.S.E.   Price **E**
Zelinsky, W. *et al.*, *Geography in a Crowded World: A Symposium on
   Population Pressures upon Physical and Social Resources in the
   Developing Lands*   O.U.P.   1971   17 years +   Price **H**

FILMS
Black Man's Burden (1971)
　　Concord　　50 min., col.　　Hire **G**
Day Before Tomorrow, The (Population explosion)
　　Concord　　30 min., col.　　Hire **G**
Feel No Shame (1971)
　　Concord　　20 min., col.　　Hire **D**
Harvest for Tomorrow? (1968) (Botswana and Kenya)
　　C.F.L. (V 722)　　19 min.　　Hire **E**
Legacy of Empire (1970) (The slave trade and immigration)
　　Concord　　20 min.　　Hire **E**
No Other Choice (1965) (The United Nations)
　　C.F.L. (V 681)　　17 min.　　Hire **D**
Not Enough (1968) (Overseas aid)　　17 years +
　　Concord　　30 min.　　Hire **E**
Out of the Darkness (1972) (Immigration)
　　Concord　　20 min., col.　　Hire **E**
Widening Gap, The (Rich and poor countries)
　　C.F.L.　　28 min.　　Hire **D**

FILMSTRIPS/SLIDES/FILMLOOPS/TRANSPARENCIES
China – Another Way. A Family in Tachai (1973)
　　V.C.O.A.D.　　12 slides, col.　　Price **E**
Community for Whom?, A (1973) (E.E.C. and the third world)
　　V.C.O.A.D.　　96 f., with tape　　Price **G**
　　　　　　96 slides, with tape　　Price **G**
Family in Jamaica, A (1972)
　　V.C.O.A.D.　　12 slides, col.　　Price **E**
Problems of Water in the Third World (1973)
　　V.C.O.A.D.　　12 slides, col.　　Price **E**
Shanty Towns (Guayaquil, Lusaka and Manila)
　　V.C.O.A.D.　　12 slides, b/w.　　Price **E**
Ten Years of U.N.E.S.C.O.　　14 years +
　　N.A.V.A.L.　　42 f., b/w.　　Price **D**
Town and Village in Northern Ghana (1973)
　　V.C.O.A.D.　　12 slides, col.　　Price **E**
Ujamaa Village in Tanzania, An (1973)
　　V.C.O.A.D.　　12 slides, col.　　Price **E**
United Nations in Asia (1960)　　14 years +
　　N.A.V.A.L.　　36 f., b/w.　　Price **D**
Walk in Bangladesh, A (1972)
　　V.C.O.A.D.　　18 slides, col.　　Price **E**

WALLCHARTS/POSTERS
Aid (1971)
　　V.C.O.A.D.　　Price **A**

Attitudes and Values (1971)
    V.C.O.A.D.   Price **A**
Charting Poverty   Secondary
   Malnutrition
   Life Expectancy
   Illiteracy
   Population Increase
    Oxfam/Christian Aid   4 charts   Price **E**
Education (1971)
    V.C.O.A.D.   Price **A**
Health (1971)
    V.C.O.A.D.   Price **A**
Photoset of Bangladesh
    Oxfam   28 photographs   Price **D**
Rich Man: Poor Man
    P.C.E.T.   Secondary   Price **D**
Rich World/Poor World (1971)
    V.C.O.A.D.   Price **A**
Trade (1971)
    V.C.O.A.D.   Price **A**
Why Bother? (U.K. trade with the third world)
    Oxfam   4 charts

GAMES/KITS/WORKCARDS

Aid Committee Game (Deciding priorities for aid)
    Oxfam   Price free
Coffee Game
    V.C.O.A.D.   Price **D**
Development Game
    Oxfam   13 years +   Price free

ORGANIZATIONS

Christian Aid
Community Service Volunteers (C.S.V.)
Freedom From Hunger Campaign (F.F.H.)
International Voluntary Service
Minority Rights Group, The
Oxfam
Save the Children Fund
Third World First
Voluntary Committee on Overseas Aid and Development (V.C.O.A.D.)
War on Want (W.O.W.)
World Development Movement (W.D.M.)

JOURNALS/PERIODICALS

Ceres
Finance and Development

Internationalist
Resurgence
Third World
VOX
World Health
World Hunger

ARTICLES

Omo-Fadaka, J., 'Industrialization and Poverty in the Third World'
    Ecologist   February 1974
Baker, R., 'Famine: the Cost of Development?'   *Ecologist*   June 1974
Sadove, R., 'Urban Needs of Developing Countries'   *Finance and*
    Development   June 1973
'Action for Tropical Africa' series   *Geographical Magazine*   October
    1970—February 1972
Johnson, D. G., 'Food for Survival'   *Geographical Magazine*
    December 1972
'Third World' series   *Geographical Magazine,*   started March 1973
Gold, E., 'Developing Countries and the Law of the Sea'   *New*
    Scientist   27 June 1974
Jackson, D., 'Third World Food Crisis'   *New Society*   16 May 1974
Knedel, P., 'Energy and Food, A Double Dilemma threatens the Third
    World'   *Plain Truth*   April 1974

BOOKS (GENERAL)

Beazley, E., *Designed for Recreation: A Practical Handbook for all Concerned with Providing Leisure Facilities in the Countryside* Faber   1969   Price **J**

Bengtsson, A., *Environmental Planning for Children's Play* Lockwood   1970   Price **H**

Bengtsson, A. (ed.), *Adventure Playgrounds*   Lockwood 1970   Price **G**

Bracey, H. E., *People and the Countryside*   Routledge   1970 Price **G**

British Waterways Board, *Leisure and the Waterways*   H.M.S.O. 1967   Price **C**

Burton, T. L., *Experiments in Recreation Research*   Allen & Unwin 1971   Price **J**

Burton, T. L., *Recreation Research Planning*   Allen & Unwin   1971 Price **H**

Clawson, M. & Knetsch, J. L., *Economics of Outdoor Recreation* Johns Hopkins   1966   Price **E/H**

Coppock, J. T., *Recreation in the Countryside: A Spatial Analysis* Macmillan   in preparation

Countryside Commission, *Coastal Recreation and Holidays. Special Study Reports*   H.M.S.O.   1969   Price **E**

Countryside Commission, *Coastal Recreation and Leisure*   H.M.S.O. Price **E**

Jackson, R. & Cosgrove, I., *Geography of Recreation and Leisure* Hutchinson   1972   Price **D/F**

Mutch, W. E. S., *Public Recreation in National Forests: A Factual Survey*   H.M.S.O.   1968   Price **C**

Patmore, J. A., *Land and Leisure*
David & Charles   1970   Price **H**
Penguin   1972   Price **D**

Pole, N., *Recreation Traffic in National Parks: Beyond the Car*   Eco-Publications   1973   Price **C**

Roberts, K., *Leisure* ('Aspects of Modern Society' series)   Longman 1970   Price **D/E**

Rubinstein, D. & Speakman, C., *Leisure, Transport and the Countryside* Fabian Society   1969   Price **B**

Sillitoe, K. K., *Planning for Leisure* (Government Social Survey) H.M.S.O.   1969   Price **E**

Smith, M. *et al.*, *Leisure and Society in Britain*   Lane   1973 Price **E/H**

Thompson, I., *Leisure*   McGraw-Hill   1968   Price **D**

The Challenge of Leisure   Civic Trust   1965   Price **C**
Colne Valley Park: A New Project   G.L.C.   1972   Price **D**

People and the Countryside   Ramblers' Association   1971
    Price **B**

BOOKS (SCHOOL)
Woolner, A. H., *Work and Leisure* ('Oxford Social Geographies' series)
    O.U.P.   1972   C.S.E.   Price **D**

FILMS
Adventure Playgrounds (1959)
    C.F.L. (UK 1784)   14 min., col.   Hire **E**
Challenge of Leisure, The (1965)   11 years +
    Concord   30 min., b/w.   Hire **F**
Land for Leisure
    B.B.C.   25 min., col.   Hire **J**
People + Leisure =. . . (1968)   11 years +
    S.P.N.R.   30 min., col.   Hire **G**
    National Benzole   Hire free
Somewhere to Play (1971) (Adventure playground in Notting Hill)
    Concord   15 min., b/w.   Hire **E**
Time Off (1969)   11 years +
    Concord   25 min., b/w.   Hire **F**
Time Off in Towns (1972) ('Places for People' series)
    B.B.C.   25 min., b/w.   Hire **H**
Vanishing Coast, The (1965)
    National Benzole   29 min., col.   Hire free
World of the Waterways, The
    British Transport   30 min., col.   Hire **E**

FILMSTRIPS/SLIDES/FILMLOOPS/TRANSPARENCIES
Bognor Regis – Seaside Resort ('Esso Geography Studies' series)
    Longman (A18)   6-slide folio   Price **D**

WALLCHARTS/POSTERS
Tomorrow and You
    P.C.E.T.   Secondary   Price **D**

GAMES/KITS/WORKCARDS
Local Leisure Resources ('Activity Factsheets' series)   C.S.E.
    Nelson   1973   Packs of 10   Price **E**
Towards Tomorrow (Social Education study kit, includes tape,
    filmstrips, workcards)
    Macmillan   1973   15–16 years   Price **K**
You and Your Community (4 audio-visual filmstrips, including one on
    Leisure)
    Coca-Cola   1974   8–13 years   Price **J**

ORGANIZATIONS

Association of River Authorities
British Caravanners' Club
British Gliding Association
British Horse Society
British Mountaineering Council
British Speleological Association
British Tourist Authority
British Waterways Board
Broads Consortium
Camping Club of Great Britain and Ireland
Caravan Club
Central Council for Physical Recreation (C.C.P.R.)
Central Rights of Way Committee
Commons, Open Spaces and Footpaths Preservation Society
Countryside Club, The
Cyclists' Touring Club
Dartington Amenity Research Trust
English Tourist Board
Fell and Rock Climbing Club of the Lake District
Holiday Fellowship
Home Counties Rambling Association
Inland Waterways Amenity Advisory Council
Inland Waterways Association Ltd.
Institute of Park and Recreation Administrators
Institution of Water Engineers
Irish Mountaineering Club
Kennet and Avon Canal Trust Ltd.
Metropolitan Public Gardens Association
Ministry of Agriculture, Government of Northern Ireland: Forestry
    Division
Motor Caravanners' Club
National Anglers' Council
National Caravan Council
National Federation of Anglers
National Playing Fields Association
National Ski Federation of Great Britain
National Trust
National Trust for Scotland
New Horizon School Camps
Northern Ireland Tourist Board
Outward Bound Trust
Ramblers' Association
River Thames Society
Royal Yacht Squadron
Scottish Anglers' Association
Scottish Council of Physical Recreation
Scottish Dinghy Association

Scottish Gliding Union
Scottish Rights of Way Society Ltd.
Scottish Tourist Board
Scottish Youth Hostels Association
Sports Council
Sports Council for Scotland
Sports Council for Wales
Ulster Council for Outdoor Organizations
Wales Tourist Board
Youth Hostels Association (Y.H.A.)
Youth Hostels Association of Northern Ireland

JOURNALS/PERIODICALS

New Society
Rucksack

ARTICLES

Goldsmith, E., 'Pollution by Tourism'   *Ecologist*   February 1974
'People at Play in the Dartmoor National Park'   *Geographical*
     Magazine   January 1970
Barrett, J. H., 'Progress on a Coastal Footpath'   *Geographical*
     Magazine   January 1970
Board, C. & Morgan, B., 'Parks for People'   *Geographical Magazine*
     June 1971
Clout, H., 'Two Homes, One Away'   *Geographical Magazine*
     November 1972
Simmons, I. G., 'Japanese Playgrounds'   *Geographical Magazine*
     May 1973
Dower, M., 'Leisure – Its Impact on Man and the Land'   *Geography*
     July 1970
Mercer, D. C., 'The Geography of Leisure'   *Geography*   July 1970
Clark, M. J., 'Conflict on the Coast'   *Geography*   April 1974
Dankenbring, W. F., 'Making the Most of your Leisure Time'   *Plain*
     Truth   April 1973
Schumacher, E. F., 'Education for Leisure and Wholesome Work'
     Resurgence   March/April 1974

BOOKS (GENERAL)

Berry, P. S., *Guide to Resources in Environmental Education* rev. edn. (An annual publication giving details of broadcasts, articles, books, etc.)   J.E.W.P.   1974   Price **B**

Berry, P. S., *National Survey into Environmental Education in Secondary Schools: Report and Recommendations* (7 regional reports also available)   Conservation Society/J.E.W.P.   1974   Price **C**

Berry, P. S., *Guide to Resources in Environmental Education,* rev. edn. *Secondary Schools: Statistical Supplement*   J.E.W.P.   1974   Price **B**

Brainerd, J., *Nature Study for Conservation: A Handbook for Environmental Education*   Collier-Macmillan   1971   Price **F**

Brown, A. E. & Martin, G. C. (eds.), *Environmental Education: The Present, and Future, Trends* (S.E.E. Occasional Papers No. 7)   S.E.E.   1972   Price **E**

Calder, N., *Nature in the Round: A Guide to Environmental Science*   Weidenfeld & Nicolson   1973   Price **G**

Carson, S. McB., *Environmental Studies: The Construction of an 'A' Level Syllabus*   N.F.E.R.   1971   Price **E**

Clegg, J. (ed.), *Teaching Science Out of Doors*   Warne   1968   Price **D**

Colton, R. W. & Morgan, R. F., *Project Environment* (Schools Council)
Education for the Environment   Price **E**
Learning from Trails   Price **E**
The School Outdoor Resource Area   Price **E**
Longman   1974/5   8–18 years

D.E.S., *Schools and the Countryside*   H.M.S.O.   1958   Price **D**

Devon Trust for Nature Conservation, *School Projects in Natural History*   H.E.B.   1972   Price **F**

Finch, I., *Nature Study and Science*   Longman   1971   Price **J**

Hammersley, A. *et al., Approaches to Environmental Studies: A Handbook for Teachers, Students and Others Interested in the World around them*   Blandford Press   1968   Price **E**

Hopkins, M. F. S., *Learning through the Environment* ('Education Today' series)   Longman   1968   Price **D**

Illich, I., *Deschooling Society*
Calder & Boyars   1971   Price **E**
Penguin   1972   Price **C**

Lambert, J. M. (ed.), *The Teaching of Ecology: A Symposium of the British Ecological Society*   Blackwell Scientific   1967   Price **F**

Lines, C. J. & Bolwell, L. H., *Teaching Environmental Studies in the Primary and Middle School*   Ginn   1971   Price **G**

Martin, G. & Turner, E. (ed.), *Environmental Studies* ('Teachers' Handbook' series)   Blond Educational   1972   Price **F**

Masterton, T. H., *Environmental Studies: A Concentric Approach*
Oliver & Boyd   1969   Price **D**
N.A.E.E., *Environmental Education* (Annual-Journal)   Heinemann
1972/3/4   Price (each) **D**
Perry, G. A., Jones, E. & Hammersley, A., *The Teacher's Handbook for Environmental Studies*, 3rd edn.   Blandford Press   1974   Price **F**
Pritchard, T. *et al.*, *Nature Trails*   Warne   1968   Price **C**
Rogers, P. (ed.), *The Education of Human Ecologists* (Symposium at Huddersfield Polytechnic)   Knight   1973   Price **G**
Schools Council, *Environmental Studies Project*
Teacher's Guide   Starting From Maps
Case Studies   Starting From Rocks
Hart-Davis   1972/3   5–13 years   Price (each) **E**
Schools Council, *Rural Studies in Secondary Schools*   Evans/Methuen
1969   Price **B**
Schwab, M. (ed.), *Teach-in for Survival*   Robinson & Watkins   1972
Price **E/F**
Searle, G., *Project Earth: An Action Guide for Young People*   Wolfe
1973   Price **E**
S.E.E., *Occasional Papers*
1. *Environmental Studies in Colleges of Education*
3. *Curriculum Development Project on Environmental Studies*
4. *Environmental Sciences at the University of East Anglia*
5. *English Literature and the Study of Environment*
S.E.E.   Price (each) **B**
Taylor, J. L. & Walford, R., *Simulation in the Classroom*   Penguin
1972   Price **C**
Tinker, J., *You and Your Environment* (Teachers' notes)   Pedigree
Petfoods   1973   Price free
U.N.E.S.C.O., *Source Book for Geography Teaching*   Longman
1972   Price **E**
Walford, R., *Games in Geography* ('Education Today' series)   Longman
1969   Price **E**
Ward, C. & Fyson, A., *Streetwork. The Exploding School* (Environmental education in towns)   Routledge   1973   Price **E/G**
Watts, D. G., *Environmental Studies*   Routledge   1969   Price **D**

Directory of Lecturers in Natural History and Nature Conservation
Council for Nature   1973   Price **C**
Education for Our Future   Conservation Society   1973   Price **B**
Environment U.S.A. A Guide to Agencies, People and Resources
Bowker   1974   Price **J**
World Directory of Environmental Education Programmes (Directory to post-secondary training in 70 countries)   Bowker   1974
Price **J**
World Directory of Environmental Research Centres (Describes over 5000 organizations throughout world involved in research on the environment)   Bowker   1974   Price **K**

BOOKS (SCHOOL)

Bainbridge, J., *Conservation* ('Evans Integrated Themes' series)
    Evans   1972   9–14 years   Price **D**
Bell, G., *What Happens When*
    1. *A By-Pass is Built*   5. *A River is Cleansed*
    2. *A Valley is Drowned*   6. *You Throw Things Away*
    3. *An Airport is Enlarged*   7. *A Village Grows*
    4. *A District is Re-born*   8. *You Explore Your District*
    Oliver & Boyd   1970   9–13 years   Price (each) **C**
Bishop, O. N., *Outdoor Biology* (3 volumes)
    Murray   1971   9–13 years   Price (each) **D**
Burton, J., *Man and His World*
    1. *Population*   3. *Pollution*
    2. *The Conservation of Wild Life*   4. *Resources*
    Blackie   1974   12–16 years   Price (each) **D/E**
Harris, A., Harrison, C. & Smithson, P., *Man's Environment* ('Visual
    Books' series)   Macdonald Educational   1972   C.S.E.
    Price **D**
Jackman, L., 'Exploring' series
    1. *The Woodland*   3. *The Hedgerow*
    2. *The Park*   4. *The Seashore*
    Evans   1970   9–13 years   Price (each) **D**
Perrott, E., *Biology: An Environmental Approach*
    The World of Life: The Biosphere   Price **D/E**
    Diversity Among Living Things   Price **D/E**
    Patterns in the Living World   Price **D/E**
    Looking into Organisms   Price **E/F**
    Man and his Environment   Price **E/F**
    Murray   1972   15 years +
Rigg, J. B., *Textbook of Environmental Study for School Scientists*
    Constable   1968   16 years +   Price **F**
Williams, R., *Environment Project Workbooks* –
    *Pollution (Air Pollution/Water Pollution/Waste Pollution/Noise
    Pollution)*
    *Conservation (Wildlife/The Countryside/Conservation in Towns/
    Population)*
    *Urban Studies (Traffic/Planning and Development/Improvements/
    New Developments)*
    Collins   13–16 years   Price **E** (per 4-copy pack)

    Science and Your Surroundings:
    A Piece of Waste Ground
    In the Park
    On the Road
    Looking into Water
    Beside the Seaside
    Ginn   1969–74   9–13 years   Price **C**

FILMS

Creative Spirit, The
  Shropshire County Council   30 min., col.   Hire E
Environmental Study, An
  Shropshire County Council   30 min., col.   Hire E
World Outside, The (Neighbourhood field studies)
  Guild (900 4497–3)   19 min., col.   Hire G

WALLCHARTS/POSTERS

You and Your Environment (Resources, pollution, landscape, ecology)
  Pedigree Petfoods   1973   Price free

GAMES/KITS/WORKCARDS

Activity Factsheets Phase 1 (1973)   C.S.E.
  1. *The Homeless*   6. *Gambling*
  2. *Old Age*   7. *Crime in Towns*
  3. *Local Pollution*   8. *Fatherless Families*
  4. *Transport Problems*   9. *The Need for New Towns*
  5. *Unemployment*   10. *Living in New Towns*
  Nelson   Sets of 10   Price (each) E
Approaches to Environmental Studies (Includes teacher's handbook and
  guides, class books, programmed learning material, slide folios,
  film loops. All items are available separately, and are listed
  elsewhere in this book)
  Blandford Press   9–13 years   Price various
Our Environment – Our Choice (7 fact/discussion sheets)
  J.E.W.P.   1972   11 years +   Price A
Study of a Village (A Schools Council Curriculum Discussion Kit,
  based on a Somerset village).
  Hart-Davis   56 slides, 2 tapes   Price K
                        20 teacher's charts   Price D

ORGANIZATIONS

Advisory Centre for Education (A.C.E.)
Association of School Natural History Societies
Central Council for Physical Recreation (C.C.P.R.)
Centre for Environmental Studies
Conservation Society, Joint Education Working Party (J.E.W.P.)
Council for Education in World Citizenship
Council for Environmental Education (C.E.E.)
Council for Social Service for Wales and Monmouthshire
Council for Urban Studies Centres (C.U.S.C.)
Duke of Edinburgh's Award Scheme
Educational Foundation for Visual Aids (E.F.V.A.)
Enterprise Youth
Environment Centre, The

Field Studies Council
Forest School Camps
Geographical Association (G.A.)
Humane Education Centre
Institute of Biology
Institution of Environmental Sciences
International Union for the Conservation of Nature (I.U.C.N.)
International Youth Federation for Environmental Studies and
      Conservation
London Co-operative Education Department
National Association for Environmental Education (N.A.E.E.)
National Association for Outdoor Education
National Council of Social Service (N.C.S.S.)
National Institute of Adult Education (N.I.A.E.)
Pictorial Charts Educational Trust (P.C.E.T.)
Prince of Wales's Committee
Public Interest Research Centre Ltd.
Regional Studies Association
Royal Society of Arts (R.S.A.)
School Natural Science Society
Schools Council
Schools Eco-Action Group (S.E.A.G.)
Scottish Committee on Education and the Countryside
Scottish Council of Social Service
Scottish Field Studies Association
Scout Association
Society for Environmental Education (S.E.E.)
Voluntary Committee on Overseas Aid and Development (V.C.O.A.D.)
Workers' Educational Association (W.E.A.)
Youth Service Information Centre

JOURNALS/PERIODICALS
Audio-Visual
Bulletin of Environmental Education (BEE)
Communication on Education Newsletter
Council for Environmental Education Newsheet
Education and Culture
Environment Film Review, The
Environmental Education
Environmental Education Report
Geography
Information for Survival
J.E.W.P. Newsletter
Journal of Biological Education
Pictorial Education
Regional Studies
Review of Environmental Education Developments (REED)

172

SACK
S.A.G.E. Newsletter
S.E.A.G. Newsletter
U.N.E.S.C.O. Courier
Visual Education
Where?
World and the School

ARTICLES

Fyson, A., 'Environmental Studies in Schools'   *BEE*   January 1973
Martin, G., 'Environmental Education'   *BEE*   May 1973
McLaren, R., 'Environmental Studies as Political Education'   *BEE*
   October 1973
Bulford, D., 'Environmental Education in Scotland – a Survey in
   1973'   *BEE*   December 1973
Forbes, J., 'Towards Co-ordinating Framework for Environmental
   Education – a Planner's View'   *BEE*   March 1974
Johnson, C., 'Environmental Education – Not so much a Subject, more
   a Way of Life'   *Biologist*   May 1972
'Environmental Studies at A-level'   *Biologist*   May 1972
Berry, P. S., 'National Survey into Environmental Education in
   Secondary Schools'   *Conservation News*   July 1974
Jones, E. L., 'An Education for Ecologists'   *Ecologist*   February
   1972
Fenwick, W. P., 'Education and the Environment'   *Ecologist*   August
   1972
Nicholls, A. D., 'Environmental Studies in Schools'   *Geography*   July
   1973
Wise, M. J., 'Environmental Studies: Geographical Objectives'
   Geography   November 1973
Elliot, J., 'Material Available for Environmental Education'   *Journal
   of Biological Education*   April 1973
Cerovsky, J., 'Environmental Education: Yes, But How?'   *Your
   Environment*   Spring 1971
Oswold, P., 'Environmental Education and the Conservationists'   *Your
   Environment*   Spring 1971
Patterson, W. C., 'Environmental Education: A Working Dossier'   *Your
   Environment*   Spring 1971
Carter, G., 'Urban Nature Trails: Pupils and Parks'   *Your Environ-
   ment*   Summer 1971

PART TWO

Sources of Teaching Material

The following sections give further details of the publishers and suppliers listed in Part One.

Suppliers and Publishers — These have been listed alphabetically, with their addresses and telephone numbers. An indication of the type of material produced in the field of Environmental Studies/Science, together with the titles of appropriate series, has also been included.

Organizations — Again, these have been listed alphabetically with addresses and telephone numbers. Some indication of their work has been included, where this is not apparent from their names. Relevant publications have also been included.

Journals and Periodicals — Most of the publishers of these have been listed in one or other of the above mentioned sections, but where they have not already appeared their addresses are quoted in this section. Details are also given of the frequency of publication, and the subscription, although this latter is subject to alteration. Subscription rates to libraries may vary from those quoted.

Additional Sources of Information — A number of valuable sources of material, including guides, classified catalogues, and Schools Council publications has been listed in this section. The items are arranged alphabetically under the name of the publisher or organization responsible.

Note: See pages vii—ix for abbreviations of suppliers, publishers and organizations listed.

1 SUPPLIERS AND PUBLISHERS

Details of other organizations supplying educational material will be found on pages 195–221.

Abelard-Schuman Ltd.
450 Edgware Road, London W2 1EG (*tel.* 01-723 0138)
Books
Academic Press Inc. (London) Ltd.
24–28 Oval Rd., Camden Town, London NW1 7DX (*tel.* 01-267 4466).
Books
Adam, Rouilly (London) Ltd.
10 Winchester Rd., Swiss Cottage, London NW3 (*tel.* 01-636 2703).
Wallcharts
Adams & Dart
1a Queen Square, Bath, Avon BA1 2HA (*tel.* 0225 27324).
Books
Addison-Wesley Publishing Co. Ltd.
West End House, 11 Hills Place, London W1R 2LR (*tel.* 01-734 8817).
Books ('Environmental Studies' series)
Advisory Centre for Education (A.C.E.)
32 Trumpington St., Cambridge CB2 1QY (*tel.* 0223 51456).
Kits
Aerofilms Ltd.
Elstree Way, Boreham Wood, Herts. WD6 1SB (*tel.* 01-953 6161).
Slides   Prints   Transparencies
Aldus Books Ltd.
Aldus House, 17 Conway St., Fitzroy Square, London W1P 6BS
(*tel.* 01-387 2811).
Books ('Interdependence in Nature' series)
Allen (George) & Unwin Ltd.
40 Museum St., London WC1A 1LU (*tel.* 01-405 8577).
Books
Angus & Robertson (U.K.) Ltd.
2 Fisher St., London WC1R 4QA (*tel.* 01-405 9547).
Books   Maps and atlases
Animals Magazine
21–2 Great Castle St., London W1N 8LT (*tel.* 01-499 4383).
Posters
Applied Science Publishers
Ripple Rd., Barking, Essex. (*tel.* 01-595 2121).
Journals
Architectural Press Ltd., The
9–13 Queen Anne's Gate, London SW1H 9BY (*tel.* 01-930 0611).
Books   Kits ('Lifescape' series)

Arnold (Edward) (Publishers) Ltd.
25 Hill St., London W1X 8LL (*tel.* 01-493 8511).
   Books ('Contemporary Biology'; 'Studies in Biology';
   'Basic Studies in Geography' series)
Arnold, E. J. & Son Ltd.
Butterley Street, Leeds LS10 1AX (*tel.* 0532-442944).
Association of Agriculture
78 Buckingham Gate, London SW1E 6PE (*tel.* 01-222 6115/6).
   Kits ('Farm Study' series)
Atlantic Educational Trust
37a High Street, Wimbledon, London SW19 5BY (*tel.* 01-947 4985).
   Periodicals
Australian News & Information Bureau (A.N.I.B.)
Canberra House, Maltravers St., London WC2 (*tel.* 01-836 2435).
   Film hire
Baker (John) (Publishers) Ltd.
4–6 Soho Square, London W1V 6AD (*tel.* 01-734 0845).
   Books
Ballantine Books Ltd.
8 King St., London WC2E 8HS (*tel.* 01-836 0718).
   Books (especially in conjunction with PAN and F.O.E.)
Bartholomew & Son Ltd.
Duncan St., Edinburgh EH9 1TA (*tel.* 031-667 6981).
   Maps and atlases
   Books
Batsford (B.T.) Ltd.
4 Fitzhardinge St., Portman Square, London W1H OAH (*tel.* 01-935
   0537).
   Books ('World Wide' series)
Bell (G.) & Sons Ltd.
York House, 6 Portugal St., London WC2A 2HL (*tel.* 01-405
   8505/6).
   Books
Black (A. & C.) Ltd.
4–6 Soho Square, London W1V 6AD (*tel.* 01-734 0845).
   Books ('Looking at Nature'; 'Picture Information Books'; 'Young
   Naturalist' series)
Blackie & Son Ltd.
Bishopbriggs, Glasgow G64 2NZ (*tel.* 041-772 1046).
   Books ('Man and His World' series)
Blackwell (Basil) & Mott Ltd.
5 Alfred St., Oxford OX1 4HB (*tel.* 0865 22146).
   Books ('Location and Links' series)
   Games ('New Ways in Geography' series)
   Workcards ('Environmental Study' series)
Blackwell Scientific Publications Ltd.
Osney Mead, Oxford OX2 OEL (*tel.* 0865 40201).
   Journals

Blandford Press Ltd.
167 High Holborn, London WC1V 6PH (*tel.* 01-836 9551).
   Books ('Approaches to Environmental Studies'; 'Rural Studies';
   'Natural History' series)
   Teaching aids ('Approaches to Environmental Studies' series)
Blond (Anthony) Ltd. *See* Holt-Blond Ltd.
Blond & Briggs Ltd.
56 Doughty St., London WC1N 2LS (*tel.* 01-405 2767/8).
   Books
Blond Educational. *See* Holt-Blond Ltd.
Bodley Head Ltd., The
9 Bow St., London, WC2E 7AL (*tel.* 01-836 9081).
   Books
Book Centre Ltd.
P.O. Box 30, North Circular Rd., Neasden, London NW10 OJE
   (*tel.* 01-459 1222).
   Book suppliers
Boulton-Hawker Films. *See* N.A.V.A.L.
Bowker Publishing Co. Ltd.
18 Bedford Row, London WC1R 4EJ (*tel.* 01-404 5881).
   Books
B.B.C. Enterprises Film Hire
25 The Burroughs, Hendon, London NW4 4AT (*tel.* 01-202 5342).
   Film hire
B.B.C. Publications
35 Marylebone High St., London W1M 4AA (*tel.* 01-580 5577).
   Books
British Film Institute (B.F.I.)
42/3 Lower Marsh, London SE1 (*tel.* 01-928 4742).
   Film hire
B.P. Film Library
15 Beaconsfield Rd., London NW10 2LE (*tel.* 01-451 1129).
   Film hire
British Transport Films
Melbury House, Melbury Terrace, London NW1 6LP (*tel.* 01-262
   3232).
   Film hire   Filmstrip hire
Brodie (James) Ltd.
15 Queen Square, Bath BA1 2IIW (*tel.* 0225 22110).
   Books
   Filmstrips
Burke Publishing Co. Ltd.
14 John St., London WC1N 2EJ (*tel.* 01-242 6724/5).
   Books
Business Books Ltd.
Mercury House, 103–119 Waterloo Road, London SE1 8UL
   (*tel.* 01-928 3388).
   Books

Butterworth & Co. (Publishers) Ltd.
88 Kingsway, London WC2B 6AB (*tel.* 01-405 6900).
Books
Calder & Boyars Ltd.
18 Brewer St., London W1R 4AS (*tel.* 01-734 1985).
Books
Cambridge Aids to Learning (Publishing) Ltd. (C.A.L.L.)
91 King St., Cambridge, (*tel.* 0223 63215).
Books
Cambridge University Press (C.U.P.)
Bentley House, 200 Euston Rd., London NW1 2DB (*tel.* 01-387 5030).
Books
Camera Talks Ltd.
31 North Row, London W1R 2EN (*tel.* 01-493 2761).
Filmstrips
Canada House Film Library
Canada House, Trafalgar Square, London SW1Y 5BJ (*tel.* 01-930 9741).
Film hire
Canfield Press. *See* Harper & Row.
Cape (Jonathan) Ltd.
30 Bedford Square, London WC1B 3EL (*tel.* 01-636 5764).
Books   Kits ('Jackdaw' series)
Careers Research Advisory Centre (C.R.A.C.)
Bateman St., Cambridge CB2 1LZ (*tel.* 0223 54445).
Games
Carousel Books. *See* Transworld.
Cassell & Collier-Macmillan Publishers Ltd.
35 Red Lion Square, London WC1R 4SG (*tel.* 01-405 5237).
Books ('Environment through Photographs' series)
Centaur Press Ltd.
Fontwell, Arundel, Sussex (*tel.* 024-368 3302).
Books
Central Electricity Generating Board (C.E.G.B.)
Sudbury House, 15 Newgate St., London EC1 7AU (*tel.* 01-248 1202).
Film hire
Central Film Library (C.F.L.)
Government Building, Bromyard Ave., Acton, London W3 7JB (*tel.* 01-743 5555).
Film hire (for C.O.I.)
Central Office of Information (C.O.I.)
Photographs Library, Hercules Rd., London SE1 7DU (*tel.* 01-928 2345).
Posters
Chapman (Geoffrey) Ltd.
35 Red Lion Square, London WC1R 4SG (*tel.* 01-242 6281).
Books

Chapman & Hall Ltd.
11 New Fetter Lane, London EC4P 4EE (*tel.* 01-583 9855).
Books
Chatto & Windus Educational Ltd.
Frogmore, St. Albans, Herts. AL2 2NF (*tel.* 0727 59101).
Books
Chatto & Windus Ltd.
40–2 William IV St., London WC2N 4DF (*tel.* 01-836 0127).
Books
C.I. Audio Visual Ltd. (C.I.A.V.)
5 Rosemont Rd., London NW3 6NG.
Kits ('Modular Learning Programme')
Civic Trust
17 Carlton House Terrace, London SW1Y 5AW (*tel.* 01-930 0914).
Books   Film hire
Clarendon Press. *See* Oxford University Press
Coca-Cola Export Corporation
Atlantic House, 7 Rockley Rd., London W14 ODH (*tel.* 01-743 9111).
Games
Collier-Macmillan. *See* Cassell & Collier-Macmillan Publishers Ltd.
Collins Educational
Kirkintilloch Rd., Bishopbriggs, Glasgow G64 2PW (*tel.* 041-772 5954).
Books ('Certificate Topics in Geography'; 'Nuffield Junior
Science Project' series).
Collins (William), Sons & Co. Ltd.
14 St. James's Place, London SW1A 1PS (*tel.* 01-493 5312).
Books ('Collins Ecology'; 'New Naturalist'; 'Fontana New
Naturalist' series)
Atlases   Wallcharts
Common Ground
Longman House, Burnt Mill, Harlow, Essex CM20 2JE (*tel.* Harlow
26721).
Filmstrips
Community Service Volunteers (C.S.V.)
237 Pentonville Rd., London N1 9NJ (*tel.* 01-278 6601).
Kits ('Sack' series)
Compton Russell Ltd. (Compton Press)
Compton Chamberlayne, Salisbury, Wilts. (*tel.* 072-270 630).
Books
Concord Film Council Ltd.
Nacton, Ipswich IP10 OJZ (*tel.* 0473 76012).
Film hire (for I.P.P.F., Shelter, Oxfam, F.P.A., etc.)
Conservation Books
28 Bearwood Rd., Wokingham RG11 4TD (*tel.* 0734 780989).
Book Suppliers
Conservation Society
12 London St., Chertsey, Surrey KT16 8AA (*tel.* 093-28 60975).
Booklets

179

Conservation Trust. *See* Conservation Society
Conservative Political Centre
32 Smith Square, London SW1P 3HH (*tel.* 01-222 9000).
Books
Constable & Co. Ltd.
10 Orange St., Leicester Square, London WC2H 7EG (*tel.* 01-930 0801/7).
Books
Coronet Books. *See* Hodder & Stoughton Ltd.
Council for the Protection of Rural England (C.P.R.E.)
4 Hobart Place, London SW1W OHY (*tel.* 01-235 9481).
Posters   Film hire   Slide hire
Countryside Commission
1 Cambridge Gate, Regent's Park, London NW1 4JY (*tel.* 01-935 5533).
Posters
David & Charles (Publishers) Ltd.
South Devon House, Railway Station, Newton Abbot, Devon TQ12 2DW (*tel.* 0626 3521/6).
Books
Davis-Poynter Ltd.
10 Earlham St., London WC2H 9LP (*tel.* 01-240 2935).
Books
Dekker (Marcel) Ltd.
14 Craufurd Rise, Maidenhead SL6 7LX (*tel.* 0628 31011).
Books
Dent (J. M.) & Sons Ltd.
Aldine House, 26 Albemarle St., London W1X 4QY (*tel.* 01-491 2970).
Books ('Pollution' series)
Deutsch (Andre) Ltd.
105 Great Russell St., London WC1B 3LJ (*tel.* 01-580 2746/9).
Books
Dinosaur Publications Ltd.
Beechcroft, Over, Cambridge CB4 5NE (*tel.* 0954 30324).
Books ('National Trust Children's Series')
Dobson (Dennis)
80 Kensington Church St., London W8 4BZ (*tel.* 01-229 0225).
Books
Duckworth (Gerald) & Co. Ltd.
43 Gloucester Crescent, London NW1 7DY (*tel.* 01-485 3484).
Books
Earth Island
20 New Cavendish St., London W1M 7LH (*tel.* 01-485 2471).
Books ('Red Alert!' series)
Ecology Bookshop. *See* Robinson & Watkins
Economics Association
Room 340, Hamilton House, Mabledon Place, London WC1H 9BH (*tel.* 01-387 6321).
Filmstrips

Eco-Publications
6 Cavendish Ave., Cambridge CB1 4US (*tel.* 0223 46005).
  Books   Posters ('Eco-posters' series)
Edinburgh University Press
22 George Sq., Edinburgh EH8 9LF (*tel.* 031-667 1011).
  Books
Educational Audio Visual Ltd. (E.A.V.)
Coal Rd., Seacroft, Leeds LS14 2AW.
  Audio-visual teaching materials
Educational Productions Ltd.
East Ardsley, Wakefield, Yorks. WF3 2JN (*tel.* 0924 823971).
  Filmstrips   Kits   Wallcharts
Educational Supply Association Ltd., The (E.S.A.)
School Materials Division, Pinnacles, P.O. Box 22, Harlow, Essex.
  (*tel.* 027-96 21131).
  Kits ('A.C.E. Study Kits')
Elek (Scientific Books) Ltd., Paul
54–8 Caledonian Rd., London N1 9RN
  Books
Elsevier. *See* Applied Science Publishers.
Encyclopaedia Britannica
Instructional Materials Division, Dolcis House, 87–91 New Bond St.,
  London W1.
  Filmstrips   Transparencies   Study prints
  Multi-media Resource Kit
English Universities Press Ltd. (E.U.P.)
St. Paul's House, Warwick Lane, London EC4P 4AH (*tel.* 01-248 5797).
  Books
Europa Publications Ltd.
18 Bedford Square, London WC1B 3JN (*tel.* 01-580 8236/8).
  Books
Evans Brothers Ltd.
Montague House, Russell Square, London WC1B 5BX (*tel.* 01-636
  8521).
  Books ('Integrated Themes'; 'Exploring' series)
Faber & Faber Ltd.
3 Queen Sq., London WC1N 3AU (*tel.* 01-278 6881).
  Books
Fabian Society
11 Dartmouth St., London SW1H 9BN (*tel.* 01-930 3077).
  Books
Field Studies Council (F.S.C.)
9 Devereux Court, Strand, London WC2R 3JR.
  Film hire
Fontana. *See* Collins (William)
Food & Agricultural Organization (F.A.O.)
Via delle Terme de Caracalla, Rome 00100, Italy.
  Wallcharts

Foulis (G. T.) & Co. Ltd.
50a Bell St., Henley-on-Thames RG9 2BJ (*tel.* 049-12 2426/7).
Books
Foulsham (W.) & Co. Ltd.
Yeovil Rd., Slough, Bucks.
Seminar Cassettes (Including 'International Report' and 'Life on Earth' series)
Foyle (W. & G.) Ltd.
119—125 Charing Cross Rd., London WC2 OEB (*tel.* 01-437 5660).
Book suppliers
Freeman (W. H.) & Co. Ltd.
58 King's Rd., Reading RG1 3AA (*tel.* 0734 583250).
Books   Games
Galt (J.) & Co. Ltd.
30 Great Marlborough St., London W1 (*tel.* 01-734 0829).
Wallcharts
Gas Council Film Library
6—7 Great Chapel St., London W1V 3AG
Film hire
Gateway Educational Films Ltd.
St. Lawrence House, 29—31 Broad St., Bristol BS1 2HF (*tel.* 0272 25351).
Film hire
General Learning Press
Kershaw House, 3 Henrietta Street, London WC2E 8LU.
Books (including 'Environment Reprints')
Geographia Ltd.
Colney St., St. Albans, Herts. (*tel.* 0727 7221).
Maps and atlases
Geographical Publications Ltd.
The Keep, Berkhamsted Place, Berkhamsted, Herts. HP4 1HQ (*tel.* 044-27 2981).
Maps and atlases ('World Land Use Survey' series)
Gerrard (T.) & Co.
Gerrard House, Worthing Rd., East Preston, Littlehampton, Sussex BN16 1AS (*tel.* 090-62 4151/3).
Posters
Gill Books (Claude)
481 Oxford St., London W1 (*tel.* 01-499 5664).
Book suppliers
Ginn & Co. Ltd.
Elsinore House, Buckingham St., Aylesbury, Bucks. (*tel.* 0296 88411).
Books ('Discovering your Environment'; 'Science and your Surroundings'; 'Social Biology' series)
Gollancz (Victor) Ltd.
14 Henrietta St., London WC2E 8QJ (*tel.* 01-836 2006).
Books

Gordon & Breach Science Publishers Ltd.
42 William IV St., London WC2N 4DF (*tel.* 01-836 5125).
Books   Journals
Granada Film Library
Manchester M60 9EA (*tel.* 061-832 7211).
Film sales (Films for hire now available from Concord and British Film Institute
Greater London Council (G.L.C.)
County Hall, London SE1 7PB (*tel.* 01-633 8849).
Books   Film hire
Griffin & George Ltd.
285 Ealing Rd., Wembley HAO 1HJ (*tel.* 01-997 3344).
Field study equipment   Filmstrips
Guild Sound & Vision Ltd.
85–129 Oundle Rd., Peterborough PE2 9PY (*tel.* 0733 63122).
Film hire   Transparencies
Hamilton (Hamish) Ltd.
90 Great Russell St., London WC1B 3PT (*tel.* 01-580 4621/6).
Books
Hamlyn Group, The
Astronaut House, Hounslow Road, Feltham, Middx. TW13 4AZ (*tel.* 01-751 8400).
Harcourt Brace Jovanovich Ltd.
24–8 Oval Rd., London NW1 7DX (*tel.* 01-485 7074/5).
Books
Harper. *See* Harper & Row Ltd.
Harper & Row Ltd.
28 Tavistock St., London WC2E 7PN (*tel.* 01-836 4635).
Books
Harrap (George G.) & Co. Ltd.
182–4 High Holborn, London WC1V 7AX (*tel.* 01-405 9935).
Books
Hart-Davis (Rupert) Ltd.
Park St., St. Albans, Herts. AL2 2NF (*tel.* 0727 59101).
Books
Heath (D.C.) (Europe) Ltd.
1 Westmead, Farnborough, Hants. (*tel.* 0252 41196).
Books
Heinemann Educational Books (H.E.B.)
48 Charles St., London W1X 8AH (*tel.* 01-493 9103).
Books
Heinemann (William) Ltd.
15–16 Queen St., London W1X 8BE (*tel.* 01-493 4141).
Books
Her Majesty's Stationery Office (H.M.S.O.)
49 High Holborn, London WC1V 6HB (*tel.* 01-928 6977).
Books
Hill (Leonard). *See* Intertext

Hodder & Stoughton Ltd.
St. Paul's House, Warwick Lane, London EC4P 4AH (*tel.* 01-248 5797).
Books
Holmes McDougall Ltd.
Allander House, 137—141 Leith Walk, Edinburgh EH6 8NS (*tel.* 031-554 9444).
Books ('This is your World'; 'This is your City'; 'Today's World'; 'Living Geography'; 'Exploring your World'; 'Design and the Environment' series)
Atlases   Posters
Holt-Blond Ltd.
120 Golden Lane, London EC1Y OTU (*tel.* 01-253 0855/8).
Books
Holt, Rinehart & Winston Ltd. *See* Holt-Blond Ltd.
Hong Kong University Press. *See* Oxford University Press
Hulton Educational Publications Ltd.
Raans Rd., Amersham, Bucks. HP6 6JJ (*tel.* 02-403 4196/8).
Books ('Environmental Studies'; 'Biological Field Studies'; 'Practical Geography' series)   *Filmstrips*
Hutchinson Educational Ltd.
3 Fitzroy Square, London W1P 6JD (*tel.* 01-387 2888).
Books ('Hutchinson University Library' series)
I.B.E.G. Ltd.
2—4 Upper Brook St., London W1Y 1AA (*tel.* 01-499 4688).
Book suppliers
Iliffe. *See* Butterworth & Co. (Publishers) Ltd.
I.C.I. Film Library.
Thames House, North Millbank, London SW1P 4QG (*tel.* 01-834 4444).
Film hire
I.W.P.C.
Water Pollution Control Dept., Aldewarke Works, Aldewarke, Rotherham S65 3SR South Yorks.
Film hire
Institution of Municipal Engineers (I.M.E.)
25 Eccleston Square, London SW1V 1NX (*tel.* 01-834 5082/3).
Books
Intermediate Technology Development Group Ltd. (I.T.D.G.)
Parnell House, 25 Wilton Rd., London, SW1V 1JS (*tel.* 01-828 5791/4).
Kits
International Planned Parenthood Federation (I.P.P.F.)
18/20 Lower Regent St., London SW1Y 4PW (*tel.* 01-839 2911).
Film hire (see Concord)   *Filmstrips*
International Textbook Co. Ltd. *See* Intertext.
Intertext
Kingswood House, Heath and Reach, Leighton Buzzard, Beds. (*tel.* 052-523 581).
Books

Irish University Press (International) Ltd.
60 Russell Square, London WC1B 4HP (*tel.* 01-637 2541/6).
Books
Italian Institute
39 Belgrave Square, London SW1 (*tel.* 01-235 1461).
Film hire
Joseph (Michael) Ltd.
52 Bedford Square, London WC1B 3EF (*tel.* 01-637 0941).
Johns Hopkins University Press, The *See* I.B.E.G. Ltd.
Kaye & Ward Ltd.
21 New St., London EC2M 4NT (*tel.* 01-283 7495/7).
Books
Kimpton (Henry) Publishers
205 Great Portland St., London W1N 6LR (*tel.* 01-580 6381).
Books
Knight (Charles) & Co. Ltd.
25 New Street Square, London EC4A 3AJ (*tel.* 01-353 3212).
Books
Knopf (Alfred) Inc.
20–4 Uxbridge St., London W8 7TA (*tel.* 01-229 9171).
Books
Lane (Allen)
17 Grosvenor Gardens, London SW1 (*tel.* 01-828 7090).
Books
Lexington Books. *See* D. C. Heath Ltd.
Liverpool University Press
123 Grove St., Liverpool L7 7AF (*tel.* 051-709 3630).
Books
Lockwood (Crosby) & Son Ltd.
Park St., St. Albans, Herts. AL2 2NF (*tel.* 0727 59101).
Books
Longman Group Ltd.
Longman House, Burnt Mill, Harlow, Essex CM20 2JE (*tel.* Harlow 26721).
Books (inc. 'Schools Council Project Environment') *Atlases*
Looking & Seeing Filmstrips. *See* Ginn
Low (Sampson), Marston & Co. Ltd. *See* Macdonald & Co.
Macdonald & Co. (Publishers) Ltd.
St. Giles House, 49/50 Poland St., London W1A 2LG (*tel.* 01-437 9844).
Books ('Visual Books' series)
Macdonald Educational. *See* Macdonald & Co.
Macdonald & Evans Ltd.
8 John St., London WC1N 2HY (*tel.* 01-242 2177/9).
Books ('Handbook' series)
MacGibbon & Kee Ltd. *See* Hart-Davis
Macmillan Education Ltd. *See* Macmillan International Ltd.

Macmillan International Ltd.
4 Little Essex St., London WC2R 3LF (*tel.* 01-836 6633).
> *Books* ('Topics in Geography'; 'Landscapes of Britain'; 'Geographical Readings' series)
> *Filmloops*   *Charts*
> *Kits* ('Topicards'; 'Social Education Kit')   *Journals*

Manchester University Press
316–324 Oxford Rd., Manchester M13 9NR (*tel.* 061-273 5539).
> *Books*

M.I.T. Press
126 Buckingham Palace Rd., London SW1W 9SD (*tel.* 01-730 9208).
> *Books*

Maybank (J. & J.) Ltd.
Maybank Wharf, Herringham Rd.,Charlton, London SE7(*tel.* 01-858 6100).
> *Leaflets* (on organization of waste collection schemes and recycling waste material)

McGraw-Hill Publishing Co. Ltd.
Shoppenhangers Rd., Maidenhead SL6 2QL (*tel.* 0628 23432).
> *Books   Film hire/purchase   Filmstrips*

Mentor Books. *See* New English Library Ltd.

M.T.P.: Medical & Technical Publishing Co. Ltd.
P.O. Box 55, St. Leonard's House, St. Leonard's Gate, Lancaster LA1 3BR (*tel.* 0524 68765).
> *Books*

Methuen Educational Ltd.
11 New Fetter Lane, London EC4P 4EE (*tel.* 01-583 9855).
> *Books* ('Get to Know'; 'The World we are Making'; 'Stand and Stare' series)

Metropolitan Water Board
Statistical Officer, Room 134, New River Head, Rosebery Ave., London EC1R 4TP.
> *Film hire*

Midwinter (Eric)
c/o Paddington Comprehensive School, Liverpool L7 3EA.
> *Games*

Miller (J. Garnett) Ltd.
1–5 Portpool Lane, London EC1N 7SL (*tel.* 01-405 7980).
> *Books*

Milliken. *See* Guild Sound & Vision Ltd.

Mills & Boon Ltd.
17–19 Foley St., London W1A 1DR (*tel.* 01-580 9074).
> *Books* ('On Location' series)

Morris (John) Documentary Films
36 Brueton Rd., Solihull, Warks. (*tel.* 021-705 6166).
> *Film hire*

Muller (Frederick) Ltd.
110 Fleet St., London EC4A 2AP (*tel.* 01-353 1040).
> *Books* ('Man and Society'; 'The World we Live in' series)

Municipal Publications Co. Ltd.
178–202 Great Portland Street, London W1N 6NH (*tel.* 01-637
   2400).
   Journals
Murray (John) (Publishers) Ltd.
50 Albemarle St., London W1X 4BD (*tel.* 01-493 4361/3).
   Books ('Biology: An Environmental Approach' series)
National Audio-Visual Aids Library (N.A.V.A.L.)
Paxton Place, Gipsy Rd., London SE27 9SR (*tel.* 01-670 4247).
   Film hire
National Benzole Film Library
15 Beaconsfield Road, London NW10 2LE (*tel.* 01-451 1120).
   Film hire
National Book League
7 Albemarle St., London 41X 4BB (*tel.* 01-493 9001).
   Book suppliers
National Coal Board Film Library (N.C.B.)
Hobart House, Grosvenor Place, London SW1X 7AE (*tel.* 01-235
   2020).
   Film hire
**National Foundation for Educational Research Publishing Co. Ltd.
   (N.F.E.R.)**
2 Jennings Buildings, Thames Ave., Windsor, Berks. SL4 1QS
   (*tel.* 075-35 69345).
   Books
National Society for Clean Air
134–7 North St., Brighton BN1 1RG (*tel.* 0273 26313).
   Books   Wallcharts
Nelson (Thomas) & Sons Ltd.
36 Park St., London W1Y 4DE (*tel.* 01-493 8351).
   Books ('Nelson Geography Studies' series)
   Workcards ('Activity Fact Sheets' series)
New English Library Ltd.
Barnard's Inn, Holborn, London EC1N 2JR (*tel.* 01-405 4614).
   Books
New Scientist
128 Long Acre, London WC2E 9QH (*tel.* 01-836 2468).
   Booklets ('Readers' series)
New Society
128 Long Acre, London WC2E 9QH (*tel.* 01-836 2468).
   Booklets ('Social Studies Readers' series)
North-Holland Publishing Co. Ltd.
100 South Hill Park, London NW3.
   Books
Oliver & Boyd
Tweeddale Court, 14 High St., Edinburgh EH1 1YL (*tel.* 031-556
   4622/4).
   Books ('What Happens When . . .' series)

Open University Press
Walton Hall, Milton Keynes, Bucks. MK7 6AA (*tel.* 090-82 4066).
Books
Ordnance Survey
Romsey Rd., Maybush, Southampton SO9 4DH (*tel.* 0703 775555).
Maps
Oriel Press Ltd.
32 Ridley Place, Newcastle-upon-Tyne NE1 8LH (*tel.* 0632 20892).
Books   Journals
Osprey Publishing Ltd.
137 Southampton St., Reading RG1 2QZ, Berks. (*tel.* 0734 85802).
Books
Oxford University Press (O.U.P.)
Ely House, 37 Dover St., London W1X 4AH (*tel.* 01-629 8494).
Books ('Oxford Social Geographies'; 'The Changing World';
'Oxford Biology Readers' series)   *Atlases*
Paladin Books. *See* Panther Books.
Pall Mall Press Ltd.
5 Cromwell Place, London SW7 2JL (*tel.* 01-589 3264).
Books
Pan Books Ltd.
33 Tothill St., London SW1 (*tel.* 01-222 7090).
Books
Panther Books Ltd.
Park St., St. Albans, Herts. (*tel.* 0727 59101).
Books
Peak Park Planning Board
Aldern House, Baslow Rd., Bakewell, Derbs. DE4 1AE (*tel.* 062-981 2881).
Kits
Pedigree Petfoods Ltd.
Education Centre, Avon House, 360—366 Oxford St., London
W1N 9HA (*tel.* 01-499 0231).
Wallchart   Booklet
Pemberton Publishing Co. Ltd.
88 Islington High St., London N1 8EN (*tel.* 01-226 7251).
Books
Penguin Books Ltd.
Bath Rd., Harmondsworth, Middx. UB7 ODA (*tel.* 01-759 1984).
Books ('Connexions'; 'Extensions' series)
Pergamon Press Ltd.
Headington Hill Hall, Oxford OX3 OBW (*tel.* 0865 64881).
Books   Atlases   Kits   Journals
Phaidon Press Ltd.
5 Cromwell Place, London SW7 2JL (*tel.* 01-589 3264).
Books
Philip (George) & Son Ltd.
12—14 Long Acre, London WC2E 9LP (*tel.* 01-836 7863).
Books   Maps and atlases   Globes   Kits ('Beaver Units' series)

Philip Alexander (George) Ltd.
Norfolk House, Smallbrook Queensway, Birmingham B5 4LT (*tel.* 021-643 8641).
Books
Philip & Tacey Ltd.
North Way, Andover, Hants. (*tel.* 0264 61171).
Wall display
Phoenix House. *See* Dent
Pictorial Charts Educational Trust (P.C.E.T.)
132 Uxbridge Rd., London W13 8QU (*tel.* 01-567 9206).
Wallcharts
Pitman Medical & Scientific Publishing Co. Ltd.
Pitman House, 39 Parker St., Kingsway, London WC2B 5PB (*tel.* 01-405 9791).
Books
Plenum Publishing Corp.
Davis House, 8 Scrubs Lane, Harlesden, London NW10 6SE (*tel.* 01-969 4727).
Books
Praeger Publishers Inc.
5 Cromwell Place, London SW7 2JL (*tel.* 01-589 3264).
Books
Prentice-Hall International Inc.
Durrants Hill Rd., Hemel Hempstead, Herts. (*tel.* 0442 58531).
Books
Priority
Harrison Jones School, West Derby St., Liverpool L7 8TP.
Kits
Priory Press Ltd.
101 Gray's Inn Rd., London WC1X 8TX (*tel.* 01-242 1598).
Books
Rank Film Library
P.O. Box 70, Great West Rd., Brentford, Middx. TW8 9HR (*tel.* 01-568 9222).
Film hire   Filmstrips
Ray (Marian)
36 Villiers Ave., Surbiton, Surrey. (*tel.* 01-390 1800).
Filmstrips
Reader's Digest Association Ltd.
25 Berkeley Square, London W1X 6AB (*tel.* 01-629 8144).
Books   Atlases
Resurgence
275 King's Rd., Kingston-upon-Thames, Surrey. (*tel.* 01-546 0544).
Books
Rivingtons (Publishers) Ltd.
Montague House, Russell Square, London WC1B 5BX (*tel.* 01-636 8521).
Books

Robinson & Watkins
19/21 Cecil Court, Charing Cross Rd., London WC2N 4HB (*tel*. 01-836
2182).
Book suppliers
Routledge & Kegan Paul
Broadway House, 68–74 Carter Lane, London EC4V 5EL
(*tel*. 01-248 4821/4).
Books ('C.S.E. General Science' series)
Royal Society for the Prevention of Cruelty to Animals (R.S.P.C.A.)
105 Jermyn St., London SW1 (*tel*. 01-930 0971).
Film hire   Slide hire
Royal Society for the Protection of Birds (R.S.P.B.)
The Lodge, Sandy, Beds. SG19 2DL (*tel*. 0767 80551).
Wallcharts   Kits   Slides
Russell (Bertrand) Peace Foundation
Bertrand Russell House, Gamble St., Nottingham NG7 4ET
(*tel*. 0602 74504).
Books
Saunders (W. B.) Co. Ltd.
12 Dyott St., London WC1A 1DB (*tel*. 01-836 1641).   *Books*
Saxon House. *See* D. C. Heath Ltd.
Schofield & Sims Ltd.
35 St. John's Rd., Huddersfield HD1 5DT (*tel*. 0484 30684).
Books ('Environmental Studies Assignment Books' series)
School Government Publishing Co. Ltd.
Darby House, Bletchingley Rd., Merstham, Redhill RH1 3DN
(*tel*. Merstham 2223).
Kits
Schoolmaster Publishing Co. Ltd.
Derbyshire House, Lower St., Kettering, Northants NN16 8BB (*tel*. 053-
687 3407).
Books
Schools Council
Field Officers Section, 160 Great Portland St., London W1N 6LL
(*tel*. 01-580 0352).
Kits
Scottish Film Council
16–17 Woodside Terrace, Glasgow G3 7XN (*tel*. 041-332 5413).
Film hire (in Scotland)
Secker (Martin) & Warburg Ltd.
14 Carlisle St., London W1V 6NN (*tel*. 01-437 2075).
Books
Seeley, Service & Cooper Ltd.
196 Shaftesbury Ave., London WC2H 8JL (*tel*. 01-836 6225).
Books
Shell Mex & B.P.
25 The Burroughs, Hendon, London NW4 4AT (*tel*. 01-202 7803).
Film hire   Wallcharts

Shire Publications Ltd.
12b Temple Square, Aylesbury, Bucks. HP20 2QN (*tel.* 0296
   83999).
   Books ('Discovering' series)
Shropshire County Council
Education Dept., Shirehall, Abbey Foregate, Shrewsbury SY2 6NF.
   Film hire
Sidgwick & Jackson Ltd.
1 Tavistock Chambers, Bloomsbury Way, London WC1A 2SG
   (*tel.* 01-242 6081/3).
   Books
Sinauer. *See* Freeman (W. H.)
Singer (Andrew)
Bottisham Park Mill, Swaffham Rd., Bottisham, Cambs. CB5 9ED
   (*tel.* 0223 811071).
   Books
Slide Centre Ltd., The
Portman House, 17 Brodrick Rd., London SW17 7DZ (*tel.* 01-672
   3221).
   Slidefolios   Audio-Visual Aids
Society for the Promotion of Nature Reserves (S.P.N.R.)
The Green, Nettleham, Lincoln.
   Film Hire (also from county trusts)
Society of Chemical Industry
14 Belgrave Square, London SW1X 8PS (*tel.* 01-235 3681).
   Books
Spearman (Neville) Ltd.
112 Whitfield St., London W1 (*tel.* 01-387 2466).
Sphere Books Ltd.
30/2 Gray's Inn Rd., London WC1X 8JL (*tel.* 01-405 2087).
   Books
Stacey (Tom) Ltd.
See Philip Alexander (George) Ltd. for school books. Enquiries for
   general books to W. H. Cork Gully & Co., 19 Eastcheap, London
   EC3.
   Books
Stanford (Edward) Ltd.
12–14 Long Acre, London WC2E 9LP (*tel.* 01-836 1321).
   Maps and atlases
Staples Press Ltd.
Park St., St. Albans, Herts. (*tel.* 0727 59101).
   Books
Stewart Film Distributors Ltd.
82-4 Clifton Hill, London NW8 OJT (*tel.* 01-624 7296).
   Film hire
Studio Vista Publishers
Blue Star House, Highgate Hill, London N19 5NY (*tel.* 01-272 7531).
   Books

Stillitron
72 New Bond St., London W1Y OQY (*tel.* 01-493 1177).
   Kits ('Programmed Learning System')
Stuart & Watkins. *See* Robinson & Watkins
Student Recordings Ltd.
King Street, Newton Abbot, Devon.
   Filmstrips   Tapes
Tavistock Publications Ltd.
11 New Fetter Lane, London EC4P 4EE (*tel.* 01-583 9855).
   Books
Technical Press Ltd., The
Freeland, Oxford OX7 2AP (*tel.* 0993-881 788).
   Books
Temple Smith (Maurice) Ltd.
37 Great Russell St., London WC1B 3PP (*tel.* 01-636 9810).
   Books
Thames & Hudson Ltd.
30/4 Bloomsbury St., London WC1B 3QP (*tel.* 01-636 5488).
   Books
Third World Publications
67 College Rd., Birmingham B13 9LR (*tel.* 021-777 9644).
   Books
Time-Life International Ltd.
Time and Life Building, 153 New Bond St., London W1
   (*tel.* 01-499 4080).
   Books ('Life Nature Library'; 'Life Science Library'; 'World's
   Wild Places'; 'Emergence of Man' series)
Times Newspapers Ltd.
New Printing House Square, London WC1X 8EZ (*tel.* 01-837 1234).
   Atlases
Toronto University Press. *See* Oxford University Press
Town & Country Planning Association (T. & C.P.A.)
17 Carlton House Terrace, London, SW1Y 5AS (*tel.* 01-930
   8903/5).
   Books   Journals
Trade & Technical Press Ltd., The
   Crown House, Morden, Surrey (*tel.* 01-540 3897).
   Books
Transworld Publishers Ltd.
Cavendish House, 57/59 Uxbridge Road, London W5 5SA (*tel.* 01-579
   2652).
   Books
Tull Graphic Ltd.
84 Teesdale St., London E2 6PU (*tel.* 01-739 2138).
   Wallcharts
Unicorn
   c/o Books, 84 Woodhouse Lane, Leeds LS2 8AB.
   Books

University of London Press Ltd.
St. Paul's House, Warwick Lane, London EC4P 4AH (*tel.* 01-248 5797).
Books
University Tutorial Press Ltd. (U.T.P.)
9–10 Great Sutton St., London EC1V ODA (*tel.* 01-253 6992).
Books
Van Nostrand Reinhold Co. Ltd.
25–8 Buckingham Gate, London SW1E 6LQ (*tel.* 01-834 3726).
Books ('Design and Planning' series)
Visual Information Service
12 Bridge St., Hungerford, Berks. (*tel.* Hungerford 2267).
Filmstrips
V.P.S. Film Library *See* Guild Sound & Vision Ltd.
Visual Publications
197 Kensington High St., London W8 6BB (*tel.* 01-937 1568).
Filmstrips
Voluntary Commitee on Overseas Aid and Development (V.C.O.A.D.)
Parnell House, 25 Wilton Rd., London SW1V 1JS (*tel.* 01-828 7611/6).
Wallcharts   Filmstrips   Slides   Tapes   Games
Wadebridge Ecological Centre
73 Molesworth St., Wadebridge, Cornwall PL27 7DS
Books
Ward Lock Ltd.
116 Baker St., London W1M 2BB (*tel.* 01-486 3271).
Books
Warne (Frederick) & Co. Ltd.
40 Bedford Square, London WC1B 3HE (*tel.* 01-580 9622).
Books ('Wayside and Woodland'; 'Observer's' series)   *Wallcharts*
Watts (Franklin) Ltd.
1 Vere St., London W1N 9HQ (*tel.* 01-493 8557/9).
Books
Wayland (Publishers) Ltd. *See* Priory Press
Books ('Project Earth' series)
Weidenfeld & Nicolson
11 St. John's Hill, London SW11 1XA (*tel.* 01-228 8888).
Books
Wiley (J.) & Sons Ltd.
Baffins Lane, Chichester PO19 1UD (*tel.* 0243 84531).
Books
Wills & Hepworth Ltd.
Beeches Rd., Loughborough LE11 OBR (*tel.* 050-93 68021).
Books ('Ladybird' series)   *Workcards   Filmstrips*
Wisconsin University Press
70 Great Russell St., London WC1B 3BY (*tel.* 01-405 0182).
Books
Wolfe Publishing Ltd.
10 Earlham St., London WC2H 9LP (*tel.* 01-240 2935).
Books

World Development Movement
25 Wilton Rd., London SW1Y 1LW (*tel.* 01-834 4795).
Books
World's Work Ltd.
The Windmill Press, Kingswood, Tadworth, Surrey (*tel.* 01-604 3511).
Books
Wyllie (Diana) Ltd.
3 Park Rd., Baker St., London NW1 (*tel.* 01-723 7333).
Filmstrips ('Environment' series)
World University Library (W.U.L.)
5 Winsley St., London W1N 7AQ (*tel.* 01-580 7941).
Books
Wykeham Publications (London) Ltd.
10–14 Macklin St., London WC2B 5NF (*tel.* 01-405 2237).
Books
Yale University Press Ltd.
20 Bloomsbury Square, London WC1A 2NP (*tel.* 01-580 2693/5).
Books

2 ORGANIZATIONS

Abortion Law Reform Society
22 Brewhouse Hill, Wheathampstead, Herts. (*tel.* 058-283 2347).
Concerned with the legal, medical and social aspects of abortion.
Publications: *A Guide to the Abortion Act*; newsletters.

Advisory Centre for Education (A.C.E.)
32 Trumpington St., Cambridge CB2 1QY (*tel.* 0223 51456).
Provides information service. Publications: *Watchword; Where?*

Alkali and Clean Air Inspectorate
Queen Anne's Chambers, 28 Broadway, London SW1H 9JU
(*tel.* 01-930 4300).
Concerned with the control of air pollution from certain
industrial processes.

All Change
12 Carlton House Terrace, London SW1.
Soon to publish details of local railway defence groups.

Alternative Society
9 Morton Ave., Kidlington, Oxford (*tel.* 08675 3413).
Organizes conferences.

Amateur Entomologists' Society
23 Manor Way, North Harrow, Middx. (*tel.* 01-863 2132).
Publishes various bulletins and handbooks on entomology.

Ancient Monuments Society
33 Ladbroke Square, London W11 3NB (*tel.* 01-221 6178).
Concerned with the study and conservation of historic structures.
Publications: *Transactions*.

Anglers' Co-operative Association
53 New Oxford St., London WC1A 1B1 (*tel.* 01-240 1339).
Fights river pollution. Publications: *Pollution Handbook*; *A.C.A.
Handbook*.

Animals in Danger Corps (A.I.D.)
Marston Court, Manor Rd., Wallington, Surrey (*tel.* 01-669 4995).
Raises money to save wildlife.

Anti-Concorde Project
70 Lytton Ave., Letchworth, Herts. (*tel.* 046-26 2081).
Opposes development and operation of supersonic aircraft.

Arboricultural Association
59 Blythwood Gardens, Stansted, Essex (*tel.* 02-7971 3160).
Concerned with tree care and education. Publishes a series of
leaflets on tree care.

Armagh Field Naturalists' Society
Brean Main St., Richhill, Co. Armagh (*tel.* Richhill 295).
Publishes annual report.

Association for Neighbourhood Councils
24 Pembridge Gardens, London W2 (*tel.* 01-980 6263).
Concerned with interests of urban parish councils.

Association for Studies in the Conservation of Historic Buildings
31–4 Gordon Square, London WC2 (*tel.* 01-387 6052).
  Publishes bi-monthly newsletter.
Association for the Preservation of Rural Scotland
1 Thistle Court, Edinburgh EH2 1DE (*tel.* 031-225 6744).
  Takes action to improve, protect and preserve countryside.
Association of Agriculture
78 Buckingham Gate, London SW1E 6PE (*tel.* 01-222 6115/6).
  Produces farm study schemes. Publications: *Association of Agriculture Journal.*
Association of British Tree Surgeons and Arborists
11 Wings Rd., Upper Hale, Farnham, Surrey (*tel.* 0251–3 5924).
  Concerned with tree repair and care.
Association of County Councils
Eaton House, 66*a* Eaton Square, London SW1W 9BH.
  (*tel.* 01-235 5173).
  Originally County Councils Association. Publishes monthly gazette.
Association of County Councils in Scotland
3 Forres St., Edinburgh EH3 6BL (*tel.* 031-225 1626).
  Protects interests of Scottish county councils.
Association of District Councils
25 Buckingham Gate, London SW1E 6LE (*tel.* 01-828 7425).
  Replaced Urban District Councils Association and Rural District Councils Association.
Association of Metropolitan Authorities
36 Old Queen St., London SW1H 9JE (*tel.* 01-930 9861).
  Represents local authorities in England and Wales (formerly Association of Municipal Corporations).
Association of School Natural History Societies
Wormholt Lodge, 76*a* Wormholt Rd., London W12.
  Publishes annual journal and newsletters.
Association of Tree Transplanters
91*a* High St., Great Missenden, Bucks. (*tel.* 0240-6 3661).
Automobile Association
Fanum House, Basing View, Basingstoke RG21 2EA (*tel.* Basingstoke 20123).
  Safeguards interests of motorists. Publications: *Drive;* various leaflets, guides, maps.
Birth Control Campaign
233 Tottenham Court Rd., London W1P 9AE (*tel.* 01-580 9360).
  Advocates family planning education, and provides information on birth control.
Botanical Society of Edinburgh
c/o Royal Botanic Garden, Inverleith Row, Edinburgh EH3 5LR
  (*tel.* 031-552 5531).
  Scotland's National Botanical Society.

Botanical Society of the British Isles
c/o Department of Botany, British Museum (Natural History), Cromwell
Rd., London SW7 5BD.
Concerned with study and conservation of flora.
British Airports Authority
2 Buckingham Gate, London SW1E 5JL (*tel.* 01-834 6621).
Owns and manages Britain's major airports.
British Arachnological Society
Pear Tree House, The Green, Blennerhasset, Carlisle CA5 3RE.
Publishes quarterly bulletin.
British Association for the Control of Aircraft Noise (B.A.C.A.N.)
30 Fleet St., London EC4 (*tel.* 034-284 2382).
Publishes various items on the effects of aircraft
noise.
British Broadcasting Corporation: Natural History Unit
Whiteladies Rd., Bristol BS8 2LR (*tel.* 0272-32211).
Responsible for B.B.C. natural history programmes. Library of
recordings and films.
British Butterfly Conservation Society Ltd.
Tudor House, Quorn, Leics.
Publishes quarterly news-sheet.
British Caravanners' Club
11 Lower Grosvenor Place, London SW1 OEY (*tel.* 01-828 9232).
British Commune Movement
2 Chapel Hill, Ashcott, Bridgewater, Somerset.
Publishes monthly journal.
British Cycling Bureau
Greater London House, Hampstead Rd., London NW1 7QP
(*tel.* 01-387 6868).
British Cycling Federation
26 Park Crescent, London W1N 4BL (*tel.* 01-636 4602).
Publishes various handbooks.
British Deer Society
Whale Moor Head, Lowther S. Park, Penrith, Cumbria
(*tel.* Hackforth 400).
Promotes conservation of deer.
British Ecological Society
Harvest House, 62 London Rd., Reading RG1 5AS.
Studies living organisms in relation to their surroundings.
Publications: *Journal of Ecology.*
British Entomological and Natural History Society
c/o The Alpine Club, 74 South Audley St., London W1.
British Field Sports Society
26 Caxton St., London SW1H ORG (*tel.* 01-222 5407).
Protects and promotes country sports.
British Gliding Association
Artillery Mansions, 75 Victoria St., London SW1 (*tel.* 01-799
7548).

British Horse Society
National Equestrian Centre, Stoneleigh, Kenilworth, Warks. CV8 2LR
(*tel.* 0203 27192/5).
Publishes textbooks and leaflets.
British Humanist Association
13 Prince of Wales Terrace, London W8 5PG (*tel.* 01-937 2341).
Pressure group with local branches. Publications include *People First* (environment statement).
British Mountaineering Council
26 Park Crescent, London W1N 4BE (*tel.* 01-637 1598).
Publishes bi-annual magazine; various leaflets; 'mountain code'.
British Naturalists' Association
Willowfield, Boyneswood Road, Four Marks, Alton, Hants. GU34 5EA
(*tel.* Medstead 3659).
Publishes magazine, leaflets and bulletins.
British Ornithologists' Union
c/o Zoological Society of London, Regent's Park, London NW1 4RY
(*tel.* 01-586 4443).
Publishes quarterly journal. Publications: *Status of Birds of Britain and Ireland.*
British Pteridological Society
46 Sedley Rise, Loughton, Essex (*tel.* 01-508 4601).
Concerned with conservation of fern flora. Publications: annual journal; newsletter.
British Railways Board
222 Marylebone Rd., London NW1 6JJ (*tel.* 01-262 3232).
British Road Federation
26 Manchester Square, London W1M 5RF (*tel.* 01-935 0221).
British Scrap Federation
33–4 Chancery Lane, London WC2A 1ER (*tel.* 01-405 0514).
Represents interests of scrap metal merchants.
British Society for Social Responsibility in Science
9 Poland St., London W1V 3DG (*tel.* 01-437 2728).
Publications: *The Social Impact of Modern Biology.*
British Speleological Association
4 Kingston Ave., Acklam, Middlesbrough, Cleveland TS5 7RS.
Concerned with caving, cave archaeology and leadmining history.
British Tourist Authority
64 St. James's St., London SW1A 1NF (*tel.* 01-629 9191).
Publishes quarterly newsletter, various books and leaflets.
British Trust for Conservation Volunteers
Zoological Gardens, Regent's Park, London NW1 4RY
(*tel.* 01-722 7112).
Provides practical voluntary work in the countryside.
British Trust for Entomology
41 Queen's Gate, London SW7.
Publishes monthly magazine.

British Trust for Ornithology
Beech Grove, Tring, Herts. (*tel.* Tring 3461).
  Concerned with collection of data for bird study. Publishes
  various field guides.
British Waste Paper Association
21 Devonshire St., London W1 (*tel.* 01-935 2081).
British Waterways Board
Melbury House, Melbury Terrace, London NW1 6JX (*tel.* 01-262 6711).
  Responsible for 2000 miles of waterway. Publishes guide books
  and maps.
Broads Consortium
Norfolk County Council, County Hall, Martineau Lane, Norwich
  NOR 47A (*tel.* 0603 22288).
  Aims to conserve natural environment of the Norfolk Broads.
Campaign for Biological Sanity
24 Abercorn Place, London NW8 (*tel.* 01-286 4366).
Camping Club of Great Britain and Ireland Ltd.
11 Lower Grosvenor Place, London SW1W OEY (*tel.* 01-828 1012).
  Publishes monthly magazine. Publications: *Camping and Outdoor
  Life*; *International Camping.*
Caravan Club
65 South Molton St., London W1Y 2AB (*tel.* 01-629 6441).
  Publishes handbooks, leaflets and posters.
Central Committee for the Architectural Advisory Panels
4 Hobart Place, London SW1W OHY (*tel.* 01-235 4771).
  Offers advice to improve standards of architectural design.
Central Council for Rivers Protection
Fishmongers' Hall, London EC4R 9EL (*tel.* 01-626 3531).
  Represents national bodies concerned with maintaining the
  purity of rivers.
Central Council of Physical Recreation (C.C.P.R.)
70 Brompton Rd., London SW3 1EX (*tel.* 01-589 3411).
  Aims to promote physical and mental health. Publications: *Sport
  and Recreation.*
Central Electricity Generating Board (C.E.G.B.)
Sunbury House, 15 Newgate St., London EC1A 7AV (*tel.* 01-248 1202).
  Statutory body.
Central Housing Advisory Committee
2 Marsham St., London SW1P 3EB (*tel.* 01-212 4023).
Central Rights of Way Committee
See Commons, Open Spaces and Footpaths Preservation Society.
Central Water Planning Unit
Reading Bridge House, Reading, Berks. (*tel.* 0734 57551).
  Statutory body.
Centre for Environmental Studies
62 Chandos Place, London WC2N 4HH (*tel.* 01-240 3434).
  Research body on urban and regional planning. Publications:
  Developing Patterns of Urbanization.

Chartered Institute of Transport
80 Portland Place, London W1N 4DP (*tel.* 01-580 5216).
Chiltern Society
Season's Watch, Bledlow Ridge, High Wycombe, Bucks.
    Concerned with history and planning of Chiltern Hills.
Christian Aid
P.O. Box 1, 2 Sloane Gardens, London SW1 (*tel.* 01-730 0614).
    Charitable body. Publications: *New Internationalist* (with
    OXFAM).
Civic Trust
17 Carlton House Terrace, London SW1Y 5AW (*tel.* 01-930 0914).
    Works for higher standards of city planning and design. Supports
    about 750 local amenity societies. Publications: numerous,
    including bi-monthly newsletter.
Civic Trust for the North East
34/5 Saddler St., Durham (*tel.* Durham 61182).
Civic Trust for the North West
56 Oxford St., Manchester M1 6EU (*tel.* 061-236 7464).
Civic Trust for Wales
6 Park Place, Cardiff CF1 3DP (*tel.* 0222 26006).
Clean Air Council for England and Wales
Queen Anne Chambers, 28 Broadway, London SW1H 9JU
    (*tel.* 01-930 4300).
    Concerned with abatement of air pollution.
Clean Air Council for Scotland
c/o Scottish Development Department, 21 Hill St., Edinburgh EH2 3JY
    (*tel.* 031-226 5208).
Coastal Anti-Pollution League Ltd.
Alverstoke, Greenway Lane, Bath BA2 4LM (*tel.* 0225 64094).
    Combats pollution of beaches by sewage. Publications: *Golden List
    of Beaches*; *Water Pollution in Coastal Areas – the layman's point
    of view*.
Commission for the New Towns
Glen House, Stag Place, London SW1E 5AJ (*tel.* 01-834 8034).
    Takes over from New Town Development Corporations after
    completion.
Commitment
42 Shirley Rd., Croydon, Surrey.
Committee for Environmental Conservation (CoEnCo)
29–31 Greville St., London EC1N 8AX (*tel.* 01-242 9647).
    Alliance of 14 national conservation organizations.
Commons, Open Spaces and Footpaths Preservation Society
166 Shaftesbury Ave., London WC2H 8JH (*tel.* 01-836 7220).
    Publishes books on law for the country lover.
Community Service Volunteers (C.S.V.).
237 Pentonville Rd., London N1 9NJ (*tel.* 01-278 6601).
    Helps young people play responsible role in the community.
    Publications: *SACK*.

Compassion in World Farming
Copse House, Greatham, Liss, Hants. (*tel.* Blackmore 285).
Conchological Society of Great Britain and Ireland
51 Wychwood Ave., Luton LU2 7HT.
>Publishes quarterly newsletter and occasional papers for students.
Conservation Corps.
See British Trust for Conservation Volunteers.
Conservation Society
12 London St., Chertsey, Surrey KT16 8AA (*tel.* 09328 60975).
>Aims to make the public more aware of the effects of the population explosion and technological developments. About 60 local branches. Publications: numerous, including *Conservation News; Good Earth.*
Conservation Society Joint Education Working Party
246 London Rd., Earley, Reading RG6 1AJ (*tel.* 0734 63650).
>Provides speakers and information service on all aspects of Environmental Education. Publications: *Guide to Resources in Environmental Education; National Survey into Environmental Education in Secondary Schools.*
Conservation Society Transport Working Party
16 Nethergreen Rd., Sheffield 11.
Conservation Youth Association
45 St. Mary's Rd., Huyton, Liverpool L36 5SR (*tel.* 051-489 5996).
>Aims to stimulate interest of young people in their environment.
Consumers' Association
14 Buckingham St., London WC2N 6DS.
>Tests quality and reliability of products. Publications: *Which?; Motoring Which?*; etc.
Convention of Royal Burghs
51 Castle St., Edinburgh 2 (*tel.* 031-225 7558).
>Represents interests of Scottish burghs.
Council for British Archaeology
8 St. Andrew's place, Regent's Park, London NW1 4LB (*tel.* 01-486 1527).
>Co-ordinating body for archaeological societies.
Council for Education in World Citizenship
93 Albert Embankment, London SE1 (*tel.* 01-735 4639).
Council for Environmental Education (C.E.E.)
24 London Rd., Reading RG1 5AQ (*tel.* 0734 85234).
>Represents over 40 organizations concerned with education and the environment. Publications: *DELTA; Outdoor Studies Code; REED; C.E.E. Newsheet.*
Council for Nature
c/o Zoological Society of London, Regent's Park, London NW1 4RY (*tel.* 01-722 7111).
>Represents 450 local natural history and conservation societies. Publications: *Habitat.*

Council for Small Industries in Rural Areas
35 Camp Rd., London SW19 (*tel.* 01-946 5101).
> Assists in the development of small firms in rural areas.

Council for the Protection of Rural England (C.P.R.E.)
4 Hobart Place, London SW1W OHY (*tel.* 01-235 9481).
> Guards the beauty of the English countryside. Publications: *Notes for the Guidance of Architectural Panels; The Houses We Build.*

Council for the Protection of Rural Wales
Meifod, Powys SY22 6DA (*tel.* Meifod 383).

Council for Urban Studies Centres (C.U.S.C.)
17 Carlton House Terrace, London SW1Y 5AS.

Council of Social Service for Wales and Monmouthshire
2 Cathedral Rd., Cardiff CF1 9XR (*tel.* 0222 21456).
> Promotion of educational, recreational, social and welfare services.

Countryside Club
109 Upper Woodcote Rd., Reading, Berks.
> Provides access to private woodlands in the home counties.

Countryside Commission (Originally National Parks Commission)
John Dower House, Crescent Place, Cheltenham, Glos. GL50 3RA (*tel.* 0242 21381).
> Statutory body responsible for the designation of National Parks, etc. Publications: *Countryside Information Directory.*

Countryside Commission for Scotland
Battleby, Redgorton, Perth PH1 3EW (*tel.* 0738 27921).

Countryside Planning: Economic Forestry Group
Forestry House, Berkhamsted, Herts.

County Naturalists' Trust.
> *See* Society for the Promotion of Nature Reserves.

Crofters Commission
4/6 Castle Wynd, Inverness (*tel.* 0463 37231).
> Statutory body.

Crusade Against All Cruelty to Animals Ltd.
Humane Education Centre, Avenue Lodge, Bounds Green Rd., London N22 (*tel.* 01-889 1595).
> Publications: *The Living World; All Living Things.*

Cumberland Countryside Conference
6 West Walls, Carlisle (*tel.* 0228 25159).
> Promotes co-operation between voluntary organizations in Cumberland.

Cyclists' Touring Club
Cotterell House, 69 Meadrow, Godalming, Surrey.
> Publishes bi-monthly magazine and various leaflets and guides.

Dartington Amenity Research Trust
Shinners Bridge, Dartington, Totnes, Devon (*tel.* 080-46 2271).
> Conducts research on recreation in the countryside.

Dartmoor Preservation Association
8 Barons Rd., Dousland, Yelverton, Devon PL20 6NG.
Publishes newsletter.
David Davies Memorial Institute of International Studies
34 Smith Square, London SW1 (*tel.* 01-222 7331).
Department of Agriculture and Fisheries for Scotland
St. Andrew's House, Edinburgh EH1 3DA (*tel.* 031-556 8501).
Publishes annual report and various leaflets.
Department of the Environment
2 Marsham St., London SW1P 3EB (*tel.* 01-212 3434).
Government department formed from the former Ministry of
Housing and Local Government, Ministry of Public Buildings
and Works, and Ministry of Transport. Publications: numerous
reports, etc.
Department of Health and Social Security (D.H.S.S.)
Alexander Fleming House, Elephant & Castle, London SE1 (*tel.* 01-407
5522).
Publications obtainable from H.M.S.O.
District Councils Association for Scotland
28 Union St., Larkhill, Lanarkshire (*tel.* Larkhall 881240).
Duke of Edinburgh's Award Scheme
2 Old Queen St., London SW1 (*tel.* 01-930 7681).
Makes awards for practical projects by young people.
Eastern Federation of Amenity Societies
c/o Feilden & Mawson, Ferry Rd., Norwich NOR 18S (*tel.* 0603
29571).
Promotes high standard of planning in Eastern England.
Educational Foundation for Visual Aids (E.F.V.A.)
33 Queen Anne St., London W1M OAL.
Provides service for schools through the National Audio-Visual
Aids Library (N.A.V.A.L.) and the Visual Educational
National Information Service for Schools
(V.E.N.I.S.S.).
Electricity Council
30 Millbank, London SW1P 4RD (*tel.* 01-834 2333).
English Tourist Board
4 Grosvenor Gardens, London SW1W ODU (*tel.* 01-730 3400).
Encourages provision of tourist facilities.
Enterprise Youth
29 Queen St., Edinburgh EH2 1JX (*tel.* 031-226 3192).
National organization for co-ordination of voluntary service in
Scotland.
Environment Centre, The
56 Oxford St., Manchester.
Maintains a library of environmental literature.
Environmental Communicators' Organization (E.C.O.)
8 Hooks Close, Watton-at-Stone, Hertford.
An association of environmental journalists.

Environmental Consortium
10/11 Great Newport St., London WC2H 7JA (*tel.* 01-836 0908/9).
Concerned with the investigation and identification of environmental problems.
Eugenics Society
69 Eccleston Square, London SW1V 1PJ.
Concerned with the study of heredity and environmental aspects of human qualities. Publications: *Journal of Biosocial Science.*
Exmoor Society
Parish Rooms, Dulverton, Somerset.
Exmoor National Park branch of C.P.R.E.
Family Planning Association (F.P.A.)
27/35 Mortimer St., London W1 (*tel.* 01-636 7866).
Publications: *Family Planning*
Farm and Food Society
37 Tanza Rd., London NW3 (*tel.* 01-435 2596).
Promotes humane and ecologically sound farming.
Farmers Union of Wales
Llys Amaeth, Queens Square, Aberystwyth (*tel.* Aberystwyth 2755).
Safeguards interests of farmers and landowners in Wales.
Fauna Preservation Society
c/o Zoological Society of London, Regent's Park, London NW1 4RY (*tel.* 01-586 0872).
Promotes conservation of wildlife throughout the world.
Publications: *Oryx.*
Federation against Aircraft Nuisance
60 Beckenham Place Park, Beckenham, Kent (*tel.* 01-658 6227).
Fell and Rock Climbing Club of the English Lake District
110 Low Ash Drive, Shipley, West Yorks. (*tel.* Shipley 51363).
Provides books, maps, information, etc.
Fermanagh Naturalists' Field Club
Crannog Rakeelan Glebe, Enniskillen, Co. Fermanagh (*tel.* Enniskillen 2375).
Concerned with practical study of natural history and archaeology.
Field Studies Council
9 Devereux Court, London WC2R 3JR (*tel.* 01-583 7471).
Teaching and research body on environmental subjects. Runs 9 centres. Publications: *Field Studies.*
Forest School Camps
3 Pine View, Fairmile Park Rd., Cobham, Surrey (*tel.* 093-26 2920).
Provides educational and character training facilities for young people.
Forestry Commission
Priestley Rd., Basingstoke RG24 9NS (*tel.* 0256 3181).
Responsible for management of large areas of forest, and provision of nature trails, forest parks, etc. Publishes various guides and booklets.

Freedom from Hunger Campaign (F.F.H.)
17 Northumberland Ave., London WC2 (*tel.* 01-930 8248).
Charitable body. Publications: *World Hunger.*
Freshwater Biological Association
The Ferry House, Far Sawrey, Ambleside, Cumbria.
Friends of the Earth Ltd. (F.O.E.)
9 Poland St., London W1V 3DG (*tel.* 01-437 6121).
Undertakes aggressive activity to restore the environment.
Publications: numerous in conjunction with Pan/Ballantine and
Earth Island.
Friends of the Lake District
27 Greenside, Kendal, Cumbria (*tel.* Kendal 20296).
Protects the natural beauty of the Lake District.
Game Conservancy
Fordingbridge, Hants. (*tel.* Fordingbridge 2381).
Undertakes research into conservation of British game.
Geographical Association (G.A.)
343 Fulwood Rd., Sheffield S10 3BP (*tel.* 0742 61666).
Organization for Geography teachers. Publications: *Geography*;
booklets, including *British Landscapes through Maps* series.
Georgian Group
2 Chester St., London SW1 (*tel.* 01-235 3081).
Concerned with the preservation of Georgian architecture.
Good Gardeners' Association
Arkley Manor, Arkley, Barnet, Herts. (*tel.* 01-449 2177).
Promotes organic gardening. Publications: *The A.B.C. of Soils,*
Humus and Health; *The Compost Gardening Book.*
Green Belt Council for Greater London
1–4 Crawford Mews, London W1H 1PT.
Concerned with the preservation of London's Green Belt.
Green Survival Campaign
Agriculture House, Knightsbridge, London SW1X 7NJ (*tel.* 01-235 5077).
Encourages the increased use of trees and plants in rural and
urban areas.
Henry Doubleday Research Association
20 Convent Lane, Bocking, Braintree, Essex (*tel.* Braintree 1483).
Promotes gardening without chemicals. Publications: *Pest*
Control without Chemicals; *Fertility without Fertilizers.*
Highlands and Islands Development Board
Bridge House, Bank St., Inverness (*tel.* 0463 34171).
Holiday Fellowship
142 Great North Way, Hendon, London NW4 (*tel.* 01-203 3381).
Encourages provision for enjoyment of open air.
Homes Before Roads
28 Grove Park Gardens, London W4 (*tel.* 01-994 0296).
Home Counties Rambling Association
7 Roche Rd., Norbury, London SW16.
Fosters knowledge and appreciation of countryside.

Housing Centre Trust
13 Suffolk St., London SW1Y 4HG (*tel.* 01-930 2881).
Works for the improvement of housing conditions. Publications: *Housing Review.*
Howey Foundation, The
2a Lebanon Rd., Croydon, Surrey CRO 6UR.
Conducts research into environmental health, pollution, conservation, etc. Publications: *Epoch.*
Humane Education Centre
See Crusade against all Cruelty to Animals Ltd.
Inland Waterways Amenity Advisory Council
Melbury House, Melbury Terrace, London NW1 6JX (*tel.* 01-262 6711).
Inland Waterways Association Ltd.
114 Regent's Park Rd., London NW1 8UQ (*tel.* 01-586 2556).
Encourages fullest use and development of Britain's waterways. Publications: *Waterways Holiday Guide.*
Institute of Biology
41 Queen's Gate, London SW7 5HU (*tel.* 01-589 9076).
Provides information service and list of speakers.
Publications: *Biologist*; *Journal of Biological Education.*
Institute of Landscape Architects
Nash House, 12 Carlton House Terrace, London SW1Y 5AH (*tel.* 01-839 4044).
Professional body.
Institute of Park and Recreation Administration
Lower Basildon, Reading RG8 9NE (*tel.* Goring-on-Thames 2314).
Professional body of officers in public parks, etc.
Institute of Petroleum
61 New Cavendish St., London W1M 8AR (*tel.* 01-636 1004).
Promotes scientific study of petroleum, including aspects of pollution.
Institute of Public Cleansing
28 Portland Place, London W1 (*tel.* 01-580 5324).
Institute of Rural Life at Home and Overseas
27 Northumberland Rd., New Barnet, Herts.
Publishes newsletter.
Institute of Water Pollution Control
Ledson House, 53 London Rd., Maidstone, Kent (*tel.* 0622 62034).
Provides information service. Publications: *Water Pollution Control.*
Institution of Environmental Sciences
14 Prince's Gate, Hyde Park, London SW7 1PU.
Learned society concerned with aspects of environmental science, including education.
Institution of Municipal Engineers (I.M.E.)
25 Eccleston Square, London SW1V 1NX (*tel.* 01-834 5082).
Professional body.

Institution of Public Health Engineers
32 Eccleston Square, London SW1V 1PB (*tel.* 01-834 3017).
Institution of Water Engineers
6/8 Sackville St., London W1X 1DD (*tel.* 01-734 5422).
Professional society of engineers, geologists, etc.
Intermediate Technology Development Group Ltd.
Purnell *House*, 25 Wilton Rd., London SW1V 1JS (*tel.* 01-828 5791/4).
Research and publications on low-cost, labour intensive technology.
Publications: *Appropriate Technology*; various manuals.
International Planned Parenthood Federation (I.P.P.F.)
18–20 Lower Regent St., London SW1 (*tel.* 01-839 2911).
Publishes a list of teaching material.
International Union for the Conservation of Nature (I.U.C.N.)
1110 Morges, Switzerland.
Publishes an educational newsletter.
International Voluntary Service
91 High St., Harlesden, London NW10 (*tel.* 01-965 1446).
International Youth Federation for Environmental Studies and Conservation
40 Pensford Ave., Kew, Surrey (*tel.* 01-876 6051).
Organizes international camps, conferences and projects for young people.
Irish Mountaineering Club
157 Stranmillis Rd., Belfast BT9 5AH (*tel.* Belfast 21282).
Publishes guide books.
Joint Committee for the Conservation of British Insects
c/o Royal Entomological Society of London, 41 Queen's Gate, London SW7.
Preparing a register of species requiring conservation.
Joint Education Working Party (J.E.W.P.)
See Conservation Society Joint Education Working Party.
Keep Britain Tidy Group
Circus House, New England Rd., Brighton BN1 4GW (*tel.* 0273 691217/8).
Produces posters, badges, etc.
Kennet and Avon Canal Trust Ltd.
The Coppice, Elm Lane, Lower Earley, Reading RG6 2UG (*tel.* 0734 82149).
Landscape Research Group
8 Cunningham Rd., Banstead, Surrey (*tel.* Burgh Heath 55932).
Emphasises ecological aspects of the environment.
Light Railway Transport League
64 Grove Ave, London W7 3ES.
Advocates the wider use of modern rapid transit systems.
Linnean Society of London
Burlington House, Piccadilly, London W1V OLQ (*tel.* 01-734 1040).
Concerned with aspects of Biology related to the interrelationships of organisms.

Local Authorities Aircraft Noise Council
Town Hall, King St., Hammersmith, London W6 9JU (*tel.* 01-748 3020).
Local Government Information Service
36 Old Queen St., London SW1H 9HZ (*tel.* 01-930 8214).
London Borough Association
Westminster City Council, Victoria St., London SW1E 6QW
    (*tel.* 01-828 8070).
London Co-operative Education Department
129 Seven Sisters Rd., London N7 7QG (*tel.* 01-263 1127).
    Organizes summer schools on environment, consumer affairs, etc.
London Society
3 Dean's Yard, London SW1 (*tel.* 01-222 1562).
    Concerned for the beauty of London.
Malacological Society of London
Department of Biology, Queen Elizabeth College, Campden Hill Road,
    London W8.
Mammal Society of the British Isles
c/o Institute of Biology, 41 Queen's Gate, London SW7.
    Publishes handbooks and wallcharts.
Marine Biological Association of the United Kingdom
The Laboratory, Citadel Hill, Plymouth PL1 2PB (*tel.* 0752 67105).
    Publishes an aquarium guide.
Maritime Trust
53 Davies St., London W1Y 1FH (*tel.* 01-629 5782).
    Charitable trust concerned with the preservation of vessels, etc.
McCarrison Society
5 Derby Rd., Caversham, Reading, Berks. (*tel.* 0734 473165).
    Doctors' whole food and preventative medicine pressure group.
Men of the Stones
The Rutlands, Tinwell, Stamford, Lincs. PE9 3UD (*tel.* 0780 3372).
    Promotes use of stone in building.
Men of the Trees
Crawley Down, Crawley, Sussex (*tel.* Copthorne 2536).
    Concerned with the planting and preservation of trees.
    Publication: *Trees.*
Metropolitan Public Gardens Association
4 Carlos Place, London W1Y 5AE (*tel.* 01-493 6617).
    Encourages the provision of open spaces and trees in London.
Ministry of Agriculture, Fisheries and Food
Whitehall Place, London SW1 (*tel.* 01-839 7711).
**Ministry of Agriculture, Government of Northern Ireland: Forestry
    Division**
Dundonald House, Upper Newtownards Rd., Belfast, BT4 3SB
    (*tel.* Belfast 650111).
    Publishes leaflets for five Forest Parks.
**Ministry of Development, Government of Northern Ireland:
    Conservation Branch**
Parliament Buildings, Stormont, Belfast BT4 3SS (*tel.* 0232 63210).

Provides speakers on the work of Ulster Countryside Committee
and Nature Reserves Committee.
**Ministry of Finance, Government of Northern Ireland: Ancient
Monuments Branch**
Churchill House, Victoria Square, Belfast BT1 4QW (*tel.* Belfast 34343).
Undertakes preservation of Ulster's historic monuments.
Minority Rights Group
Benjamin Franklin House, 36 Craven St., London WC2N 5NG
(*tel.* 01-930 6659).
Attempts to secure justice for groups suffering discrimination.
Motor Caravanners' Club
22 Chiswick High Road, London W4 (*tel.* 01-944 3158).
National Anglers' Council
17 Queen St., Peterborough PE1 1PJ (*tel.* 0733 4084).
Publishes quarterly newsletter.
National Anti-Fluoridation Campaign
36 Station Rd., Thames Ditton, Surrey KT7 ONS.
National Association for Environmental Education (N.A.E.E.)
Education Office, County Hall, Bedford (*tel.* 0234 63222).
Association of teachers and lecturers concerned with education
and the environment. Publications: *Environmental Education*;
newsletter.
National Association for Outdoor Education
Buckden House Outdoor Centre, Buckden, Skipton, North Yorks.
BD23 5JA.
Provides information service, and publishes bulletin and news-
letter.
National Association of Boys' Clubs
17 Bedford Square, London WC1B 3JJ (*tel.* 01-636 5357).
Responsible for Boys' Clubs Conservation Force and League of
Young Adventurers.
National Association of Local Councils
100 Great Russell St., London WC1B 2HU (*tel.* 01-636 4066).
Promotes interests of parish councils.
National Book League
7 Albemarle St., London W1X 4BB (*tel.* 01-493 9001). Provides
exhibitions of books, display materials, etc. Publications:
Environment, Resources and Man.
National Caravan Council Ltd.
Sackville House, 40 Piccadilly, London W1V OND (*tel.* 01-734 3681).
Represents the British caravan industry and provides advice on
caravan parks.
National Coal Board (N.C.B.)
Hobart House, Grosvenor Place, London SW1X 7AE (*tel.* 01-235
2020).
National Council for Voluntary Youth Services (N.C.V.Y.S.)
26 Bedford Square, London WC1B 3HU (*tel.* 01-636 4066).
Encourages co-operation within the Youth Service.

National Council of Social Service (N.C.S.S.)
26 Bedford Square, London WC1B 3HU (*tel.* 01-636 4066).
Co-ordinates work of county community councils.
National Council of Women (N.C.W.)
36 Lower Sloane St., London SW1 (*tel.* 01-730 0619).
National Council on Inland Transport
396 City Rd., London EC1V 2QA (*tel.* 01-837 9145).
National Farmers Union
Agriculture House, Knightsbridge, London SW1 (*tel.* 01-235 5077).
Represents all sectors of the agricultural and horticultural
industry.
National Federation of Anglers
Haig House, 87 Green Lane, Derby (*tel.* 0332 362000).
Provides information service on rivers, lakes, etc.
National Federation of Community Associations
26 Bedford Square, London WC1B 3HU (*tel.* 01-636 4066).
Represents 600 local community and neighbourhood associations.
National Federation of Young Farmers' Clubs
Y.F.C. Centre, National Agricultural Centre, Kenilworth, Warwickshire
CV8 2LG (*tel.* 0203 56131).
Publishes newsletter.
National Housing and Town Planning Council
11 Green St., London W1Y 4ES (*tel.* 01-629 7107).
Publishes monthly magazine.
National Industrial Materials Recovery Association
9 Sea Road, Bexhill-on-Sea, Sussex (*tel.* Bexhill 5018/9).
Promotes use of redundant or waste materials.
Publications: *Industrial Recovery.*
National Institute of Adult Education (N.I.A.E.)
35 Queen Anne St., London W1M OBL (*tel.* 01-580 3155).

NATIONAL PARK AUTHORITIES
Each provides information centres and a variety of guides, etc.
Brecon Beacons National Park
County Hall, Brecon (*tel.* Brecon 2311).
Countryside and National Park Committee
Northumberland County Council, County Hall, Newcastle-
upon-Tyne (*tel.* 0632 24593).
Dartmoor National Park Committee
Devon County Council, County Hall, Topsham Rd., Exeter
(*tel.* 0392 77977).
Exmoor National Park Joint Advisory Committee
County Hall, Taunton (*tel.* 0823 3451).
Lake District Planning Board
County Hall, Kendal, Cumbria (*tel.* Kendal 1000).
North York Moors National Park Planning Committee
County Hall, Northallerton (*tel.* Northallerton 3123).

Peak Park Planning Board
Aldern House, Baslow Rd., Bakewell DE4 1AE (*tel.* Bakewell 2881).
Pembrokeshire National Park Committee
Pembrokeshire County Council, County Offices, Haverfordwest (*tel.* Haverfordwest 3131).
Snowdonia Park Joint Advisory Committee
County Offices, Penarlag, Dolgellau, Gwynedd (*tel.* Dolgellau 341).
Yorkshire Dales National Park Joint Advisory Committee
County Hall, Wakefield (*tel.* 0924 75234).
National Playing Fields Association
57*b* Catherine Place, London SW1E 6EY (*tel.* 01-834 9274).
Provides information service.
National Ports Council
Commonwealth House, 1–19 New Oxford St., London WC1A 1DZ (*tel.* 01-242 1200).
National Pure Water Association (N.P.W.A.)
225 Newtown Rd., Worcester WR5 1JB (*tel.* 0905 22456).
Water pollution and purification pressure group.
National Ski Federation of Great Britain
118 Eaton Square, London SW1 (*tel.* 01-235 8227).
National Society for Clean Air
134/7 North St., Brighton, Sussex BN1 1RG (*tel.* 0273 26313).
Developed the idea of smokeless zones. Publications: *Clean Air Yearbook*; *Smokeless Air*.
National Trust for Places of Historic Interest or Beauty
42 Queen Anne's Gate, London SW1H 9AS (*tel.* 01-930 0211).
Publishes guide books and leaflets, including *The Continuing Purpose*; *The What to See Atlas*; *The National Trust*.
National Trust for Scotland
5 Charlotte Square, Edinburgh EH2 4DU (*tel.* 031-225 2184).
Publishes newsletter.
National Union of Students — Conservation Project
3 Endsleigh St., London WC1 (*tel.* 01-387 1277).
Publications: *Communus*.
National Water Council
1 Queen Anne's Gate, London SW1 (*tel.* 01-930 3100).
Statutory body, set up by Water Act 1973.
Natural Environment Research Council (N.E.R.C.)
Alhambra House, 29/33 Charing Cross Rd., London WC2H 0AX (*tel.* 01-930 9232).
Publications: *N.E.R.C. News Journal.*
Nature Conservancy Council (Great Britain)
19–20 Belgrave Square, London SW1X 8PY (*tel.* 01-235 3241).
Provides scientific advice on flora and fauna, and establishes nature reserves. Publications: numerous, including *Nature in Focus*; *Journal of Environment Management.*

New Horizon School Camps
92 Shortlands Rd., Kingston-upon-Thames, Surrey (*tel.* 01-546 3217).
Provides young people with an opportunity of camping in wilder
parts of countryside.
New Towns Association
Glen House, Stag Place, London SW1 (*tel.* 01-828 1103).
Association of New Town Development Corporations.
New Villages Association, The
3 Salubrious, Broadway, Worcs. WR12 7AU.
Works for the establishment of new villages based on the
principles of self-sufficiency.
Noise Abatement Society
6–8 Old Bond St., London W1 (*tel.* 01-493 5877).
Publications: *Law on Noise*; *Feasibility Study on Third London
Airport*; *Noise News Digest*; *Quiet Please*.
Noise Advisory Council
Queen Anne's Chambers, 28 Broadway, London SW1H 9JU (*tel.* 01-930
4300).
Consultative body.
Northern Ireland Bird Records Committee
Flat 5, 116 Holywood Rd., Belfast BT4 1NY.
Northern Ireland Ornithologists Club
20 Ardvarna Crescent, Belfast BT4 2GJ (*tel.* 0232 68524).
Provides information service on its various projects.
Northern Ireland Tourist Board
River House, 48 High St., Belfast BT1 2DS (*tel.* 0232 31221).
North of Scotland Hydro-Electricity Board
16 Rothesay Terrace, Edinburgh 3 (*tel.* 031-225 1361).
Northwestern Naturalists' Union
91 Stanley Rd., Cheadle Hulme, Greater Manchester SK8 6PL (*tel.* 061-
485 5617).
Publishes quarterly newsletter.
Offa's Dyke Association
March House, Wylcwm St., Knighton, Powys (*tel.* Knighton 328).
Publishes guide-book and maps.
Outward Bound Trust
Iddesleigh House, Caxton St., London SW1 (*tel.* 01-222 2926).
Provides courses for students in mountaineering and seamanship.
OXFAM
274 Banbury Rd., Oxford (*tel.* 0865 56777).
Charitable body.
Publications: *New Internationalist* (with Christian Aid).
Pedestrians' Association for Road Safety
166 Shaftesbury Ave., London WC2H 8JH (*tel.* 01-836 7220).
Protects rights of pedestrians. Publications: *Arrive*.
People
69 Hertford St., Coventry.
Political movement concerned with the environment.

Pictorial Charts Educational Trust (P.C.E.T.)
132 Uxbridge Rd., London W13 8QU (*tel.* 01-567 9206).
Publishes six charts at the beginning of each school term.
Pilgrim Trust
Millbank House, 2 Great Peter St., London SW1 (*tel.* 01-222 4231).
Concerned with the preservation of buildings and countryside.
Political and Economic Planning
12 Upper Belgrave St., London SW1 (*tel.* 01-235 5271).
Population Stabilization
6 St. Mark's Place, London W11 (*tel.* 01-229 4950).
Prince of Wales's Committee
15 Wellfield Court, Bangor, Gwynedd. (*tel.* 0248 4559).
Voluntary committee concerned with improvement of the environment in Wales.
Professional Institutions Council for Conservation
12 Great George St., Parliament Square, London SW1P 3AD (*tel.* 01-839 5600).
Concerned with planning, management and development of natural resources.
Public Interest Research Centre Ltd.
Munro House, 9 Poland St., London W1V 3DG (*tel.* 01-734 0314).
Pure Rivers Society
74 Dagenham Avenue, Dagenham, Essex RM9 6LH.
Publishes various pamphlets.
Pye Research Centre
Walnut Tree Manor, Haughley, Stowmarket, Suffolk IP14 3RS (*tel.* 044-970 444/5).
Has taken over the farms of the Soil Association.
Railway Invigoration Society
BM-RIS, London WC1V 6XX (*tel.* 01-405 0463).
Concerned with the retention and modernization of railway services.
Ramblers' Association
1/4 Crawford Mews, York St., London W1H 1PT (*tel.* 01-262 1477).
Secures right of public access to open country.
Publications: *Rucksack.*
Red Deer Commission
Elm Park, Island Bank Rd., Inverness (*tel.* Inverness 31751).
Responsible for conservation and control of red deer in Scotland.
Regional Studies Association
Newcombe House, 45 Notting Hill Gate, London W11 (*tel.* 01-727 8252).
Publications: *Regional Studies*; newsletter.
Rescue
Rutland House, 25a The Tything, Worcester (*tel.* 0905 20651).
Trust for British Archaeology.
Research Institute for Consumer Affairs
43 Villiers St., London WC2 (*tel.* 01-930 3360).
Tests consumer products.

River Thames Society
2 Ruskin Ave., Kew, Richmond, Surrey (*tel.* 01-876 1520).
Promotes amenities of River Thames.
Route Naturalists Field Club
Blackrock Cottage, Runkerry, Bushmills, Co. Antrim.
Concerned with archaeology and natural history of Northern
Ireland.
Royal Agricultural Society of England
National Agricultural Centre, Kenilworth, Warks. CV8 2LG (*tel.* 0203
56151).
Provides information service.
Royal Automobile Club
83–85 Pall Mall, London SW1 (*tel.* 01-930 4343).
Motorists' organization.
Royal Commission on Environmental Pollution
Church House, Great Smith St., London SW1P 3BL (*tel.* 01-222 6991).
Publishes an annual report.
Royal Entomological Society of London
41 Queen's Gate, London SW7 (*tel.* 01-584 8361).
Publishes handbooks on British insects.
Royal Forestry Society of England, Wales and Northern Ireland
102 High St., Tring, Herts. (*tel.* 0442-82 2028).
Provides information service. Publication: *Journal of Forestry.*
Royal Geographical Society (R.G.S.)
1 Kensington Gore, London SW7 2AR (*tel.* 01-589 5466).
Information service includes map library.
Publications: *Geographical Journal.*
Royal Institute of British Architects (R.I.B.A.)
66 Portland Place, London W1 (*tel.* 01-580 5533).
Publishes journal.
Royal Institution of Chartered Surveyors (R.I.C.S.)
12 Great George St., London SW1P 3AD (*tel.* 01-839 5600).
Royal Scottish Forestry Society
26 Rutland Square, Edinburgh, EH1 2BU (*tel.* 031-229 3651).
Publications: *Scottish Forestry.*
Royal Society for the Protection of Birds (R.S.P.B.)
The Lodge, Sandy, Beds. SG19 2DL (*tel.* 0767 80551).
Manages about 40 reserves. Teaching material available from
Education Department. Publications: *Bird Life*; *Birds*; *Farming
and Wildlife; R.S.P.B. Teachers' Newsletter.*
Royal Society of Arts (R.S.A.)
6–8 John Adam St., London WC2N 6EZ (*tel.* 01-839 2366).
Liaison between arts and sciences, including preservation of the
countryside.
Royal Society of Health
13 Grosvenor Place, London SW1X 7EN (*tel.* 01-235 9961).
Royal Town Planning Institute
26 Portland Place, London W1N 4BE (*tel.* 01-636 9107).

Royal Yachting Squadron
5 Buckingham Gate, London SW1 (*tel.* 01-828 9296).
Publishes half-yearly magazine.
Salmon and Trout Association
Fishmongers' Hall, London EC4 (*tel.* 01-626 3531).
Guards interests of game fisheries and fishermen.
Save the Children Fund
29 Queen Anne's Gate, London SW1 (*tel.* 01-930 2461). Charitable body.
Save the Village Pond Campaign
111—13 Lambeth Rd., London SE1 (*tel.* 01-582 0185).
School Natural Science Society
2 Bramley Mansions, Berrylands Rd., Surbiton, Surrey (*tel.* 01-399 9424).
Publishes journal.
Schools Action Group for the Environment (S.A.G.E.)
c/o Dr. Challoner's Grammar School, Amersham, Bucks.
Publishes newsletter.
Schools Council
160 Great Portland St., London W1 (*tel.* 01-580 0352).
Projects include Integrated Science, Nuffield Secondary Science,
General Studies Project and Project Environment.
Schools Eco-Action Group (S.E.A.G.)
53 The Ridge, Orpington, Kent BR6 8AQ.
Publishes monthly newsletter.
Scottish Anglers' Association
117 Hanover St., Edinburgh 2 (*tel.* 031-664 1740).
Protects interests of anglers.
Scottish Civic Trust
24 George Square, Glasgow G2 1EF (*tel.* 041-221 1466).
Publications: *Environment Scotland*; *Environment — a Basic
Human Right.*
Scottish Committee on Education and the Countryside
c/o Scottish Education Department, St. Andrew's House, Edinburgh
(*tel.* 031-556 6591).
Similar to Council for Environmental Education.
Scottish Council of Physical Recreation
4 Queensferry St., Edinburgh EH2 4PB (*tel.* 031-225 5544).
Publishes brochures.
Scottish Council of Social Service
18/19 Claremont Crescent, Edinburgh EH7 4QD (*tel.* 031-556 3882).
Similar to N.C.S.S.
Scottish Counties of Cities Association
City Chambers, High St., Edinburgh (*tel.* 031-225 2424).
Represents Edinburgh, Glasgow, Aberdeen and Dundee.
Scottish Countryside Activities Council
Carrick Cottage, 15 Main St., Dundonald, Kilmarnock, Ayrshire
KA2 9HF (*tel.* 056-385 406).
Representative body of a number of Scottish countryside leisure
organizations.

Scottish Development Department
St. Andrew's House, Edinburgh EH1 3DD (*tel.* 031-556 8545).
Government department concerned with environmental
planning.
Scottish Dinghy Association
Ayton House, Abernethy, Perth (*tel.* Abernethy 242).
Co-ordinating body for Scottish sailing clubs.
Scottish Field Studies Association
Forelands, 18 Marketgate, Crail, Fife KY10 3TL (*tel.* Crail 343).
Scottish Gliding Union
Portmoak, Scotlandwell, Kinross (*tel.* Scotlandwell 243).
Scottish National Housing and Town Planning Council
Council Chambers, Monkdyke, Alexandra Drive, Renfrew,
Renfrewshire (*tel.* 041-886 2387).
Concerned with the provision of houses of good standards.
Scottish Ornithologists' Club
21 Regent Terrace, Edinburgh EH7 5BT (*tel.* 031-556 6042).
Publishes quarterly journal and annual report.
Scottish Rights of Way Society Ltd
32 Rutland Square, Edinburgh EH1 2BZ (*tel.* 031-556 3942).
Publications: *The Cairngorm Passes*; *A Walker's Guide to the
Law of Right of Way in Scotland*.
Scottish Tourist Board
23 Ravelston Terrace, Edinburgh EH4 3EU (*tel.* 031-332 2433).
Provides information service.
Scottish Wildlife Trust
8 Dublin St., Edinburgh EH1 3PP (*tel.* 031-556 4199).
Publishes booklets on nature trails, reserves, etc.
Scottish Woodland Owners' Association
6 Chester St., Edinburgh EH3 7RD (*tel.* 031-226 3475).
Publishes newsletter.
Scottish Youth Hostels Association
7 Glebe Crescent, Stirling FK8 2JA (*tel.* 0786 2821).
Publishes guidebooks, maps and handbooks.
Scout Association
25 Buckingham Palace Rd., London SW1 (*tel.* 01-834 6005).
Many publications, including monthly magazine, news-sheets,
etc.
Seabird Group
c/o Zoological Society of London, Regent's Park, London NW1 4RY
(*tel.* 01-586 4443).
Concerned with the study and protection of British seabirds.
Shelter
86 Strand, London WC2R OEQ (*tel.* 01-836 2051).
National Campaign for the Homeless.
Small Industries Council for Rural Areas of Scotland
27 Walker St., Edinburgh EH3 7HZ (*tel.* 031-225 2846).
Provides advisory service to small rural firms.

Snowdonia National Park Society
Dyffryn Mymbyr, Capel Curig, Bettws-y-Coed, Gwynedd (*tel.* Capel Curig 234).
Publishes newsletter.
Society for Environmental Education (S.E.E.)
16 Trinity Rd., Enderby, Leicester LE9 5BU (*tel.* 053-729 4396).
Arranges courses and conferences on Environmental Education.
Publications: *S.E.E. Journal*; newsletter; occasional papers.

SOCIETY FOR THE PROMOTION OF NATURE RESERVES (S.P.N.R.)
The Green, Nettleham, Lincoln.
Establishes nature reserves and county nature trusts (*see below*).
Publications: *Conservation Review*; *Conservation Code Handbook*.
Bedfordshire and Hunts. Naturalists' Trust
23 St. Cuthbert's St., Bedford.
Berkshire, Bucks. and Oxon Naturalists' Trust (B.B.O.N.T.)
Shirburn Lodge, Christmas Common, Watlington, Oxford OX9 5HU.
Cambridgeshire and Isle of Ely Naturalists' Trust
1 Brookside, Cambridge CB2 1JF.
Cheshire Conservation Trust
2 Pear Tree Lane, Acton Bridge, Northwich, Cheshire.
Cornwall Naturalists' Trust
Mount Pleasant, Tehidy, Camborne, Cornwall.
Derbyshire Naturalists' Trust
25 Rykneld Way, Littleover, Derby DE3 7AT.
Devon Trust for Nature Conservation
2 Pennsylvania Rd., Exeter EX4 6BQ.
Dorset Naturalists' Trust
Island View, 58 Pearce Ave., Parkstone, Poole, Dorset BH14 8EH.
Durham County Conservation Trust
Robin Hood Farm, Brompton on Swale, Richmond, N. Yorks.
Essex Naturalists' Trust
Fingringhoe Wick Nature Reserve, Fingringhoe, Colchester, Essex.
Gloucestershire Trust for Nature Conservation
Church House, Standish, Stonehouse, Glos. GL10 3EU.
Hampshire and Isle of Wight Naturalists' Trust
King John's Lodge, Romsey, Hants. SO5 8BT.
Herefordshire and Radnorshire Nature Trust
Community House, 25 Castle St., Hereford.
Herts. and Middlesex Trust for Nature Conservation
325 Ware Rd., Hertford.
Kent Trust for Nature Conservation
P.O. Box 29, Maidstone, Kent.
Lake District Naturalists' Trust
5 Annisgarth Close, Bowness-on-Windermere, Cumbria.

SOURCES OF TEACHING MATERIAL

Lancashire Naturalists' Trust
Samlesbury Hall, Samlesbury, Lancs. PR5 OUP.
Leicestershire and Rutland Trust for Nature Conservation
1 West St., Leicester.
Lincolnshire Trust for Nature Conservation
The Manor House, Alford, Lincs. LN13 9DL.
Norfolk Naturalists' Trust
72 The Close, Norwich NOR 16P.
Northamptonshire Naturalists' Trust
2 Stanfield Rd., Duston, Northampton NN5 6EZ.
Northumberland Wildlife Trust
Hancock Museum, Barras Bridge, Newcastle-upon-Tyne NE2 4PT.
Nottinghamshire Trust for Nature Conservation
Shire Hall, High Pavement, Nottingham NG1 1HR.
Shropshire Conservation Trust
32 Kennedy Rd., Shrewsbury SY3 7AB.
Somerset Trust for Nature Conservation
Strangmans, Heale, Curry Rivel, Langport, Somerset.
Staffordshire Nature Conservation Trust
5 Harrowby Drive, Newcastle, Stoke-on-Trent.
Suffolk Trust for Nature Conservation
Estates Dept., County Hall, Ipswich IP4 2JS.
Surrey Naturalists' Trust
Centre for Adult Education, University of Surrey, Guildford, Surrey.
Sussex Naturalists' Trust
Woods Mill, Henfield, Sussex.
Warwickshire Nature Conservation Trust
c/o County Museum, Warwick.
Wiltshire Trust for Nature Conservation
4 Peppercombe Close, Urchfont, Devizes, Wilts.
Worcestershire Nature Conservation Trust
Foxhill, Ullenhall, Henley-in-Arden, Warwickshire.
Yorkshire Naturalists' Trust
20 Castlegate, York YO1 1RP.
Wales:
Brecknock County Naturalists' Trust
Byddwn, Llanhamlach, Powys.
Glamorgan County Naturalists' Trust
Pengwern, Llanblethian, Cowbridge, South Glam. CF7 7EY.
Monmouthshire Naturalists' Trust
40 Melbourne Way, Newport, Gwent NPT 3RF.
North Wales Naturalists' Trust
154 High St., Bangor, Gywnedd.
West Wales Naturalists' Trust
4 Victoria Place, Haverfordwest, Dyfed.
Society for the Protection of Ancient Buildings
55 Great Ormond St., London WC1N 3JA (*tel.* 01-405 2646).
Publishes information on the preservation of old buildings.

Society of Antiquaries of London
Burlington House, Piccadilly, London W1V OHS (*tel.* 01-734 0193).
Society of Sussex Downsmen
93 Church Rd., Hove, Sussex (*tel.* 0273 71906).
Concerned with the preservation of the character of the Sussex Downs.
Soil Association
Walnut Tree Manor, Haughley, Stowmarket, Suffolk IP14 3RS (*tel.* 044-970 235/7).
Concerned with the relation between soil, plants, animals and man. Publications: *Span*; *Journal of the Soil Association.*
Southwestern Naturalists' Union
Shorton Manor, Shorton, Paignton, Devon (*tel.* 0803 50519).
Supplies material on natural history.
Sports Council
70 Brompton Rd., London SW3 1EX (*tel.* 01-589 3411).
Publishes quarterly magazine.
Sports Council for Scotland
4 Queensferry St., Edinburgh EH2 4PB (*tel.* 031-225 5544).
Sports Council for Wales
Sophia Gardens, Cardiff, CF1 9SW (*tel.* 0222 397571).
Survival
19 Carleton Rd., London N7 (*tel.* 01-609 1819).
Campaigns for legislation on over-population and pollution.
Survival International Ltd.
See Minority Rights Group.
Third World First
4 Marston Ferry Rd., Oxford. (*tel.* 0865 54006).
Concerned with the development of the third world. Publications: *Internationalist.*
Town and Country Planning Association (T. & C.P.A.)
17 Carlton House Terrace, London SW1Y 5AS (*tel.* 01-930 8903/5).
Fights for 'humanity in planning', safeguards green belts, promotes new towns. Publications: *Town and Country Planning*; *Bulletin of Environmental Education (BEE)*; *Planning Bulletin.*
Traffic Trust
5 New Bridge St., London EC4V 6HL (*tel.* 01-353 3112).
Founded 1971.
Transport and Road Research Laboratory
Old Wokingham Rd., Crowthorne RG11 6AU (*tel.* 03446 3131).
Government research body.
Transport Reform Group
2 Hyde Park St., London W2.
Transport Studies Society
99 Andrewes House, London EC2Y 8AY.
Transport Trust
18 Ramillies Place, London W1V 2BA (*tel.* 01-734 3590). Founded 1971.

SOURCES OF TEACHING MATERIAL

Transport Users' Consultative Committees
3/4 Great Marlborough St., London W1V 2EA (*tel.* 01-734 0056).
Transport 2000
9 Catherine Place, London SW1E 6DX (*tel.* 01-828 6650).
Alliance of three railway unions and environmental groups.
Ulster Council of Outdoor Organizations
4 Nendrum Gardens, Belfast BT5 5LZ (*tel.* 0232 654110).
Provides an information service on various organizations concerned with outdoor activities.
Ulster Society for the Preservation of the Countryside
West Winds, Carney Hill, Holywood, Co. Down (*tel.* Holywood 2300).
Publishes half-yearly magazine and newsletter.
United Nations Association (U.N.A.)
93 Albert Embankment, London SE1 (*tel.* 01-735 0181).
Vegetarian Society (U.K.) Ltd.
53 Marloes Rd., London W8 6LD (*tel.* 01-937 7739).
Promotes vegetarianism. Publications: *The Vegetarian.*
Voluntary Committee on Overseas Aid and Development (V.C.O.A.D.)
Parnell House, 25 Wilton Rd., London SW1V 1JS (*tel.* 01-828 7611/6).
Distributes material on behalf of a number of charitable organizations. Publications: *VOX*; *The Development Puzzle.*
Wales Tourist Board
Welcome House, Llandaff, Cardiff CF5 2YZ (*tel.* 0222 567701/10).
War on Want (W.O.W.)
467 Caledonian Rd., London N7 9BE (*tel.* 01-609 0211).
Charitable body.
Watch
32 Trumpington St., Cambridge CB2 1QY (*tel.* 0223 51456).
Club for young people concerned over environmental matters. Sponsored by A.C.E. and *Sunday Times.* Publications: *Watchword.*
Water Pollution Research Laboratory
Elder Way, Stevenage, Herts. SG1 1TH (*tel.* 0438 2444).
Provides an information service. To become part of new Water Research Centre (1974). Publications: *Notes on Water Pollution.*
Water Research Association
Ferry Lane, Medmenham, Marlow, Bucks. SL7 2HD (*tel.* Hambleden 282).
Central research body of water supply industry in U.K.
Welsh Railways Action Committee
Mor Awel, Stryd Fawr, Tywyn, Gwynedd.
Wildfowl Trust
Slimbridge, Gloucester GL2 7BT (*tel.* 045-389 333).
Concerned with the scientific study of wildfowl in their natural state.
Wildlife Observation Society
105 Jermyn St., London SW1 (*tel.* 01-837 2422).
Encourages the study of natural history among members of R.S.P.C.A.

Wildlife Youth Service
Wildlife, Marston Court, Manor Rd., Wallington, Surrey (*tel.* 01-669
5995).
    Education service of W.W.F.   Publications: *Animals Magazine;*
    newsletter.
Workers' Educational Association (W.E.A.)
Temple House, 9 Upper Berkeley St., London W1H 8BY (*tel.* 01-402
5608/9).
    Publications: *Background Notes on Social Studies.*
World Development Movement (W.D.M.)
25 Wilton Rd., London SW1V 1LW (*tel.* 01-834 4795).
    Political consortium of charities.
World Health Organization (W.H.O.)
    Publications obtainable through H.M.S.O.
World Population Society
c/o The American University, Washington, D.C. 20016, U.S.A.
    Organizes national and international meetings, publishes journals,
    and encourages research on all aspects of the population problem.
World Wildlife Fund (W.W.F.)
29–31 Greville St., London EC1N 8AX (*tel.* 01-404 5691).
    Assists in the conservation of Wildlife and wild places. Publica-
    tions: *World Wildlife News; Annual Yearbook.*
Yorkshire Field Studies
Westlands, Westfields, Kirkbymoorside, York YO6 6AG (*tel.* Kirkby-
    moorside 648).
Young Crusaders
    See Crusade against All Cruelty to Animals Ltd.
Young Liberals (Fight the Urban Crisis)
69 Blackfriars Rd., London SE1 (*tel.* 01-928 2883).
Youth Hostels Association (Y.H.A.)
Trevelyan House, St. Albans, Herts. (*tel.* 0727 55215).
    Provides field study facilities at certain hostels.
Youth Hostels Association of Northern Ireland
Bryson House, 28 Bedford St., Belfast BT2 7FE (*tel.* 0232 24733).
Youth Service Information Centre
37 Belvoir Rd., Leicester (*tel.* 0533 51769).
    Provides information service.
Zoological Society of London
Regent's Park, London NW1 4RY (*tel.* 01-722 3333).
    Undertakes research in zoology and provides an information
    service. Publications: numerous, including *International Zoo*
    Yearbook.

3   JOURNALS AND PERIODICALS

Agriculture
Produced monthly by the Ministry of Agriculture, Fisheries and Food.
H.M.S.O.
Subscription: £1.20 *p.a.*

All Living Things
Journal of the Junior Section of the Crusade Against All Cruelty to
Animals, the Young Crusaders.
Subscription: 20p *p.a.*

Ambio
A Journal of the Human Environment: Research and Management.
6 times *p.a.*   Universitetsforlaget, P.O. Box 307, Blindern, Oslo 3,
Norway.
Subscription: $19 *p.a.*

Animals Magazine
Monthly.   Animals Magazine.
Subscription: £3.95 *p.a.*

Appropriate Technology
Quarterly.   Intermediate Technology Development Group.
Subscription: £2 *p.a.*

Architectural Journal
Weekly.   Architectural Press Ltd.
Subscription: £8 *p.a.*

Arrive
Pedestrians' Association for Road Safety.

Association of Agriculture Journal
Association of Agriculture.
Subscription: 50p *p.a.*

Atmospheric Environment
Monthly.   Pergamon.
Subscription: £26 *p.a.*

Audio-Visual
Monthly.   P.O. Box 109, Croydon CR9 1QH (*tel.* 01-688 7788).
Subscription: £3.25 *p.a.*

Background Notes on Social Studies
Quarterly.   W.E.A.
Subscription: 63p *p.a.*

Biological Conservation
Quarterly.   Applied Science Publishers.
Subscription: £8.10 *p.a.*

Biologist
Quarterly.   Institute of Biology.
Subscription: £2 *p.a.*

Bird Life
R.S.P.B.
Subscription: 60p *p.a.*

Birds
Bi-monthly.   R.S.P.B.
Subscription: free to members.
Birds and Country Magazine
Quarterly.   79 Surbiton Hill Park, Surbiton, Surrey (*tel.* 01-399 7809).
Subscription: 90p *p.a.*
Bird Study
Quarterly.   British Trust for Ornithology.
Subscription: £4 *p.a.*
Bulletin of Environmental Education (BEE)
Monthly.   T. & C.P.A.
Subscription: £3 *p.a.*
Ceres
Bi-monthly.   F.A.O.
Subscription: £2 *p.a.*
Clean Air
Quarterly.   National Society for Clean Air.
Subscription: £1.10 *p.a.*
Commission on Education Newsletter
I.U.C.N.
Subscription: free.
Communus
9 times *p.a.*   N.U.S. Conservation Office.
Subscription: £1.40 *p.a.*
Compost Science
Bi-monthly,   73 Molesworth St., Wadebridge, Cornwall, PL27 7DS.
Subscription: £2.70 *p.a.*
Conservation News
Bi-monthly.   Conservation Society.
Subscription: free to members.
Conservation Review
Published in Spring and Autumn.   S.P.N.R.
Subscription: free to members.
Council for Environmental Education Newsheet
Monthly.   C.E.E.
Subscription: free to schools and colleges; otherwise 40p *p.a.*
Countryside
3 times *p.a.*   British Naturalists' Association.
Subscription: 75p *p.a.*
Courier
See UNESCO Courier.
Crisis Paper
Published occasionally.   Atlantic Educational Publishers.
Subscription: 75p for 7 issues.
Design
Monthly.   Design Council, 28 Haymarket, London SW1Y 4SU
     (*tel.* 01-839 8000).
Subscription: £5.10 *p.a.*

Ecologist, The
10 times *p.a.*   Now includes *Information for Survival.*   73
    Molesworth St., Wadebridge, Cornwall, PL27 7DS (*tel.* 020 881
    2296/7).
    Subscription: £4.75 *p.a.* (£4.25 to members of the Conservation
    Society and F.O.E.).
Ecology of Food and Nutrition
Quarterly.   Gordon & Breach.
    Subscription: £5.50 *p.a.*
Education and Culture
3 times *p.a.*   Council of Europe, 67006 Strasbourg, CEDEX.
    Subscription: free to those with professional responsibilities in
    education.
Effluent and Water Treatment Journal
Monthly.   Thunderbird Enterprises.
    Subscription: £6 *p.a.*
Energy Policy
Quarterly.   I.P.C. House, 32 High St., Guildford, Surrey
    (*tel.* 0483 71661).
    Subscription: £14 *p.a.*
Enviro-Bulletin
Monthly.   Pollution Research Bureau, 59 Skinner St., London EC1.
    Subscription: £2 *p.a.*
Environment
Monthly newspaper concerned with the built environment in northern
    England.
17 Ridgmont Rd., Bramhall, Greater Manchester (*tel.* 061-428
    9507).
    Subscription: £1.50 *p.a.*
Environment and Industry
Monthly.   Current Publications, Longwood, Maidenhead Court Park,
    Maidenhead, Berks.
Environment Film Review, The
c/o Ecologist, 73 Molesworth St., Wadebridge, Cornwall.
    Subscription: $20 *p.a.*
Environment This Month, The
Monthly.   P.O. Box 55, St. Leonard's House, Lancaster.
    Subscription: £18 *p.a.*
Environmental Education
Annually.   N.A.E.E.
    Subscription: free to members.
Environmental Education Report
Monthly.   Environmental Educators Inc., 1621 Connecticut Ave., N.W.,
    Washington, D.C., 20009, U.S.A.
    Subscription: $25 *p.a.*
Environmental Pollution
Quarterly.   Applied Science Publishers.
    Subscription: £8 *p.a.*

Environmental Pollution Management
Monthly.   680 Garrett Lane, London SW17 ONP.
Environmental Studies
Gordon & Breach.
   Subscription: £5.50 per volume (4 issues).
Environmental Times
Annually.   Gordon & Breach.
   Subscription: £3.50 *p.a.*
Epoch
Quarterly.   Howey Foundation.
   Subscription: £2 *p.a.*
Family Planning
Monthly.   F.P.A.
   Subscription: £1.80 *p.a.*
Field Studies
Annually.   F.S.C.
   Subscription: £2 *p.a.* (including membership of F.S.C.).
Finance and Development
Quarterly.   International Monetary Fund, Washington, D.C., 20431,
   U.S.A.
   Subscription: free to appropriate institutions.
Freshwater Biology
Bi-monthly.   Blackwell Scientific.
   Subscription: £12 *p.a.*
Geographical Journal
Quarterly.   R.G.S.
   Subscription: £6.30 *p.a.*
Geographical Magazine
Monthly.   128 Long Acre, London WC2E 9QH (*tel.* 01-836 2468).
   Subscription: £5.10 *p.a.*
Geography
Quarterly.   Geographical Association.
   Subscription: free to members.
Good Earth
Bi-monthly.   Conservation for Survival.   18 Cofton Lake Rd.,
   Birmingham B45 8PL.
   Subscription: 50p *p.a.* (bulk orders for schools £3.50 per 100
   copies).
Habitat
Council for Nature
Human Ecology
An Interdisciplinary Journal   Quarterly.   Plenum.
   Subscription: $17.20 *p.a.* (Individuals) $32.80
   (Libraries).
Industrial Recovery
Published monthly.   National Industrial Materials Recovery
   Association.
   Subscription: £5 *p.a.*

Information for Survival
Originally published separately, then with *Towards Survival* (1973),
    now amalgamated with *The Ecologist* (1974).
International Journal of Environmental Studies
Quarterly.   Gordon & Breach.
    Subscription: £5.50 *p.a.*
Internationalist
3 times *p.a.*   Third World First.
    Subscription: 85p *p.a.*
J.E.W.P. Newsletter
About 3 times *p.a.*   J.E.W.P.
    Subscription: free on receipt of s.a.e.
Journal of Animal Ecology
3 times *p.a.*   Blackwell Scientific.
    Subscription: £14 *p.a.*
Journal of Applied Ecology
3 times *p.a.*   Blackwell Scientific.
    Subscription: £14 *p.a.*
Journal of Biological Education
Bi-monthly.   Institute of Biology.
    Subscription: £4.45 *p.a.* (£2.25 to members).
Journal of Biosocial Science
Bi-monthly,   Eugenics Society.
    Subscription: £20 *p.a.*
Journal of Ecology
3 times *p.a.*   Published for the British Ecological Society.   Blackwell
    Scientific.
    Subscription: £14 *p.a.*
Journal of Environment Management
Quarterly.   Nature Conservancy Council.
    Subscription: £6.50.
Journal of Forestry
Royal Forestry Society of England.
Journal of the Institute of Public Health Engineers
Quarterly.   Municipal Publications.
    Subscription: £3 *p.a.*
Journal of the Institution of Municipal Engineers
Monthly.   I.M.E.
    Subscription: £6 *p.a.*
Journal of the Soil Association
Quarterly.   Soil Association.
    Subscription: £1 *p.a.*
Journal of Urban Analysis
Half-yearly.   Gordon & Breach.
    Subscription: £3.70 *p.a.*
Kingfisher
Concerned with conservation of bird life.   Penna Press, St. Albans,
    Herts.

Living World, The
Crusade Against All Cruelty to Animals.
Subscription: 7½p per copy.
Mammal Review
Quarterly.*   Blackwell Scientific.
Subscription: £8 *p.a.*
Marine Pollution Review
Monthly.   Macmillan.
Subscription: £3.50 *p.a.*
National Geographic Magazine
Monthly.   National Geographic Society.
Subscription: £3.88 *p.a.* (to Barclays Bank International Ltd.,
168 Fenchurch St., P.O. Box 115, London EC3P 3HP).
Natural History
Box 553, Planetarium Station, New York, NY 10024, U.S.A.
Subscription: £4 *p.a.*
Nature
Weekly.   Macmillan.
Subscription: £14 *p.a.*
Naturopa
3/4 times *p.a.*   Published for the Council of Europe.   Nature
Conservancy Council.
Subscription: free.
N.E.R.C. News Journal
Quarterly.   N.E.R.C.
Subscription: free.
New Internationalist
Monthly.   R.P.S. Ltd., Victoria Hall, London SE10 8BP.
Subscription: £3.85 *p.a.* (£3.50 by banker's order).
New Scientist
Weekly.   128 Long Acre, London WC2E 9QH (*tel.* 01-836 2468).
Subscription: £9.75 *p.a.*
New Society
Weekly.   128 Long Acre, London WC2E 9QH (*tel.* 01-836 2468).
Subscription: £8 *p.a.*
Noise and Vibration Bulletin
Monthly.   Multi-Science.
Subscription: £10.50 *p.a.*
Noise Control and Vibration Reduction
8 times *p.a.*   Trade & Technical Press.
Subscription: £5.40 *p.a.*
Noise News Digest
Monthly.   Noise Abatement Society.
Subscription: £5.25 *p.a.*
Operculum
Bi-monthly. Includes material on water pollution.   P.O. Box 82,
University of Queensland, St. Lucia, Queensland, Australia.
Subscription: $A5 *p.a.*

Oryx
3 times *p.a.*   Fauna Preservation Society.
   Subscription: £3 *p.a.*
Outlook
Quarterly.   P.O. Box 27, Broad Quay, Bristol, BS99 7AX.
   Subscription: 60p *p.a.*
Pictorial Education
Monthly.   Evans Bros.
   Subscription: £4.25 *p.a.*
Plain Truth ('A magazine of understanding')
Monthly. Includes frequent articles on population, energy, etc.
   P.O. Box 111, St. Albans, Herts.
   Subscription: free.
Planning Bulletin
Weekly.   T. & C.P.A.
   Subscription: £3 *p.a.*
Planning Outlook
Half-yearly.   Oriel Press.
   Subscription: £1.25 *p.a.*
Pollution
Monthly.   4 High St., Alton, Hants.
   Subscription: £13 *p.a.*
Pollution Control
Monthly.   Hermes House, Blackfriars Rd., London SE1.
Pollution Monitor
Bi-monthly.   Speedway House, Quarry Hill, Tonbridge, Kent.
Pollution Monthly
Monthly.   176 Wymering Mansions, London W9.
   Subscription: 4p per copy.
Pollution Technology International
Incorporates *Waste Disposal.*
276 The Corn Exchange, Fennel St., Manchester M4 3HF.
   (*tel.* 061-832 4607/8).
Population Studies
3 times *p.a.*   Population Investigation Committee.
   Subscription: £4.50.
Public Cleansing
Monthly.   Institute of Public Cleansing.
   Subscription: £2.10 *p.a.*
Quiet Please
Noise Abatement Society.
Reclamation Industries International
6 times *p.a.*   Maclaren Publishers Ltd., P.O. Box 109, Davis House,
   69/77 High St., Croydon CR9 1QH.
   Subscription: £5.50 *p.a.*
Regional Studies
Quarterly.   Regional Studies Association.
   Subscription: £10 *p.a.*

Resurgence (Journal of the 4th World)
Bi-monthly.   275 King's Road, Kingston-upon-Thames, Surrey.
Subscription: £2.50 *p.a.*
Review of Environmental Education Developments (REED)
Quarterly.   C.E.E.
Subscription: 80p *p.a.*
R.S.P.B. Teachers' Newsletter
Quarterly.   R.S.P.B.
Subscription: free.
Rucksack
Quarterly.   Ramblers' Association.
Subscription: free to members.
Sack
Published twice each school term.   C.S.V.
Subscription: £8 *p.a.*
S.A.G.E. Newsletter
S.A.G.E.
Scottish Forestry
Quarterly.   Royal Scottish Forestry Society.
Subscription: £2 *p.a.*
S.E.A.G. Newsletter
Monthly.   S.E.A.G.
Subscription: 50p *p.a.*
Smokeless Air
Quarterly.   National Society for Clean Air.
Span
Monthly.   Soil Association.
Subscription: 5p per copy.
Third World
Monthly.   Fabian Society.
Subscription: £3 *p.a.*
Towards Survival
Monthly journal of survival politics.   79 Sutton Ave., Eastern
   Green,
   Coventry CV5 7ER.
Subscription: £2.40 *p.a.*
Town and Country Planning
Monthly.   T. & C.P.A.
Subscription: £3 *p.a.*
Transportation Planning and Technology
Quarterly.   Gordon & Breach.
Subscription: £5 *p.a.*
Trees
3 times *p.a.*   Men of the Trees.
Subscription: £2.10 *p.a.*
Undercurrents. Magazine of radical science and people's technology.
6 times *p.a.*   275 Finchley Road, London NW3.
Subscription: £2 *p.a.*

UNESCO Courier
Monthly.   H.M.S.O.
  Subscription: £1.30 *p.a.*
Vegetarian, The
Monthly.   Vegetarian Society (U.K.) Ltd.
  Subscription: 5p per copy.
Visual Education
Monthly.   33 Queen Anne St., London W1M OAL (*tel.* 01-636 5742).
  Subscription: £2.40 *p.a.*
Vox
Monthly.   V.C.O.A.D.
  Subscription: 80p *p.a.*
Watchword
Advisory Centre for Education.
  Subscription: 50p *p.a.*
Water and Waste Treatment
Monthly.   103 Brigstock Rd., Thornton Heath, Surrey.
  Subscription: £6.30 *p.a.*
Water Pollution Abstracts
Monthly.   H.M.S.O.
  Subscription: £3.45 *p.a.*
Water Pollution Control
Bi-monthly.   Institute of Water Pollution Control.
  Subscription: £10 *p.a.*
Water Pollution Research
Annually.   H.M.S.O.
  Subscription: £1.15 *p.a.*
Water Research
Monthly.   Pergamon.
  Subscription: £40 *p.a.*
Where?
Monthly.   A.C.E.
  Subscription: £3.75 *p.a.*
Which?
Monthly.   Consumers' Association.
  Subscription: £2.50 *p.a.* (£4 with quarterly *Motoring Which?*)
World and the School
3 times *p.a.*   Atlantic Educational Publishers.
  Subscription: £1.50 *p.a.*
World Health
Monthly.   W.H.O., obtainable through H.M.S.O.
  Subscription: £1.20 *p.a.*
World Hunger
Bi-monthly.   F.F.H.
  Subscription: free.
World of Wildlife
Weekly.   49 Russell Square, London WC1B 4HP.
  Subscription: £10.40 *p.a.*

World Survey
Monthly.   Atlantic Educational Publishers.
   Subscription: £1.90 *p.a.*
World Wildlife News
World Wildlife Fund.
Your Environment
Quarterly.   Unit 4, Sewell St. Industrial Colony, London E13 8AT
   (*tel.* 01-552 8956)   *Note:* This has not been published since
   Summer 1973.
   Subscription: £2 *p.a.*

4   ADDITIONAL SOURCES OF INFORMATION

Conservation Books publish a classified list of environmental books
  Conservation Books   Price free
Conservation Society publishes a *Guide to Resources in Environmental Education.* Material listed includes details of radio and television broadcasts, and articles published in a wide range of periodicals
  J.E.W.P.   Price **B**
Council for Environmental Education publishes a *Directory of Environmental Literature and Teaching Aids*
  C.E.E.   Price **D**
Claude Gill Books publish a classified list of environmental books
  Gill Books   Price free
Griffin & George Ltd. publish *Field Studies,* a handbook for field work. This is a priced catalogue of equipment, but also includes valuable advice and suggestions
  Griffin & George   Price free
International Planned Parenthood Federation publishes a *Resource List on Population*
  I.P.P.F.   Price free
National Book League publishes an annotated list entitled *Environment, Resources and Man*
  National Book League   Price **C**
George Philip & Son Ltd. publish two valuable sources of information:
  Fullard, H. (ed.), *Geographical Digest* (an annual publication giving the latest available statistics on population, production, trade, etc.)
  Philip   Price **E**
Hancock, J. C. & Whiteley, P. F., *The Geographer's Vademecum* (a guide to sources of material for the Geographer, arranged by topic and country)
  Philip   Price **D**
Portola Institute has produced *The Last Whole Earth Catalogue* (Subtitled 'Access to Tools', this unusual publication includes reference to much material of value to work on the environment)
  Penguin (1971)   Price **E**
Schoolmaster Publishing Co. Ltd. publish a *Treasure Chest for Teachers*
  Schoolmaster Publishing Co.   Price **D**
Schools Council General Studies Project have so far published units and catalogues on:

China (1972)	*Africa* (1973)
Conflicts (1972)	*Planning and Design* (1973)
Crime (1972)	*Genetics and Evolution* (1973)
Economics (1972)	*Living in Britain: 1* (1973)
Education (1972)	*Living in Britain: 2* (1973)
Environment 1972)	*Nazi Germany* (1973)
Family (1972)	*Towns* (1973)

Popular Arts (1972)   *Supplements: 1* (1973)
Population (1972)   *Supplements: 2* (1973)
Science and Responsibility (1972)
Teaching and Learning (1972)
This material, which is suitable for 16–18 year olds, is available on subscription. Details from: Publishing Manager, Longman Group Ltd and Penguin Books Ltd., 9–11 The Shambles, York (tel. York 20801)
Schools Council Project Environment plans to publish:
Education for Environment (1974)   (Project handbook)
Learning from Trails (1974)   8–13 years
The School Outdoor Resource Area (1974)
Production Ecology (1974/5)   17 years +
Ethics and Environment (1974/5)   17 years +
Teachers handbook, 9 topic books and slide packs, covering Population; Food; Water; Pollution; Land Use and Planning; Man and Other Creatures; Resource Use and Recycling; Environmental Quality; Man in Nature
Longman   Prices to be announced
Voluntary Committee on Overseas Aid and Development publishes *The Development Puzzle*. This is a loose-leaf source book for teaching about the Developing Countries
V.C.O.A.D.   Price **D**
Wilson, R. W. has compiled a new edition of *Useful Addresses for Science Teachers*
Arnold (1974)   Price **J**

PART THREE

Background Information

1   SCHOOL EXAMINATIONS

Examinations in Environmental Studies and associated subjects are now
set by a number of examination boards. Outline details of these are
given below. Further details can be obtained from the addresses given.

C.S.E. EXAMINATIONS (Mode I)

Environmental Science
This examination, which was first set in 1971, consists of three papers
covering most aspects of the physical, natural and human environment.
Candidates are required to submit a short report on a suitable topic.

> Metropolitan Regional Examinations Board, 23/24 Henrietta St.,
> London WC2E 8ND.

Environmental Studies
This subject, which is examined by continuous assessment, places
particular emphasis on ecology and aspects of agriculture, horticulture
and forestry. Candidates are expected to produce a practical work book.

> East Anglian Examinations Board, The Lindens, Lexden Rd.,
> Colchester CO3 3RL.

G.C.E. EXAMINATIONS (Ordinary Level)

Rural Environmental Studies
First examined in 1973, this syllabus covers the physical landscape,
ecology and natural history, production systems, and the changing
outdoors, with the emphasis on rural environments. The examination
consists of one written paper, with no provision for the assessment of
course work or a special study.

> University of London, Schools Examinations Department,
> 66–72 Gower St., London WC1E 6EE.

Environmental Science
This was first examined in 1970. The syllabus is divided into six
sections — Astronomy, Geology, Meteorology, Physics, Chemistry and
Biology. Although termed 'Environmental Science' the emphasis is on
the 'science' with relatively little consideration of 'environmental'
aspects. The examination consists of two written papers.

> University of Cambridge, Local Examinations Syndicate,
> Syndicate Buildings, 17 Harvey Rd., Cambridge CB1 2EU.

Environmental Studies
This Ordinary (Alternative) level examination was first set in 1971, and
consists of two papers, plus a special study. The syllabus emphasises

the importance of fieldwork, and includes work on the natural, social and production aspects of the environment.

The Associated Examining Board, Wellington House, Station Road, Aldershot GU11 1BQ.

Applied Geography

This syllabus, which was first set in 1973, concentrates on man's influence on the environment in Britain and the developing countries.

Southern Universities Joint Board for School Examinations, Cotham Rd., Bristol BS6 6DD.

Environmental Studies

This subject was first set on a restricted basis in 1971. The examination consists of two written papers and an assessment of course work. The syllabus covers most aspects of the human and physical environment, including ecology and conservation.

Oxford Delegacy of Local Examinations, Summertown, Oxford OX2 7BZ.

G.C.E. EXAMINATIONS (Advanced Level)

Geography

Since 1970 this examination has included an alternative between Paper 2 (regional geography) and Paper 3 (population geography; settlement geography; agriculture, forestry and fisheries; conservation of natural resources).

University of Cambridge Local Examinations Syndicate, Syndicate Buildings, 17 Harvey Rd., Cambridge CB1 2EU.

Environmental Studies

The 'Wiltshire' syllabus was examined for the first time in 1974. The examination will consist of two written papers and a fieldwork study. The syllabus includes the local and national environment, and man's management of his environment.

Associated Examining Board, Wellington House, Station Road, Aldershot GU11 1BQ.

Environmental Studies

The 'Hertfordshire' syllabus will be examined for the first time in 1975. It will include work on ecosystems and the relationships between man and his environment. The candidates will also be expected to submit a suitable field study.

University of London, Schools Examinations Department, 66–72 Gower St., London WC1E 6EE.

INTERNATIONAL BACCALAUREATE (Subsidiary Level)

Environmental Studies

This syllabus emphasizes the geographic, economic and biological aspects of the relationships between man and his environment.

International Baccalaureate Office, 1 Rue Albert-Gos, 1206 Geneva, Switzerland.

2   UNIVERSITY AND POLYTECHNIC COURSES

Increasingly universities and polytechnics are offering courses which
are either wholly or partly environmental in character. Prospective
students are advised, however, to study the appropriate university
prospectuses carefully, since courses carrying the title 'environmental'
vary consierably in content. For example, courses in 'Environmental
Design' may relate to architecture, planning, and the interior mechanics
of buildings, while those in 'Environmental Engineering' often refer to
the discharge of effluents and environmental control.

'Environmental Studies' generally refers to the social, economic and
historical aspects of the environment, and 'Environmental Science' to
the sciences of the natural environment, often including farming
techniques.

Aston, University of
The Biology of Man and his Environment (part of the B.Sc. Combined
   Honours Degree).
Birmingham University
Biological Sciences and Geography (3 year course, leading to the B.Sc.
   Joint Honours Degree).
Bradford University
Environmental Science (4 year course, commencing in 1973).
Brunel University
M. of Technology (in environmental pollution).
Cardiff University College
Interdepartmental Course on Environmental Studies (part of the
   General Degree Scheme).
East Anglia, University of
Environmental Sciences (3 year course, leading to the B.Sc. Honours
   Degree).
Edinburgh University
Environmental Conservation (leading to the M.Sc. Degree).
Exeter University
Environmental Chemical Engineering (leading to the B.Sc. Honours
   Degree).
Huddersfield Polytechnic
Human Ecology (4 year sandwich course, commencing in 1974, leading
   to C.N.A.A. degree).
Keele University
Biology and Economics (part of a 4 year course, leading to the B.A.
   Honours Degree).
Lancaster University
Environmental Sciences (3 year course, leading to the B.A. Honours
   Degree).
Leeds University
Environmental Pollution (leading to the M.Sc. Degree).

236

Leicester University
Environmental Studies (Water Resources) (part of the Combined
Studies programme, commencing in 1973).
Liverpool (Institute of Extension Studies)
Diploma in Environmental Management.
London University (Wye College)
Rural Environmental Studies (3 year course, leading to the B.Sc.
Honours Degree).
Newcastle-upon-Tyne University
Natural Environmental Control (3 year honours degree course,
commencing in 1973).
North London Polytechnic
Geography (leading to B.Sc. Honours Degree. Can include Environ-
mental Management and Ecology).
Open University
Urban Development (part of the Faculty of Social Studies and
Technology).
Oxford Polytechnic
Ecology and Behaviour (leading to membership of the Institute of
Biology). *Note:* also available at a number of other colleges.
Oxford University
Human Sciences (includes population studies, human ecology and urban
geography).
Plymouth Polytechnic
Applied Ecology (leading to C.N.A.A. degree).
Environmental Sciences (3 year course, commencing in 1973, leading
to the B.Sc. Honours Degree).
Reading, University of
Diploma in Environmental Studies in Education.
Salford University
Environmental Sciences (leading to the B.Sc. Degree).
Sheffield University
Natural Environmental Science (commencing in 1973, leading to the
Special Honours Degree).
Natural Environmental Science with Landscape Studies (leading to the
Combined Honours Degree).
Southampton University
Certificate Course in Environmental Science.
Economics with Ecology.
Environmental Sciences (3 year course, leading to the B.Sc.HonoursDegree).
Stirling University
Technological Economics (Biology) (leading to the B.Sc. Degree).
Strathclyde University
Environmental Engineering.
Ulster, New University of
Environmental Science (leading to the B.Sc. Degree).
History of Resource Management (leading to the B.A. Degree).
Human Ecology (leading to the B.Sc. Degree).

3 GLOSSARY OF ENVIRONMENTAL TERMS

The figures in brackets at the end of the following entries refer to the
sections in Part One where further information can be obtained on
each entry. For example, further information on *leaching* can be
obtained by consulting Part One, Section 4: Soils and Soil Erosion.

Amphibian
Creature that can live on land or water. (3)
Annual
Plant which completes its growing cycle within one year. (3)
Artificial selection
Process of breeding plants/animals to obtain qualities required by man.
(2, 3)
Atmosphere
Layer of gases (especially nitrogen and oxygen) surrounding the earth.
(1, 21)
Biennial
Plant which requires two seasons to complete its growth cycle. (3)
Bilharzia
Disease common in irrigated regions and spread by a parasitic fluke.
(2, 5, 24)
Biocide
Agent that kills organisms. (2, 3, 19)
Biogeography
Geography of plant and animal life. (2, 3)
Biology
The science of life. (2, 3)
Biological control
Control of pests, etc. by the use of other organisms (e.g. mosquitoes
and fish). (2, 3)
Biomass
Total weight of living material within an ecosystem. (2)
Biomes
Larger communities, occupying major regions and sharing common
tolerance to regional climate (*cf.* Natural Regions). (2)
Biosphere
Layer of soil, water and air, within which all life exists, and of which
it forms part. (1, 2, 4, 5)
Biotic community
Species which have similar tolerances for climate, soil, water, topo-
graphy, etc. (2, 3)
Biotic potential
Maximum number of new individuals that can be produced by a
particular population in a given unit of time. (2)
Biotic succession
Process of growth and change (i.e. pioneer community > middle
successional community > climax community). (2)

Birth control
Deliberate prevention or restriction of conception. (8)
Birth rate
Ratio of births to total population. (7)
Campos
Open plains of central Brazil. (*See also* Savanna). (2, 3)
Carbon monoxide (Co)
Colourless, odourless and toxic gas. Major factor in air pollution in
    urban areas. (21)
Carcinogenic
    Cancer-producing.
Carnivores
Flesh-eating animals. (*See also* Consumer). (2, 3)
Carrying capacity
When population of species has reached limits of its environment.
    (2, 7)
Chernozem
Fertile soil found in temperate regions (e.g. black earths of Ukraine).
    (4)
Chlorophyll
Green pigment in all plants except fungi. Important in the process of
    photosynthesis. (2)
Climax vegetation
Stable plant community, in equilibrium with existing natural
    environment. (*See also* Biological succession). (2, 3)
Colombo Plan
Aid to developing countries of the Commonwealth. (27)
Commensalas
Two or more types of organism that live together with mutual
    benefits. (2, 3)
Coniferous forest
Evergreen, cone-bearing trees. (*See also* Taiga). (3)
Conservation
Protection and restoration of the environment by maintaining a natural
    balance. (25)
Consumers
Organisms that feed on producer organisms. (*See also* Herbivores *and*
    Carnivores). (2, 3)
Contour ploughing
Method of preventing soil erosion by ploughing horizontally. (4)
Conurbation
Continuously built-up area, resulting from the amalgamation of a group
    of nearby towns (e.g. Ruhr). (10)
Crustaceans
Aquatic animals having a hard shell. (3)
Death control
Control of population by famine, war, disease, etc. (8)
Death rate
Mortality rate per 1000 of the population. (7)

Deciduous
Type of plant which sheds leaves at the end of the growing season. (3)
Derelict land
Land which has been ruined by industrial and mining operations.
   (*See also* Reclamation). (24)
Desalinization
Process of removing salt, etc. from sea water, or from soil after
   reclamation. (15, 24)
Developing countries
Countries with a low 'per caput' income (i.e. 'Geneva 77'). (27)
Development Areas
Specified regions receiving government assistance for encouraging new
   industrial development (e.g. Merseyside). Originally Depressed or
   Distressed Areas. (26)
Diatom
Minute form of plankton. (2, 3)
Dry farming
Growing crops without irrigation in regions of low rainfall. (24)
Ecology
Study of the relationship between plants and animals and their
   environment. (2)
Ecosystems
Subdivisions of the biosphere. Each is a combination of a biotic
   community and its physical environment. (2)
Edaphic
Related to the soil. (4)
Effluent
Liquid sewage or industrial waste. (23)
Endemic
Belonging to a given geographic region (biome). (2)
Environment
Surroundings in which an organism exists (note physical environment,
   human environment, etc.). (1, 5)
Epidemiology
The study of diseases of a population.
Epiphyte
Plant living on, but not feeding off, another. (2, 3)
Eutrophication
Process of enrichment by nutrients of river on lake, causing oxygen
   deficiency. (20)
Exotic
Something originating outside a particular region. (2, 3)
Fauna
Animal life of a region. (3)
Fish Farming
Technique of cropping fish (e.g. in paddy fields of south east Asia). (13)
Flora
Plant life of a region. (3)

Food chain
Means of passing energy from one organism to another in an ecosystem
(i.e. producer organisms > consumers > reducer organisms). (2)
Food pyramid
See also Food chain. Proceeding up the chain, organisms get larger,
but fewer. (2)
Food web
Interconnected food chains. (2)
Fossil fuels
Fuels formed by the decay of organic material (e.g. oil, natural gas,
coal). Represent stored solar energy. (16)
Genus
Group of closely related plant/animal species. (2, 3)
Geosphere
Solid, non-organic part of the earth. (1, 5)
Geothermal power
Power obtained from the earth's natural heat (e.g. hot springs). (16)
Green belt
Region of open country surrounding a built-up area (especially a
conurbation) in which further development is strictly controlled. (12)
Greenhouse effect
Ability of the atmosphere to pass incoming (short-wave) solar radiation,
but to block out-going (long-wave) radiation. (21)
Green revolution
Rapid increase in yields of cereals brought about by the development of
new hybrid strains. (13)
Habitat
Environment of a place inhabited by an organism. (1, 2, 3)
Halophyte
Salt-loving plant. (2, 3)
Herbicide
Agent used to kill plants. (2, 3)
Herbivores
Creatures which eat grass, herbs, leaves, etc. (*See also* Consumers). (2, 3)
Hybrid
Off-spring resulting from a cross between parents of different species. (2, 3)
Hydroponics
Process of growing crops without soil, usually in a solution of minerals
and salts. (13)
Hydrological cycle
See Water cycle. (15, 20).
Hydrosphere
Water portion of the earth (i.e. lakes, oceans, rivers, water vapour,
etc.). (1, 15, 20)
Hygrophyte
Water-loving plant (e.g. mangrove). (2, 3)
Hygroscopic particle
Particle which readily attracts moisture. (15, 20)

Indigenous
Living naturally in an area. (2, 3)
Insectivores
Primitive mammals that feed on insects. (3)
Insolation
Energy received from the sun. (1, 16)
Inversion
Meteorological condition in which temperature increases with altitude. Provides ideal conditions for smog, etc. (21)
Irrigation
Artificial application of water for cultivation in areas with low or seasonal rainfall. (13, 24)
Kwashiorkor
Disease caused by malnutrition. (13, 27)
Laterite
Highly leached (and hence infertile) soil, reddish in colour, found in the tropics. (4)
Leaching
Removal of minerals, humus, etc. from soil by the downward movement of moisture in wet areas. (*See also* Podzol *and* Laterite). (4)
Limnology
Scientific study of lakes. (15, 20)
Lithosphere
Earth's crust. (1, 5)
Llanos
Tropical grasslands of Venezuela. (*See also* Savanna). (2, 3)
Mammals
Animals which suckle their young. (3)
Megalopolis
Vast urban sprawl (especially along the north-east coast of U.S.A.).
Millionaire cities
Cities with a population of over one million. (10)
Molluscs
Shell-fish. (3)
Monoculture
Cultivation of a single crop (e.g. wheat) over a wide area. (13)
Mutation
Basic inheritable change in the gene of an organism. (2)
National Park
Region officially designated for some form of protection against development because of its natural beauty (e.g. Snowdonia, Yellowstone). (11, 12, 25)
Natural regions
Regions with similar climates, resulting vegetation and human responses (e.g. equatorial forests). (2, 3)
Natural selection
Agent of evolutionary change which ensures that an organism possessing advantageous adaptations produces more offspring than those without. (2, 3)

242

Natural vegetation
Spontaneous plant growth, unaffected by man. (2, 3)
New town
Deliberately designated urban development, intended to relieve the
    population pressure in large cities (e.g. Crawley). (12)
Overpopulation
Population too great to be supported by the natural and industrial
    output of a region. (7, 8)
Paleoecology
Study of the relationships between ancient organisms and their
    environment. (2)
Pampas
Temperate grasslands of Argentina and Uruguay. (2, 3)
Parasite
Organism living and feeding on another (e.g. mistletoe). (2, 3)
Particulates
Small particles in the atmosphere (e.g. dust, salt, soot) causing poor
    visibility. Essential in the rain-making process. (*See also* Hygro-
    scopic particles). (15, 21)
Pathogen
Organism that causes disease. (2)
Pedology
Study of soils. (4)
Perennial
Plants lasting more than two years. (3)
Permafrost
Continuously frozen ground. (4)
Photosynthesis
Production of carbohydrates by green plants from CO_2 in the
    atmosphere and hydrogen from soil water, using solar energy.
    (*See also* Chlorophyll). (2)
Pisciculture
Culture and growing of fish. (*See also* Fish farming). (13)
Plankton
Minute animal and vegetable organisms found in the sea (e.g. diatoms
    and protozoans). (2)
Podzol
Infertile leached soil, developed under coniferous forests or heathland.
    (4)
Polder
Land at or below sea level, reclaimed from the sea (e.g. Zuider Zee).
    (24)
Pollution
Contamination of air, water, land, etc. by the accumulation of material
    (e.g. smoke, radioactivity, chemicals, sewage, etc.) at a faster
    rate than natural processes can remove it. (19, 20, 21, 22)
Population explosion
Rapid growth of population, especially since the industrial revolution.
    (7, 8)

Prairies
Almost treeless temperate grasslands of North America. (2, 3)
Predators
Animals which live by preying on others. (*See also* Carnivores).

Producer organisms
First stage in a food chain (i.e. green plants). (2, 3)
Productivity
Rate at which an ecosystem produces new organic material and, through this, stores energy. (2)
Radioactivity
Property of certain chemical elements to emit radiation which may be harmful to organisms. (16, 21)
Radio-carbon dating
Method of determining the age of a substance by measuring the amount of radio-carbon in the carbon it contains.
Reafforestation
Replanting of a previously-existing forested area after clearance by man or fire. (14, 24)
Reclamation
(*a*) Process of gaining or regaining land (e.g. by drainage, irrigation, etc.). (24) (*b*) Process of reclaiming raw materials. (*See also* Recycling). (23).
Recycling
Process of recovering raw materials (e.g. metal, paper, etc.), re-processing and re-using. (23)
Reducer organisms
Final stage in food chain (i.e. creatures of breakdown and decay). (2, 3)
Reptiles
Cold-blooded animals. (3)
Resources
Raw materials. (14, 16)
Ribbon development
Spread of an urban area along the main lines of communication. Especially associated with the growth of conurbations. (9, 10)
Robber economy
Removal or extraction of non-renewable resources (e.g. minerals, fossil fuels). (14, 16, 26)
Rural depopulation
Movement of population from a rural area to an urban region. (7, 10)
Saprophyte
Plant (e.g. fungus) living on decayed vegetable matter. (2, 3)
Savanna
Tropical grassland consisting of grass and scattered trees or shrubs. (2, 3)

Selva
Equatorial forest region of the Amazon Basin. (2, 3)
Shifting cultivation
Primitive method of cultivation used especially in the tropics. (13)
Silviculture
Care and growth of trees. (14)
Sleeping sickness
Tropical disease transmitted by the tse-tse fly. (2)
Smog
Combination of smoke and fog. (21)
Soil erosion
Destruction and removal of topsoil faster than natural soil-forming
    processes can replace it. (4)
Solum
    See Topsoil. (4)
Steppe
Treeless temperate grasslands of central Asia. (2, 3)
Strip cropping/Strip cultivation
Cultivation of crops in alternate strips to combat soil erosion. (4, 13)
Symbiosis
Close-knit association of two organisms that cannot normally live
    together. (2)
Taiga
Coniferous forests of U.S.S.R. (2, 3)
Top soil
Uppermost horizon of the soil. (4)
Town and country planning
Controlled development of the urban and rural landscape. (*See also*
    Green belt and New towns). (12)
Threshold temperature
Temperature below which active plant growth ceases. (2, 3)
Transpiration
Loss of water vapour from the leaf surface of a plant. (2, 3)
Tropophyte
Plant adapted to seasonal change (i.e. wet/dry or hot/cold). (2, 3)
Troposphere
Lowest layer of the atmosphere, below the tropopause, in which most
    weather conditions occur. (1, 21)
Tundra
Barren, treeless wastes found within polar regions, between the
    coniferous forests and the Arctic Ocean. (2, 3)
Turbidity
Amount of sediment suspended in a liquid. (20)
Underpopulation
Population which is less than that which could be supported, and
    which is less than that which may be economically desirable. (7)
Urbanization
Growth of towns. (10)

Veld(t)
Temperate grasslands of southern Africa. (2, 3)

Water cycle
Continuous process of evaporation, cooling, condensation, precipitation. (15, 20)

Xerophyte
Plant adapted to conditions of drought (e.g. cactus). (2, 3)

Do-it-Yourself Teaching Programme

By careful use of the information in this source book, many schemes of work can be prepared on subjects suitable for general studies or more specialized examination syllabuses (*see pages* 234–235). The following is therefore only one possible way in which a complete teaching programme may be devised, together with a number of sample programmes on common environmental topics.

GENERAL APPROACH

1 *Initial preparation of background material:*
(a) Contact organizations concerned with the subject (they may be able to provide valuable background information and advice).
(b) Read suitable reference/textbooks (to help in the preparation of up-to-date notes and/or worksheets).
(c) Consult appropriate journals and periodicals (for more specific information on particular aspects of the subject).

2 *Class reading:*
Selected from suitable textbooks and (especially for sixth-form work) recent articles.

3 *Visual aids:*
To introduce the subject and/or reinforce particular points (may be films, filmstrips, wallcharts, etc.).

4 *Preparation of wall display:*
Using wallcharts and posters, as well as cuttings from newspapers, magazines, etc.

5 *Practical classwork:*
This may involve the use of workcards, study kits, experiments, simulation games, etc.

6 *Practical fieldwork:*
Most environmental topics lend themselves admirably to this approach. Many suggestions will be found by consulting Part One, Section 6: Field Studies.

7 *Record of work:*
This is probably best contained in a loose-leaf folder or file, and should include newspaper cuttings, class notes, completed worksheets, field notes, sketch maps, photographs, etc.

8 *Follow-up work:*
Because of the very nature of environmental work, one subject tends to
lead on naturally to many others. The important thing is to emphasize
the *inter-relationships* that occur between man and the many elements
of the natural environment.

SAMPLE PROGRAMME: CONSERVATION
Suitable for upper primary and lower secondary school classes.

Background material:
(*a*) Organizations (e.g. Conservation Society; Countryside Commission;
C.P.R.E.; I.U.C.N.; Keep Britain Tidy Group; National Trust).
(*b*) Books (e.g. Curry-Lindhal, *Conservation for Survival*; Dasmann,
Environmental Conservation; Joffe, *Conservation*; Nicholson, *The
Environmental Revolution*).
(*c*) Journals/Periodicals (e.g. *Conservation Review*; *The Ecologist*;
Nature in Focus).

Class reading:
e.g. Bainbridge, *Conservation.*

Visual aids:
(*a*) Films (e.g. *Conservation and Balance in Nature*).
(*b*) Filmstrips (e.g. 'Conservation is Everybody's Business' series;
'Conserving our Natural Resources' series).

Wall display:
e.g. *National Parks* posters; *Conservation.*

Practical classwork:
e.g. *Conservation Game.*

Follow-up work:
(*a*) Soil conservation (Sections 4, 25).
(*b*) Nature conservation (Sections 3, 25).
(*c*) Conservation of resources (Sections 14, 16, 25).
(*d*) Conservation of buildings (Sections 10, 25).
(*e*) Reclamation (Section 24).

SAMPLE PROGRAMME: POLLUTION
Suitable for C.S.E. group.

Background material:
(*a*) Organizations (e.g. Conservation Society; Howey Foundation;
Institute of Public Health Engineers).
(*b*) Books (e.g. Andrews, *Guide to the Study of Environmental Pollution*; Barr, *The Assaults on our Senses*; Bourne, *Pollute and be
Damned*; Carson, *Silent Spring*; Graham, *Since Silent Spring*;
Mellanby, *The Biology of Pollution*).
(*c*) Journals/Periodicals (e.g. *The Ecologist*; *Environmental Pollution*;
Epoch; *Nature in Focus*; *Pollution Monthly*).

Class reading:
e.g. Baker & Bushel, *The Unclean Planet*; Jackson, *Conservation and Pollution.*

Visual aids:
(*a*) Films (e.g. *After the Torrey Canyon*; *Environment in the Balance*).
(*b*) Slides (e.g. *Dangerous Litter*; *Extraction, Conservation, Pollution*).

Wall display:
e.g. *Pollution.*

Practical classwork:
e.g. Activity Factsheet on *Local Pollution*; 'Pollution' and 'Pollution Control' Modular Learning Programmes.

Follow-up work:
(*a*) Water/sea pollution (Section 20).
(*b*) Air pollution (Section 21).
(*c*) Noise pollution (Section 22).
(*d*) Waste disposal (Section 23).
(*e*) Pollution in Britain (Sections 19–23).

SAMPLE PROGRAMME: MAN AND HIS ENVIRONMENT
Suitable for G.C.E. 'O' level group.

Background material:
(*a*) Organizations (e.g. Conservation Society; G.A.; Soil Association).
(*b*) Books (e.g. Arvill, *Man and Environment*; Ehrlich, *Population, Resources, Environment*; Stamp, *Applied Geography*).
(*c*) Journals/Periodicals (e.g. *The Ecologist*; *New Scientist*; *Your Environment*).

Class reading:
e.g. Harris, Harrison & Smithson, *Man's Environment*; Robson, *Man and his Environment*; Sauvain, *Man and Environment.*

Visual aids:
(*a*) Films (e.g. *Shadow of Progress*; *Environment in the Balance*; 'Earth and Mankind' series).
(*b*) Filmstrips (e.g. 'Caring for the Countryside' series).

Wall display:
e.g. *Man Takes Control.*

Practical classwork:
e.g. *Man and his Environment.*

Follow-up work:
(*a*) Population (Sections 7, 8).
(*b*) Pollution (Sections 19–23).
(*c*) Conservation (Section 25).

SAMPLE PROGRAMME: WORLD POPULATION PROBLEM

Suitable for sixth form or further education.

Background material:
(*a*) Organizations (e.g. Conservation Society; Eugenics Society; I.P.P.F.; Population Stabilization).
(*b*) Books (e.g. Barham, *The Cancer of the Earth*; Borgstrom, *The Hungry Planet*; Cipolla, *The Economic History of World Population*; Ehrlich, *The Population Bomb*; Parsons, *Population Versus Liberty*).
(*c*) Journals/Periodicals (e.g. *The Ecologist*; *Your Environment*).

Class reading:
(*a*) Books (e.g. Flew, *An Essay on the Principle of Population*; Beaujeu-Garnier, *The Geography of Population*), plus those listed above.
(*b*) Articles (e.g. Johnson, 'The People Plague').

Visual aids:
(*a*) Films (e.g. *A Fable*; 'The Population Problem' series).
(*b*) Filmstrip (e.g. *Population and Resources: Part I*).
(*c*) Transparencies (e.g. *The Population Explosion*).

Wall display:
e.g. *F.A.O. Charts*; *Population Growth*.

Practical classwork:
e.g. 'Population' Modular Learning Programme.

Follow-up work:
(*a*) Britain's population (Section 7).
(*b*) Population control (Section 8).
(*c*) Food production (Section 13).
(*d*) Urbanization (Section 10).

Stop Press

1. General Environmental Topics

Monteith, J. L., *Principles of Environmental Physics* (Contemporary Biology)   Arnold   1973   Price **G/J**

van Tassel, A. J., *Our Environment: Outlook for the 1980s*   Lexington   1974   Price **J**

Whole Earth Epilog (Successor to *Last Whole Earth Catalog*)   Penguin   1974   Price **E**

Fawcett, R., *Problems* ('The World in Focus' series; includes conservation, overpopulation, water shortage, etc.)   Macmillan   (in preparation)   C.S.E.   Price **D**

Sealey, L., *Our World Encyclopaedia* (10 volumes and index)   Macmillan   1974   10–14 years   Price **J**

2. Ecology

Jackman, L., *The Beach* (Natural cycle of life on seashore)   Evans   1974   Price **F**

Pollock, N. C., *Animals, Environment and Man in Africa*   Saxon House   1974   Price **H**

Simmons, I. G., *The Ecology of Natural Resources*   Arnold   1974   Price **G/J**

5. Man and Environment

Insel, P. M. & Moos, R. H. (eds.), *Health and the Social Environment. Issues in Social Ecology*   Lexington   1974-in preparation

Man and his World
   1. *Confrontation*   Price **E**
   2. *Interaction*   Price **E**
      Macmillan   1973   11–14 years

6. Field Studies

Proctor, E., *Nature Themes* (Nature and its relationship with geography, meteorology, geology and conservation)   Evans   1974-in preparation   Price **D**

7. Population Growth and Distribution

Kuznets, S., *Population, Capital and Growth*   Heinemann   1974   Price **G**

8. Population Control
Blaikie, P., *Family Planning in India. A Socio-Geographical Approach*
Arnold   1975-in preparation   Price **J**

10. Urbanization
Rothenberg, J. & Heggie, I. G., *Transport and the Urban Environment*
Macmillan   1974   Price **J**

12. Planning
Alden, J. & Morgan, R., *An Introduction to Regional Planning*
Intertext   1974-in preparation   Price **J**
Cherry, G. E., *The Evolution of British Town Planning*   Intertext
1974   Price **J**
Hall, P., *Urban and Regional Planning*   Penguin   1974   Price **E**

14. Raw Materials
Simmons, I. G., *The Ecology of Natural Resources*   Arnold   1974
Price **G/J**

15. Water Supply
Funnell, B. M. & Hey, R. D., *The Management of Water Resources in
England and Wales*   Saxon House   1974   Price **H**

16. Energy and Power Supplies
Connery, R. H. & Gilmour, R. S., *The National Energy Problem* (U.S.A.)
Lexington   1975-in preparation
Scott, D. L., *Pollution in the Electric Power Industry. Its control and
Costs*   Lexington   1974   Price **H**
Energy: The Nuclear Alternative   (1974)
Towards Survival.   23 min. col.   Hire **J**

17. Industrialization
Devereux, M. P., *Industries in Britain* ('Sample Study' series)
Macmillan   1973   C.S.E./G.C.E.   Price **D**

18. Transport
Cantilli, E. J., *Programming Environmental Improvement in Public
Transportation*   Lexington   1974   Price **J**
Farris, M. T. & McElhiney, P. T. (eds.), *Modern Transportation.
Selected Readings*, 2nd edn.   Houghton Mifflin   1973   Price **G**
O'Flaherty, C. A., *Highways*, 2nd edn.
    Volume 1   Price **G/J**
    Volume 2   Price **H/J**
    Arnold   1974
Pryke, R. & Dodgson, J., *The Rail Problem: An Alternative Strategy*
Robertson   1975-in preparation   Price **H**

252

Rothenberg, J. & Heggie, I. G. (eds.), *Transport and the Urban Environment*   Macmillan   1974   Price **J**

Stratford, A., *Airports and the Environment* (A study of air transport development and its impact on the social and economic well-being of communities)   Macmillan   1974   Price **J**

Stratford, A., *Air Transport Economics in the Supersonic Era*, 2nd edn.   Macmillan   1973   Price **K**

Devereux, M. P. & Evans, C., *Ports in Britain* ('Sample Study' series)   Macmillan   (in preparation)   C.S.E./G.C.E.   Price **D**

19. Pollution (General)

Benn, F. R. & McAuliffe, C. A., *Chemistry and Pollution*   Macmillan   1974   Price **J**

Dick, D. T., *Pollution, Congestion and Nuisance. The Economics of Nonmarket Interdependence*   Lexington   1974   Price **J**

21. Air Pollution

Bibbero, R. J. & Young, I. G., *Systems Approach to Air Pollution Control*   Wiley   1974-in preparation   Price **K**

Mabey, R., *The Pollution Handbook* ('Extensions' series; A.C.E./Sunday Times clean air and water surveys)   Penguin   1974   8–13 years   Price **D**

22. Noise

Anthrop, D. E., *Noise Pollution*   Lexington   1974   Price **J**

23. Waste Disposal

Recycling.
Concord.   21 min., col.   Hire **G**

26. Economic, Social and Political Aspects

Bain, J. S., *Environmental Decay. Economic Causes and Remedies*   Eurospan   1973   Price **G**

Dasgupta, A. K., *Economic Theory and the Developing Countries*   Macmillan   1974   Price **F/H**

Richardson, H. W., *The Economics of Urban Size*   Saxon House   1974   Price **H**

Rivers, P., *Politics by Pressure* (Growth of pressure groups)   Harrap   1974   Price **G**

27. Developing Countries

Dasgupta, A. K., *Economic Theory and the Developing Countries*   Macmillan   1974   Price **F/H**

28. Leisure

Simmons, I., *Rural Recreation in the Industrial World*   Arnold   1974   Price **J**

253

Toyne, P., *Recreation and Environment* ('Aspects of Geography' series)
    Macmillan   (in preparation)   17 years+   Price **C**

29. Environmental Education

Environmental Studies Worksheets (24 sheets and teacher's notes) –
    1. *Roads and Traffic*   4. *Recreation*
    2. *Shops and Shopping*   5. *Houses and Buildings*
    3. *School*   6. *Travel*
    Collins   9–13 years   Price **D** each set

Suppliers and Publishers

Eurospan Ltd.
Kershaw House, 3 Henrietta St., London WC2E 8BR (*tel.* 01-240 0856)
    Books
Houghton Mifflin Publishers Ltd.
3 Henrietta St., London WC2E 8LU (*tel.* 01-240 0856)
    Books
Robertson, Martin
17 Quick St., London N1 8HL (*tel.* 01-837 7502)
    Books

Organizations

British Nuclear Energy Society
1–7 Great George St., London SW1 (*tel.* 01-839 3611)
International Solar Energy Society
Royal Institution, 21 Albemarle St., London W1X 4BS
Nature Conservancy Council (England)
1 Cambridge Gate, Regent's Park, London NW1 4JY

Journals and Periodicals

Environment and Behaviour
Quarterly.   Sage Publications Ltd., 44 Hatton Garden, London
    EC1N 8ER (*tel.* 01-242 7723)
    Subscription: £5.40 *p.a.*
Journal of Biogeography
Quarterly.   Blackwall Scientific Publications
    Subscription: £10 *p.a.*
Science for People
6 times *p.a.*   9 Poland Street, London W1V 3DG
    Subscription £1 *p.a.*
Seed   Journal of Organic Living
Monthly.   269 Portobello Rd., London W11. (*tel.* 01-229 4723)
    Subscription £2.40 *p.a.*